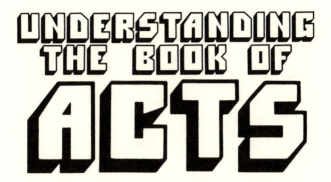

UNDERSTANDING THE BOOK OF ACTS

by
Charles F. Baker
President Emeritus – Grace Bible College
Grand Rapids, Michigan

Grace Bible College Publications
Grand Rapids, Michigan 49509

UNDERSTANDING THE BOOK OF ACTS

Library of Congress Cataloging in Publication Data

Baker, Charles F.
  Understanding the Book of Acts

  Includes bibliographical references and index.
  1. Bible. N.T., Acts — Commentaries. I. Bible. N.T., Acts. English. 1981. II. Title.
BS2625.3.B32   226'.607   81-1561
ISBN 0-912340-03-7   AACR2

Printed in the United States of America
By Grace Mission Press

*"**Understandeth** thou what thou readest?" "How can I, except some man should guide me?*

*"The eyes of your **understanding** being enlightened; that ye may know what is the hope of his calling, and, what the riches of the glory of his inheritance in the saints, and what is the exceeding greatness of his power to us-ward who believe, according to the working of his mighty power, which he wrought in Christ when he raised him from the dead, and set him at his own right hand in heavenly places, far above all principality, and power and might, and dominion, and every name that is named, not only in this world, but also in that which is to come: and hath put all things under his feet, and gave him to be the head over all things to the church, which is his body, the fulness of him that filleth all in all."*

*"Wherefore be ye not unwise, but **understanding** what the will of the Lord is."*

AREA OF UNITED STATES COMPARED WITH THAT OF NEW TESTAMENT BIBLE LANDS

Table of Contents

SECTION THREE: THE GOSPEL TO THE GENTILES THROUGH
PAUL, Chapters 13:1 - 28:31

This book is dedicated to my many students of past years with whom I had the privilege and joy of sharing the great doctrinal and dispensational truths of God's inerrant Word.

Foreword

Understanding the Book of Acts is a companion volume to *Understanding the Gospels* by the same author. Mr. Baker's main thesis is that the Book of Acts is primarily the record of God's offer of the Messianic Kingdom to the nation of Israel, the rejection of that offer, and the final setting aside of national Israel. The first half of Acts is seen as a continuation of the Kingdom ministry begun by Jesus Christ in the Gospel records to none but the Jews only. The latter part is seen as a transition, or a turning away from the long-prophesied Israelitish program to a new and hitherto unrevealed dispensation concerning the Church which is called the Body of Christ. A new Apostle by the name of Paul is separated for this distinctive ministry in chapter 13. While going to the Jews first throughout the Roman world, his ministry is characterized by pronouncing spiritual blindness upon unbelieving Jews, followed by a turning to the Gentiles. The Book ends with the final pronouncement and final turning.

Mr. Baker correlates the epistles written by Paul during and after the Acts Period with the text. The new spiritual order under Paul is developed, showing both the differences and similarities between Israelitish and Body programs.

Since the author believes that a proper understanding of Acts and Pauline theology will answer many of the questions being raised by Charismatics today, anyone who has these questions unresolved should find satisfying reading in *Understanding the Acts*.

Jack T. Dean, Ph.D.
President
Grace Bible College

Preface

Every sincere minister of the Word of God trusts that he has been led by the Spirit of God in the exposition of that Word. The author of this volume on Acts has studied and taught the Word for over fifty years and he shares in this hope that his words are the result of the Spirit's enlightenment. However, expositors have not all agreed on the interpretation of this portion of inspired Scripture, and it is to be expected that not all who read this book will agree with the writer's conclusions in every detail. But whether the reader agrees little or much, it is the writer's prayer that all who read may be motivated to put these views to the Scriptural test to see whether or not these things be so.

The author is firmly committed to the plenary inspiration and inerrancy of the entire Bible in its original writings. The book has been written from the premillennial and dispensational viewpoint. Its chief objective is to trace the progressive revelation of truth from the resurrection ministry of Christ to the setting aside of national Israel and the establishment of the full-blown dispensation of the grace of God.

The author is indebted to several of his colleagues who have gone over the original manuscript and have offered helpful suggestions, many of which have been incorporated into the finished product. Special thanks are due Pastor Vernon A. Schutz, Prof. Dale DeWitt, Pastor Clarence Kramer, Prof. Samuel R. Vinton, Jr., and Dr. Jack Dean.

Introduction

As we approach the study of the Book of Acts we should bring with us the basic principles which are set forth in the Gospels, since Acts is but a continuation of what was begun in the Gospels. The following facts and principles will be helpful in understanding the events in the Book of Acts.

The Kingdom of which the Gospels speak was only near at hand while Jesus was on earth. It had not yet been established. The disciples were taught to pray that it might be established (Matt. 4:17; 6:10).

Before the Kingdom could come Jesus had to be rejected by the rulers of Israel (Mk. 8:31; Lk. 18:31-34). It is plainly stated that He must *first* suffer before the glory associated with the Kingdom could come (Lk. 24:26; 1 Pet. 1:11).

Jesus must not only suffer and die and rise from the dead before the Kingdom could be established, but He must go back to heaven and receive His Kingdom and then return to earth to establish it. This fact is clearly taught in the parable of Lk. 19:11-27.

In His earthly ministry Jesus was sent only to the lost sheep of the house of Israel (Matt. 15:24). He commanded His disciples also not to go to the Gentiles, but rather to go to the lost sheep of the house of Israel (Matt. 10:5,6).

By limiting His earthly ministry to Israel, Jesus was not ruling out Gentile participation in the Kingdom. He was simply carrying out the provisions of the Abrahamic Covenant that all of the Gentile nations would ultimately be blessed through the multiplied seed of Abraham (Gen. 22:17,18). Since the Gentiles were to be blessed through the instrumentality of Israel, it was only logical that Israel must first be blessed before she could bless the other nations. In speaking to a Gentile woman who had come to Jesus for help He said, "The children (of Israel) must first be filled: for it is not fitting to take the children's bread and to cast it unto the dogs" (the Gentiles). He told the Samaritan woman the same thing: "Salvation is of the Jews" (John 4:22).

Jesus declared: "The kingdom shall be taken from you (the then present rulers of Israel), and given to a nation bringing forth the fruits thereof" (Matt. 21:43). He did not say that it would be given to the Church, or to Gentile nations, but to "a nation." Since Jesus also said to His disciples, "Fear not, little flock; for it is your Father's good pleasure to give you the kingdom," (Lk. 12:32), it is evident that His band of disciples were to comprise this new nation of Israel, to whom the kingdom would be given. Jesus promised that in that kingdom, the Twelve Apostles would sit on twelve thrones, judging the twelve tribes of Israel (Matt. 19:28).

Is it any wonder, then, that the main question that was uppermost in the minds of the disciples at the opening of Acts was: "Lord, wilt thou at this time restore again the kingdom to Israel?" (Acts 1:6). The Lord did not answer their question directly, because there were certain conditional elements, as well as secrets of the Divine purpose, which would determine the answer to the question. He simply told them, "It is not for you to know the times or the seasons, which the Father hath put in his own power."

As we go into the study of the Acts we will find in the first three chapters what we call the offer of the Kingdom to Israel. There is the promise if Israel repents of the crucifixion of Jesus and receives Him as Messiah, God will send Him back and there will be ushered in the times of restoration and refreshing spoken of by all the prophets of old. But it may be asked, If Jesus had predicted the rulers of Israel would reject Him, that they would persecute and put to death His followers, and that God would send the Roman army to destroy and trample under foot the city of Jerusalem, in what sense could there be a genuine or realistic offer to these upon whom judgment had already been pronounced? This is a good question, and one that deserves very close scrutiny.

Our God is long-suffering and merciful. He recognized that there was an element of ignorance on the part of the rulers who put Jesus to death (cf. Lk. 23:34; Acts 3:17; 1 Tim. 1:13). Therefore God poured out His Holy Spirit and divinely enlightened them concerning the Messiahship of Jesus, thus giving them another opportunity to repent. The rulers were now without excuse in continuing to reject Jesus. God could now righteously judge and condemn them. But those individual Jews who did repent, and there were several thousand who did, were saved. We must distinguish between God's dealings with individuals and with the nation. The nation was judged when God finally destroyed Jerusalem and its temple.

Although this judgment had been predicted, God in His sovereign grace offered to send Jesus back and bring in the times of restoration if they would only repent. But they did not repent. From the many prophetic utterances in Scripture we should have expected that God would have sent His judgment; would have brought in the Great Tribulation; would have sealed the elect remnant of Israel (Rev. 7:3,4); would have saved a great multitude of Gentiles (Rev. 7:9-14); would have purged out the rebels in Israel (Ezek. 20:38); and would have brought back Jesus as King of kings to establish His Millennial

Kingdom (Matt. 24:21-30). But although Jerusalem was finally destroyed, none of these other events occurred. It seems evident that the prophetic program was interrupted.

Paul explains why the prophetic program was interrupted. In the secret counsels of God there was a purpose which He had never before made known to the sons of men (Col. 1:24-27). That purpose, called the *mystery* or *secret,* was to call out from the world the heavenly Church, the Body of Christ, completely separate and distinct from Israel and her earthly Kingdom. When He has completed His purpose in this present dispensation, we believe He will resume His purpose with Israel.

The Book of Acts presents the Transition from the ministry of the Twelve Apostles to Israel to the ministry of the Apostle Paul for the Body of Christ. The first half of the book deals primarily with Israel, and the second half with the transition to Paul. We must go to his epistles, however, to learn the distinctive truths concerning the Body of Christ.

Numerous evangelical scholars have commented on the transitional character of the Acts. The following quotations are given in support of this view.

J. Sidlow Baxter has this to say about Acts: "In the light of our findings we affirm once again that this book, the Acts of the Apostles, is primarily an account of the renewed offer of Messiah-Jesus and the long-promised 'kingdom of heaven' to the nation of Israel."[1]

"The period covered by the Acts, we repeat, was a suspense period. So long as the kingdom was being re-offered to the nation the return of the Lord could have happened without delay upon the fulfillment of the conditions . . . Would Israel respond, repent, receive? That was the suspense point."[2]

Here are Sir Robert Anderson's views on the Book of Acts:

"Every one recognizes that the advent of Christ marked a signal 'change of dispensation,' as it is termed: that is, a change in God's dealings with men. But the fact is commonly ignored that the rejection of Christ by the favored people, and their fall in consequence from the position of privilege formerly held by them, marked another change no less definite and important (Rom. xi. 15). And yet this fact affords the solution of many difficulties and a safeguard against many errors. As indicated in these pages, it gives the clue to the right understanding of the Acts of the Apostles—a book which is primarily the record, not, as commonly supposed, of the founding of the Christian Church, but of the apostasy of the favored nation. But it also explains much that perplexes Christians in the teachings of the Gospels."[3]

"And we have turned to the Acts of the Apostles to find how fallacious is the popular belief that the Jerusalem Church was

Christian. In fact, it was thoroughly and altogether Jewish. The only difference, indeed, between the position of the disciples during the 'Hebraic period' of the Acts, and during the period of the Lord's earthly ministry, was that the great fact of the Resurrection became the burden of their testimony. And finally we have seen how the rejection of that testimony by the favored nation led to the unfolding of the Divine purpose to deprive the Jew of his vantage-ground of privilege and to usher in the Christian dispensation."[4]

"In a word, if 'To the Jew first' is characteristic of the Acts of the Apostles as a whole, 'To the Jew only' is plainly stamped upon every part of these early chapters, described by theologians as the 'Hebraic section' of the book. The fact is clear as light. And if any are prepared to account for it by Jewish prejudice and ignorance, they may at once throw down this volume, for it is here assumed that the apostles of the Lord, speaking and acting in the memorable days of Pentecostal power, were Divinely guided in their work and testimony."[5]

"Suppose again that the Epistles (of Paul) were there, but the Acts of the Apostles left out, how startling would appear the heading 'To the Romans,' which would confront us on turning from the study of the Evangelists! How could we account for the transition thus involved? How could we explain the great thesis of the Epistle, that there is no difference between Jew and Gentile, both being by nature on a common level of sin and ruin, both being called by grace to equal privileges and glory? The earlier Scriptures will be searched in vain for teaching such as this. Not the Old Testament merely but even the Gospels themselves are seemingly separated from the Epistles by a gulf. To bridge over that gulf is the Divine purpose for which the Acts of the Apostles has been given to the Church. The earlier portion of the book is the completion and sequel to the Gospels; its concluding narrative is introductory to the great revelation of Christianity."[6]

The views presented above are in contrast to the traditional concept that the Book of Acts begins with the casting away of the Jewish nation and the establishing of the Christian Church. The fact that the Apostles did not go to the Gentiles immediately is attributed to Jewish prejudice against the Gentiles. For example, one commentator states: "Peter had not gotten over the stingy bigoted notion of his countrymen,"[7] as an explanation why God had to give Peter a vision to free him from his prejudice. This view not only unjustly judges men who were filled with the Holy Spirit; it contradicts the plain statements of the book that God was sending salvation first of all to the Jews and that He was offering to send Jesus back to establish Israel's Kingdom if they would only repent. A proper understanding of these issues is crucial to a correct interpretation of the book as a whole.

INTRODUCTION

Note Page

1   3. – J. Sidlow Baxter, *Explore the Book* (Grand Rapids, Zondervan Publishing House, 1972), VoL VI, p. 41.

2   3. – Ibid., p. 48

3   3. – Sir Robert Anderson, *The Silence of God* (London, Pickering and Inglis, fourth impression, n.d.), p. 177.

4   4. – Ibid., pp. 84, 85.

5   4. – Ibid., pp. 76, 77.

6   4. – Ibid., p. 54, 55.

7   4. – Matthew Henry, *An Exposition of the Old and New Testament* (New York, Fleming H. Revell Co., n.d.), VoL VI., Acts 10.

Chronology of the Acts Period

The Book of Acts covers a period of transition from the prophesied Jewish Kingdom order to the unprophesied order of the present dispensation. For that reason it is important to recognize the points in time at which changes occur. There is a problem, however, and that is that scholars do not agree on the dates and the order of events, especially in the first half of the book.

We know that the book opens ten days before the Jewish feast of Pentecost, or forty days after the resurrection of Christ (Acts 1:3). However, we cannot be sure of the year. The two most commonly held dates for the crucifixion are 30 and 33 A.D. The Bible is not specific on the exact time of Christ's birth or of His age. Luke in his Gospel gives certain information about political conditions at the time of the birth, (Lk. 2:1,2), from which it is estimated the year was between 6 and 4 B.C. Luke also tells us that Jesus was about thirty years of age when He began His ministry, and since His ministry lasted between three and four years, this would bring His death up to about 30 A.D. However, Hoehner[1] defends quite convincingly the date of 33 A.D.

On a casual reading of the first eleven or twelve chapters of Acts one might suppose all of these events happened within the space of a year or two. However, a considerably longer period of time is involved. For example, scholars place the conversion of Saul anywhere from two to seven years after the opening of the book, and the conversion of Cornelius three to seven years after Saul's conversion.[2] There are some events of secular history, the dates of which are known quite accurately, mentioned in Acts, such as the famine of Acts 11, and the proconsulate of Gallio in Acts 18, which help in dating events in Acts. Also Paul mentions two specific periods, one of three years after his conversion, and another fourteen years after that event in Gal. 1 and 2. But even with these two dates which are related to two of his visits to Jerusalem there are problems.

Paul in Galatians tells us that immediately after his conversion he went into Arabia, then returned to Damascus, and after three years went to Jerusalem to see Peter, with whom he stayed fifteen days. He also saw James, the Lord's brother, but did not see any of the other apostles. Luke in Acts says nothing about Paul going to Arabia, but states that immediately after his conversion he preached Jesus as the Son of God in the synagogues at Damascus, after which the Jews plotted to kill him, but he was saved by being let down in a basket through a window in the wall of the city. He then came to Jerusalem where Barnabas received him and took him to the apostles. After speaking boldly to the Grecians (Greek-speaking Jews), they plotted to kill him, so the brethren took him down to Caesarea and sent him to Tarsus. Because of the difficulty in reconciling these two accounts, some have supposed they refer to two separate visits to Jerusalem. However, when Paul speaks about seeing none of the other apostles, he probably meant that he did not have an extended visit with any of them as he did with Peter and James.

    Paul goes on in Galatians to tell us that fourteen years later he went up to Jerusalem again, taking Barnabas and Titus with him, to settle the question of the relation of the Gentile believers to the law of Moses and circumcision. Since Paul mentions only two visits to Jerusalem and since Acts describes Paul's second visit as taking place in Acts 11, it would appear on the surface that the Galatians 2 visit is identical with that of Acts 11, and that the Galatian epistle was written before Paul's third visit in Acts 15, for he would surely have mentioned the Council of Acts 15 if that event had already taken place. This interpretation of the facts is known as the South Galatian theory. The name "Galatia" was apparently used in two different senses in the first century. It was used geographically to describe the country of Galatia in the northern part of the central plateau of Asia Minor, and it was also used politically to designate a large Roman province which included not only the country of Galatia but also parts of Pontus, Phrygia, Pisidia, Lycaonia, and Isauria. Thus, the South Galatian theory holds that the Galatian epistle was addressed to the churches he established in Perga, Antioch in Pisidia, Iconium, Lystra, and Derbe on his first missionary journey. This theory would logically make Galatians the first epistle which Paul wrote.

    As the name implies, the North Galatian theory holds that the epistle was addressed to churches in Galatia proper, which area Paul did not visit until his second missionary journey. On that journey he revisited the churches in the south which he had established on his first journey, and then we read that when he had gone throughout Phrygia and the region of Galatia, he bypassed Asia and Bithynia and Mysia, and came to Troas (Acts 16:6-8). Then on his third missionary journey he went over all the country of Galatia and Phrygia in order, (Acts 18:23). According to the North Galatian theory, Paul wrote Galatians after this second visit to the north, shortly after writing the Corinthian epistles. The Northern theory identifies the visit of Galatians 2 with Paul's third visit to Jerusalem, that of Acts 15.

Although the South Galatians theory is widely held by scholars today, the view does pose a number of serious problems. If Phrygia was a part of Galatia, why does Luke state that Paul went over all the country of Galatia and Phrygia, (Acts 16:6; 18:23)? This implies that Phrygia was separate and distinct from Galatia. Then there is the problem of reading a great deal into the Acts 11 visit which is not there. The purpose of the Acts 11 visit was to carry famine relief to the Jewish brethren in Judea and it was delivered to the elders at Jerusalem. Barnabas and Saul are the only two mentioned as messengers. When we try to read Gal. 2:1-10 into this visit, we are confronted with numerous problems. Here Paul says nothing about bringing famine relief to Jerusalem, but states his purpose was to communicate to the Jewish Apostles that gospel which he preached among the Gentiles. There is no mention of apostles in Acts 11, but they are prominent in Gal. 2. Titus went with Paul and Barnabas in Gal. 2, but he is not mentioned in Acts 11. In fact, there is a serious question whether Titus was a prominent leader in the church at Antioch. The leaders at Antioch are named in Acts 13:1, but Titus is not in the list. Then, it would seem strange that if Paul had just delivered these relief supplies for the poor saints in Jerusalem that the apostles there would have asked Paul "to remember the poor," (Gal. 2:10). Then further, if the visit of Gal. 2 took place in Acts 11, there is the problem of reconciling the fact that Gal. 2 indicates that Paul had had a widespread Gentile ministry up to that time, when in fact he had not yet been separated unto the ministry for which God had called him (Acts 13:2). There is no record that prior to his first missionary journey Paul had had conflicts with Jewish believers who wanted to impose circumcision on the Gentile believers. In fact, we don't even read of Gentile believers in connection with Paul before Acts 11. It was after his first missionary journey that certain Jewish believers came down from Judea and started teaching the Gentiles at Antioch they had to be circumcised in order to be saved, and it was this fact that precipitated the visit to Jerusalem to settle this matter with the Jerusalem apostles. Finally, there is the question of why the church at Antioch would send Paul and Barnabas back to Jerusalem to settle the question of circumcision in Acts 15, if they had already sent them for that purpose in Acts 11 and had already settled the matter.

The main argument in favor of identifying the Gal. 2 visit with that of Acts 11 is that Paul mentions but two visits in Galatians, whereas if the Acts 15 visit is intended in Gal. 2, it is said that Paul should have mentioned three visits. In other words, Paul omitted the Acts 11 visit in writing to the Galatians. This objection can be answered by asking Paul's motive for mentioning any visits to

Jerusalem. He spoke of these visits in an attempt to prove that he did not get his message of the gospel for the Gentiles from those who were apostles before him, but that he received it directly from Christ. Since the Acts 11 account mentions no contact whatsoever with the apostles in Jerusalem, there would be no reason for Paul's mentioning this visit to prove his point. Therefore we have taken the position, because of the above stated evidences, that the visit of Gal. 2 is to be identified with that of Acts 15.

It should be pointed out that the South Galatian theory does not necessarily force its advocates to identify the Gal. 2 visit with that of Acts 11, although most advocates of this theory do so. One can still hold to the Acts 15 view, as outlined above, and at the same time believe that those addressed were in the southern area of Asia Minor, and that Galatians was written at a later date.

We have mentioned that several dates from secular history are known quite accurately. The date of the famine in Judea when Claudius was emperor of Rome has been set at 45 - 46 A.D. This would fix the date of the first preaching to Gentiles at Antioch in Acts 11. The church at Antioch had been established by Jews who were scattered by the persecution that arose over the stoning of Stephen. We are explicitly told that these Jewish believers preached to none but the Jews only. Hence, the churches they established were entirely Jewish in constituency. Then we are told that certain ones from Cyprus and Cyrene came to Antioch and started preaching to the Greeks. This would be twelve to fifteen years after Pentecost. Those who suppose that the new Gentile dispensation began at Pentecost must be hard put to explain why such a long time elapsed before the Gentile preaching began. One explanation offered is that these Spirit-filled apostles were such bigoted Jews and haters of the Gentiles that they were disobedient to the Lord's command and refused to carry out His commission. Such an argument is self-contradictory on the surface, and is itself contradicted by the fact that these Jewish apostles and believers rejoiced greatly when they received news of the salvation of the Gentiles. It is apparent that during those early years of Acts God was dealing only with the Jews.

Another date from secular history is the procounselship of Gallio in Achaia (Acts 18:12) from 51 to 52 A.D.[3] This was when Paul was in Corinth on his second missionary journey. This would place the beginning of that journey at about 49 or 50 A.D., and since the Council of Acts 15 was held just a few months before that, the same date would apply to that Council. If Paul's conversion took place fourteen years before that Council, it must have occurred around 35 or 36 A.D. To place Paul's conversion fourteen years before his second visit to Jerusalem in Acts 11, would push the date back to 31 or 32 A.D., which would be before Pentecost for those who hold the date for Pentecost at 33 A.D. If we follow the chronological order of the Acts, Paul went to Jerusalem three years after his conversion, and then after that we have the record of the conversion of Cornelius. Adding three years to the date of Paul's conversion would date the conversion of Cornelius at 38 or 39 A.D., or about five or six, or eight or nine years after Pentecost, depending upon how we date Pentecost.

The events of the latter half of Acts, as far as chronology is concerned, are much easier to date, due to the information contained in Paul's epistles written during this time. We will not, therefore, go into a detailed examination of that period. There follows what we believe to be a fairly accurate chronology of some of the major events of the Acts period, along with the dating of Paul's epistles, and a brief note on the post-Acts chronology of Paul's ministry.

CHRONOLOGICAL SUMMARY
OF THE ACTS PERIOD

DATE   EVENTS

30 A.D. — Opening Events; Day of Pentecost; Peter's sermons, Acts
           1-6.
32 A.D. — Stoning of Stephen, Acts 7.
33 A.D. — Disciples scattered; they preach in Judea and Samaria,
           Acts 8.
35 A.D. — Conversion of Saul, Acts 9. He ministers in Damascus to
           the Jews who seek to kill him. After three years he
           escapes from the city and goes to Jerusalem.
           Sometime during those three years he went to
           Arabia and returned to Damascus, (Gal. 1:16-18).
38 A.D. — Saul's first visit to Jerusalem after his conversion. He stays
           15 days with Peter, according to Gal. 1:18. This
           fact is not mentioned in Acts. After preaching
           boldly to the Greek-speaking Jews, they seek to
           kill him. The disciples take him to Caesaria and
           send him back to Tarsus.
38-45 A.D. — Saul preaches in Syria and Cilicia, (Gal. 1:21). No
           record in Acts of his ministry during these years.
40 A.D. — Peter goes on preaching tour to Lydda, Joppa, and
           Caesaria, where Cornelius, Peter's first Gentile
           convert, is saved, Acts 9:32-10:48.
45 A.D. — Reception of Gentile converts into the Jewish church at
           Antioch, Acts 11:19-21. Barnabas is sent to investi-
           gate the situation. He goes to Tarsus to find Saul;
           brings him back to minister at Antioch, Acts
           11:22-26.
46 A.D. — Barnabas and Saul sent to Jerusalem with famine-relief
           from the church at Antioch. This is Saul's second
           visit to Jerusalem after his conversion, Acts
           11:27-30; 12:25.
47-48 A.D. — Saul and Barnabas sent on first missionary journey,
           Acts 13:1-14:25. They went to Cyprus, where
           Saul's name is changed to Paul; then to Perga, to
           Antioch in Pisidia, where Paul for the first time
           officially turns from the Jews to the Gentiles. They
           continue to Iconium and Lystra, and then retrace
           their steps to Antioch in Syria.

49 A.D. — Paul goes to Jerusalem for his third visit, this time to settle the question of Gentile freedom from the Mosaic Law and Circumcision, Acts 15:1-29; Gal. 2:1-10. He and Barnabas return to Antioch with a letter for the Gentiles, accompanied by Judas and Silas, Acts 15:30-35.

50-52 A.D. — Paul's second missionary journey. Going from Antioch he traveled through Cilicia, Lycaonia, Galatia, to Troas, Philippi, Thessalonica, Berea, Athens, and Corinth, Acts 15:36-18:18.

51 A.D. — Gallio becomes proconsul of Achaia in July, cf. Acts 18:12.

51 A.D. — Paul writes the Thessalonian epistles from Corinth, 1 Thess. 3:1, 2 cf., Acts 18:5.

52 A.D. — After spending a year and a half in Corinth, he stopped briefly in Ephesus and then hasted to Jerusalem to keep the feast. This was his fourth visit since his conversion. He then returned to Antioch, Acts 18:18-22.

52 A.D. — Paul begins his third missionary journey. He went over all the country of Galatia and Phrygia, and having passed through the interior of Asia Minor, he came to Ephesus, where he labored for three years, cf. Acts 20:31.

54 A.D. — Paul wrote 1 Corinthians from Ephesus, cf. 1 Cor. 16:5-8.

55 A.D. — Paul departed from Ephesus to go to Macedonia, and having gone over those parts he came into Greece. It is probable that he went as far as Illyricum, cf. Rom. 15:19, which may have taken another year. While in Macedonia he wrote 2 Corinthians. He then went back to Corinth, cf. 2 Cor. 2:12,13, from which place it is thought he wrote Galatians.

56 A.D. — Paul wrote Romans, cf. Rom. 15:25.

57 A.D. — Leaving Corinth, Paul went through Macedonia to Philippi, and thence to Troas, Acts 20:3-6. Taking a ship from Troas he sailed for Judea in order to keep the feast of Pentecost in Jerusalem.

57 A.D. — Paul's arrival and arrest in Jerusalem.

57-59 A.D. — Paul kept in prison at Caesarea, Acts 24:27.

59 A.D. — Paul begins his trip to Rome for his trial.

60 A.D. — Paul arrives in Rome, after the shipwreck and the winter in Malta, Acts 28:1-11.

60-61 A.D. — Paul writes Ephesians, Philippians, Colossians, and Philemon while awaiting his trial.

61 A.D. — Paul's trial before Caesar and his acquittal and release from prison. This bring us to the end of the Book of Acts.

POST-ACTS CHRONOLOGY

61-64 A.D. — Paul's final journeys. Acts does not state that Paul was acquitted, but there is strong evidence that he was. In Phil. 1:19,24,25, written while awaiting his trial, Paul expresses great confidence that he will be delivered and spared for further ministry with them. And in Phile. 22, written at the same time, Paul asks Philemon to arrange lodgings for him, as he expects to be given back to the believers through their prayers. Again, in Phil. 2:19-24 Paul dispatches Timothy to Philippi and states: "But I trust in the Lord that I also myself shall come shortly."

There is no record in Acts that Paul established a church in Crete, yet in Tit. 1:5 he states that he had left Titus in charge of the work in Crete. This visit of Paul and Titus to Crete must have occurred after the end of the Acts. Likewise, in Tit. 3:12 we learn that Paul had determined to spend the winter in Nicopolis and wanted Titus to meet him there. Again there is no mention of Nicopolis in the Book of Acts. We believe that 1 Timothy and Titus were written after Paul's release from prison and tell of his subsequent ministry. Paul was not in prison when he wrote these two epistles.

2 Timothy was written when Paul was again in prison in Rome. He knows now that his execution is imminent. We don't know where or why he was arrested, but some commentators think it might have been at Troas, for he had left his winter garment, along with his books and parchments there, and this suggests that he might have been unable to take these things with him when he was whisked away by the authorities. We do know that the terrible persecution of the Christians by Nero had scattered the believers from Rome and that at Paul's first defense in court there was no one to witness in his behalf: all had forsaken him. Only Luke remained faithful to the very end. We can

only hope that Timothy was able to reach Rome and cheer Paul's heart before his execution.

65 A.D. — Outbreak of the Jewish War.

70 A.D. — Jerusalem sacked by Titus; thousands of Jews were slain, and the city was completely destroyed.

NOTE: Some of the dates in this chronology are only approximate, and may vary by as much as two or three years.

CHRONOLOGY

Note Page

1   6. — Howard W. Hoehner, *Chronological Aspects of the Life of Christ* (Grand Rapids, Zondervan Publishing House, 1977).

2   6. — The following books contain chronological tables of the Acts period: *Chronology of the Life of Paul* by George Ogg; *Bible Handbook* by Henry Halley; *The Companion Bible,* Appendix 180; *The Greek Testament,* Vol. II, by Henry Alford; *The Acts of the Apostles* by F.F. Bruce; *Jerusalem to Rome* by Homer A. Kent, Jr.

3   9. — George Ogg, *Chronology of the Life of Paul* (London, Epworth Press, 1968), pp. 104-111.

SECTION ONE

The Gospel to the Jews Only

Chapters 1-9

I. PRE-PENTECOST EVENTS, 1:1-26.

A. *Introduction to the Book,* 1:1-5. The "former treatise," of which Luke speaks is the Gospel of Luke. It would seem that the "present treatise" must have been composed shortly after the last event recorded in it (Paul's imprisonment in Rome), otherwise we would have expected that Luke would have told us of further events in Paul's life and ministry, for he was apparently released from prison and continued his missionary journeys until his final imprisonment and execution. This would mean that Luke wrote his Gospel sometime during the Acts period.

Luke alone tells us that the period between the resurrection and the ascension was forty days. We are not told where Jesus was during those forty days; only that He did appear to His disciples several times during that period. However, while the fortieth day marked the last appearance of Jesus on earth, it was not the last time He was seen. Stephen saw Him at the right hand of God while he was being stoned to death (Acts 7:55,56), and Paul states that "last of all he was seen of me," (1 Cor. 15:8). Paul did not receive his revelations simply through the prophetic gift of the Holy Spirit, but by the personal appearance of the Lord Jesus who revealed to Paul the glorious truths which are embodied in his epistles (Gal. 1:12).

It has been said that the resurrection of Jesus Christ is one of the best attested facts in ancient history. Luke says He showed Himself alive by "many infallible proofs." One example of this can be seen in Luke 24:39-43. Apart from the resurrection of Christ there could be no salvation. That is why such great emphasis is placed upon it throughout Acts and the epistles (Rom. 4:25; 10:9; 1 Cor. 15:1-4, 14-19).

The Apostles were to wait in Jerusalem for the promised sending of the Holy Spirit. They did not tarry there until they became spiritual enough to receive the Spirit. God had a time-table with Israel, and ten days after Christ spoke these words the feast of Pentecost occurred, which typically had pointed forward to this great event. Pentecost means "fifty or fiftieth." This feast came fifty days after Passover (Lev. 23:15-21). God has never commanded anyone since Acts 1:4 to tarry in order to receive the Holy Spirit. People today receive the Holy Spirit and are sealed by the Holy Spirit the very moment they believe the Gospel (Eph. 1:13 – N.I.V.).

B. *The Final Commission,* 1:6-8. What is sometimes called "the Great Commission" is to be found at the end of each of the four Gospels. Actually during the forty days Christ commissioned the Apostles on several occasions. The question which the Apostles asked just before the giving of this final order is very revealing. Jesus had already told them to go into all the world and preach the Gospel, and that those who believed and were baptized would be saved, but those who did not believe would be lost. What did the disciples believe this witness of theirs would lead up to? Their question gives the answer. "Lord, wilt thou at this time restore again the Kingdom to Israel?" This is why we call this the Kingdom Commission. Jesus had taught them that He was going to restore the Kingdom to Israel and He told them to pray for that Kingdom to come. Was it now finally time for the Kingdom to be realized? Jesus could not answer their question at that time, for there was a very important condition which had to be fulfilled before that Kingdom could come. It was not for them to know the times and seasons which the Father had put in His own power. As we shall see in the third chapter, that condition was Israel's national repentance and acceptance of Jesus Christ as their Messiah and King. It would seem that by the time Paul wrote his first epistle there was further knowledge about the times and seasons, for by that time the Jews had given their final answer of rejection of Christ (1 Th. 2:14-16; 5:1).

Several descriptions of what would happen at Pentecost are given. Here Jesus says they will receive power. Three verses earlier He said they would be baptized with the Holy Spirit. In Luke 24:49 He said they would be endued with power from on high. There is no statement or intimation that they would be baptized into the Body of Christ (1 Cor. 12:13). The baptism at Pentecost was an enduement with power to witness and to perform miraculous works. This power, as we shall see, was an open, manifest, physical display of power.

The apostles were to bear witness to the same Kingdom Gospel they had been proclaiming while Christ was on earth. There was to be a definite order of progression. They were to begin at Jerusalem, the capital of Israel, where the Temple was

located, and then cover all Judea, next cover the northern
kingdom, Samaria, and finally to the Gentiles in the uttermost
parts of the earth. This plan was strictly in keeping with
Christ's earlier instruction: "the children (of Israel) must first
be filled before the Gentiles were to be blessed" (Mk. 7:27).
That is the reason Christ forbad His disciples to preach at that
time to the Gentiles (Matt. 10:5,6). There is no such
stipulated order given in the epistles addressed to the Church
of this dispensation.

C. *The Ascension,* 1:9-11. Just as the resurrection was bodily in
character, so was the ascension into heaven. He was taken up
bodily. The disciples saw Him ascend bodily into heaven.
Luke in his Gospel tells us the place from which He ascended
(Lk. 24:50). Bethany was a village fifteen furlongs from
Jerusalem at the Mount of Olives (Lk. 19:29). The angels told
the disciples that Jesus would return from heaven just as they
had seen Him go into heaven. The O.T. prophet tells us that
when Jesus returns His feet will stand on the Mount of Olives
(Zech. 14:4). It is interesting to note that when the glory
departed from the temple in the days of Ezekiel, the glory
cloud departed from its place between the cherubim to the
threshold of the temple; and then departed from the temple,
and from the city itself to the mount on the east of Jerusalem,
which is the Mount of Olives (Ezek. 9:3; 10:4; 11:23). Ezekiel
also foretold the return of the glory of the Lord, that it would
come from the east of Jerusalem, enter the gate on the east of
the city, enter and fill the temple (Ezek. 43:1-5). Jesus Christ
is the Glory of God. Rejected, as in Ezekiel's day, He left the
temple, went out to the Mount of Olives and ascended into
heaven. Some day He will return to that same Mount and
enter Jerusalem and establish His glorious Kingdom with
Israel.

D. *Successor of Judas Chosen,* 1:12-26. Putting together the
account of Matt. 27:3-10 with the Acts account we learn that
Judas in deep remorse after betraying Jesus went out and
hanged himself. His decomposing body must have fallen on
the rocks below and burst open. Judas did not personally
purchase the field which became a burying place for strangers,
but the thirty pieces of silver, the betrayal money, which he
returned to the priests, was used by them for this purpose. It
was blood money and the priests could not return it to the
temple treasury.
    On returning to Jerusalem the eleven apostles with the
other disciples, about one hundred and twenty in all, met in

an upper room. After fellowshipping in prayer Peter arose and stated that the Scripture had to be fulfilled which predicted Judas' betrayal of Jesus (Ps. 41:9), and that the Psalms also instructed that another man should be appointed to take the place of Judas (Ps. 69:25; 109:8). Therefore it was necessary to appoint one to fill out the number of Twelve Apostles—one who had been with them from the baptism of John to the time of the ascension. Two men were nominated; they cast lots, and the lot fell on Matthias.

There are those who think Peter made a mistake in this action and that later on God corrected it by appointing Paul as the Twelfth Apostle. But nothing could be farther from the truth. Paul is never identified as one of the Twelve in Scripture. Acts 2:14 and 6:2 clearly include Matthias as one of the Twelve. Would the Holy Spirit who inspired the Scripture have recognized him as an apostle if he were not? Paul plainly distinguishes himself as separate from the Twelve (1 Cor. 15:5). Peter was evidently divinely enlightened in interpreting these Psalms concerning Judas. Jesus had breathed upon them, giving them the Holy Spirit (John 20:22). Can we imagine him blundering under such circum-stances? Paul could not have measured up to the qualifications for the Twelfth Apostle, for he had never been with the other apostles during Christ's ministry.

Some suppose that Peter was depending upon chance instead of the Holy Spirit in casting lots. But over a hundred times in the Bible the means by which God made known His will to Israel was by casting lots. (See Lev. 16:8; Josh. 18:6,8; Neh. 10:34; Prov. 16:33.) Even in the coming kingdom the land is going to be divided by lot (Ezek. 45:1; 47:22; 48:29). There is no statement that God ever changed this method for His people Israel.

The Twelve are going to sit on twelve thrones judging the twelve Tribes in the Kingdom. Paul will not be on one of those Israelitish thrones. He will be with the heavenly Body of Christ. It is a serious mistake to confuse Paul with the Twelve. Paul is the one new Apostle of the one New Man, the Church which is the Body of Christ.

II. PETER'S MINISTRY IN JERUSALEM, 2:1-7;60.

A. *The Day of Pentecost,* 2:1-13. Just as Christ was put to death at the time of the Passover Feast when the passover lambs were sacrificed, just so the Holy Spirit came upon these believing Israelites fifty days later at the Feast of Pentecost.

The Holy Spirit was not poured out because the disciples had attained a state of super-spirituality, but simply because the set time for His coming had arrived. They were to tarry in Jerusalem, not in order that the Holy Spirit might come, but because it was His time to come.

This outpouring of the Spirit which is called a baptism with the Spirit was something that had been promised to Israel since the days of Moses. Every year for 1500 years Israel had celebrated this feast which looked forward to this most important event. This long-promised event should not be confused with another work of the Spirit which is also called a baptism and which results in the formation of the Body of Christ (1 Cor. 12:13). This latter work of the Spirit had never been promised, but is related to that which Paul calls a mystery or secret. This latter work of the Spirit is what we might call "non-experiential." When the Spirit baptizes a person into the Body of Christ upon believing the Gospel, the believer does not sense or feel any experience. The only way he knows it has occurred is that Paul's epistles tell him the Spirit has done this work. But in contrast to this, the baptizing work of the Spirit at Pentecost was completely experiential. There was the sound of a mighty rushing wind, such as that of a tornado; there was the visible appearance of a flame of fire which separated into smaller flames and which sat upon each of the believers. And then there was the miraculous gift of tongues or languages, so that when the disciples spoke the Jews from over the whole known world heard them speaking in the languages in which they had been born. With such great contrasts between these two works of the Spirit it is difficult to understand how anyone could confuse them.

Pentecost had great significance for Israel. While Christ was on earth the Holy Spirit had not yet been given (John 7:39). The rulers rejected Christ in ignorance (Lk. 23:34), and now God sends the Holy Spirit to enlighten them so that what they do is no longer in ignorance. Peter develops this theme in his second sermon in chapter 3, as we shall see when we come to that section. Pentecost was a miraculous demonstration of signs and wonders. God's manner of dealing with Israel was always through outward signs and wonders, from the day He brought them out of Egypt. God's dealings through signs are mentioned about 140 times in the Bible (Deut. 26:8 cf. 1 Cor. 1:22; 14:22). God does not work through signs in this dispensation of faith today. He does not cause the sun to stand still while we fight our enemies, or turn walking sticks into serpents, or cause the clocks to run backwards, or give

His servants power to call up swarms of frogs or flies or lice, or to turn the rivers into blood. But Jesus in His commission to these disciples just a few days before Pentecost said: "And these signs shall follow them that believe; In my name they shall cast out demons; they shall speak with new tongues; they shall take up serpents; and if they drink any deadly thing, it shall not hurt them; they shall lay hands on the sick, and they shall recover" (Mk. 16:17,18). Also Pentecost was one feast the Jews did not want to miss. They came from great distances to be in Jerusalem on this notable day. Fourteen different countries are mentioned from which these Jews came. Thus it was an occasion when the greatest number of Jews could be reached with the Gospel of the Kingdom. And through the gift of tongues every Jew could clearly understand the message for he heard it in the language of the country in which he was born.

Surely these Jews were now without excuse if they rejected Jesus as their Messiah. God authenticated the message by signs and wonders. The Old Testament is replete with promises concerning this outpouring of the Holy Spirit (cf. Isa. 32:15; 44:3; Ezek. 36:26,27; 37:14; 39:29; Joel 2:28,29). The prophet had also predicted that God would speak to Israel in other tongues, as a sign of their kingdom promises, (Isa. 28:11,12), as Paul himself reminds us in 1 Cor. 14:21. The outpouring of the Spirit, the speaking in tongues, and the removal of the physical effects of sin through miraculous healings were all a foretaste of the coming Kingdom. The writer to the Hebrews not only interprets the miracles of Pentecost as a foretaste of the coming millennial age, but he shows the impossibility of renewing to repentance those who were thus enlightened by the Holy Spirit.

"For it is impossible for those who were once enlightened, and have tasted the heavenly gift, and were made partakers of the Holy Spirit, and have tasted the good word of God, and the powers of the age to come (the millennial kingdom), if they shall fall away, to renew them again unto repentance, seeing they crucify to themselves the Son of God afresh, and put Him to an open shame" (6:4-6).

When the multitude of Jews came together and witnessed all that God was doing on that day, we read that they were amazed and were in doubt of what the meaning of all of this could be. But others in the crowd accused the disciples of being drunk with new wine. This accusation gave Peter the opportunity to preach his famous Pentecostal sermon.

B. *Peter's Sermon at Pentecost,* 2:14-42.

1. *Those Addressed:* "Ye men of Judah, and ye that dwell at Jerusalem " (v. 14).
"Ye men of Israel " (v. 22).
"Men and brethren " (v. 29).
"The promise is to you and your children " (v. 39).

It is abundantly clear that no Gentiles were addressed by Peter. It is true that there were some proselytes present, but these were Gentiles who had become Jews by religion, (cf. 1:10). Such adherents are not to be confused with Gentiles as such. It was possible for Gentiles to become Jews (cf. Esther 8:17).

2. *Time of the Sermon:* The third hour of the day," (v. 15), that is, nine o'clock in the morning. Peter states this fact in proof that the disciples were not drunk. People do not get drunk the first thing in the morning. Paul says, "They that be drunken are drunken in the night" (1 Thess. 5:7).

3. *Pentecost the Fulfillment of Prophecy:* Peter states very plainly, "This is that which was spoken by the prophet Joel." He does not say, "This is somewhat similar to what Joel prophesied." If Pentecost was what Joel predicted, then it is plain that Pentecost was the beginning of the last days, those days which would immediately precede the coming of the Lord to judge the world and to establish His glorious kingdom. There are those who say that Peter supposed what was happening was predicted by Joel, but actually he was mistaken, for God was instead beginning something brand new which none of the prophets knew anything about, namely, the beginning of an entirely new dispensation of the Church which is the Body of Christ. We must leave it up to the individual student to decide whether Peter, filled with the Holy Spirit, was mistaken. One thing is certain: God was not fulfilling prophecy and beginning the Body of Christ at the same time.

The question arises, if God was fulfilling Joel's prophecy, why did not the signs appear in the heavens and why did Christ not come back to establish His Kingdom? The answer should not be difficult to find. It was evidently because the rulers of Israel hardened themselves in their unbelief and opposition to Christ. Again, this aspect of the narrative will be developed more fully in considering Peter's second sermon.

4. *The Resurrection of Christ Attested:* Both Peter and Paul (Acts 13:35) quoted Ps. 16:10 as Scriptural evidence of the resurrection of Christ. Peter accuses Israel of having slain Christ by wicked hands, but on the other hand states that His death was according to the determinate counsel and foreknowledge of God. The fact that God fore-ordained that His Son should be delivered up to death in no way relieves the guilt of those who perpetrated the deed. There are those who would make man an irresponsible puppet in God's hand if God foreordained or foreknew whatever comes to pass. If man has no freedom of choice he has no responsibility, and if he has no responsibility then he cannot in justice be held account-able for his deeds. But man will be held accountable and will be judged. Christ said concerning His betrayer: "Good were it for that man if he had never been born" (Mk. 14:21).

Although it was possible for man to put Christ to death, it was not possible that death could hold Him as its captive. The primary reason is that He was the Son of God. But the reason Peter gives is that the Word of God expressly declared that God would not leave His soul in Hades, nor allow His flesh to see corruption. If we think of hell as the lake of fire, then Hades, the word used here, is an entirely different place. Christ's soul did not go to the lake of fire. As far as we know no one has yet been cast into the lake of fire. Christ's soul went to Hades, the unseen place of the dead. After the final resurrection of the unsaved dead Hades will be cast into the lake of fire (Rev. 20:14).

After Peter has used Ps. 16 as evidence of the resurrection of Christ he goes on to show that David could not have been speaking about himself when he wrote that Psalm, for he says that David has been dead and buried for a thousand years and that his tomb with David's moldering body is right here in the city of David. Therefore David, being a prophet, spoke about the resurrection of Christ. When Peter states that David has not ascended into the heavens, he is not saying that David's soul is sleeping with his body in the grave. He is speaking about a bodily ascension into heaven. No one could ascend thus into heaven until after the resurrection. Thus the resurrection and ascension of Jesus Christ become the main burden of the Apostles' preaching.

5. *The Invitation:* At the end of an evangelistic sermon an

invitation is usually given. In this case the audience asked
for it. When they heard that this Jesus whom they had
crucified as a blasphemer had been raised from the dead
and had ascended to the right hand of God and had been
made both Lord and Messiah, they cried out: "Men and
brethren, what shall we do?" Peter's answer is plain and
concise: "Repent (change your mind), and be baptized
every one of you in the name of Jesus Christ for the
remission of sins, and ye shall receive the gift of the Holy
Spirit. For the promise is unto you and to your children,
and to all that are afar off, even as many as the Lord our
God shall call." Peter's answer is almost identical with that
of John the Baptist, except that, between John and Peter,
Christ's death and resurrection have taken place (cf. Lk.
3:3-14).

Practically all Christians agree that Jesus Christ is the
Savior, but there is great difference of belief on how one
receives that salvation. Acts 2:38 becomes a very
important text in this regard. Some contend for baptismal
regeneration. That is, they believe that water baptism has
in itself the power to convey salvation. Others, that while
baptism is essential to salvation, baptism does not effect
salvation, but is only like a door which one must pass
through to reach Christ who does the saving. Still others
say that in the light of Paul's epistles we cannot take Acts
2:38 literally, but that we must understand Acts 2:38 to
mean that one must believe and receive the Holy Spirit
before he is a candidate for baptism. Others, using the
same basic premise, argue that the baptism in this verse
must be Holy Spirit baptism, since the baptism in this
verse effects salvation and from Paul's writings we know
that water baptism cannot accomplish this result. Finally,
there are those who interpret Acts 2:38 in the light of
God's covenant dealings with the nation of Israel. At the
time of Acts 2:38 Israel was still in active covenant
relationship with God. There was a vast difference between
Israelites and Gentiles (cf. Eph. 2:11,12). Peter in Acts
3:25 plainly states that those he was addressing were
"children of the covenant." Under the covenant the nation
of Israel enjoyed a special place of privilege and priority
over other nations of the earth. They were called the elect,
the chosen people of God, whereas Jesus referred to
Gentiles as dogs (Mk. 7:27). Peter, as John the Baptist did
before him, was calling these covenant people back to a
right relationship with God, so that He would not suspend
His covenant relationship with them. Under the covenant

God gave Israel various sacrifices and ceremonial washings, which are called baptisms in the New Testament (cf. Heb. 9:10 where divers washings should be translated "various baptisms"). The animal sacrifices and the various baptisms did not save the Israelites, in the sense that we today usually think of salvation as a regenerating work of changing a spiritually dead sinner into a living Child of God. However these sacrifices and other rituals were demanded by God and if they were not performed, such individuals were cut off from the covenant people. For examples see Gen. 17:14; Ex. 12:15,19; 31:14; Lev. 7:20; 17:4,9,10; 19:8; 23:19; Num. 9:13; 15:30,31; 19:13,20. The Israelites practised these things, not in order to become children of the covenant, but because they were children of the covenant. But individually, if they did not practise them they would be cut off from the covenant. This is what was happening in Acts 2:38. The nation had crucified their Messiah. Peter is calling them to repent of this deed and to be baptized in order to be cleansed; otherwise they would be cut off along with what he calls "this untoward or perverse generation." Those who refused baptism were cut off from the covenant. Acts 2:38 plainly teaches Jews had to be water-baptized before they could receive the Holy Spirit. Only the extremely ritualistic would agree with such preaching for today. Applying this verse to the present is a grave mistake that has brought great doctrinal confusion into Christendom. We do not need to change Paul's teachings for the Body of Christ to conform to Acts 2:38, nor do we have to change Acts 2:38 to agree with Paul's teaching. We should leave both intact and let both mean exactly what they say. Paul's theology for this dispensation is not covenant theology.

Two further remarks should be made on this section. The promise of v. 39 is confined to Israel. "Those that are far off" are not Gentiles but the scattered children of Israel. The reference is to Dan. 9:7: "O Lord, righteousness belongeth unto thee, but unto us confusion of faces, as at this day; to the men of Judah, and to the inhabitants of Jerusalem, and unto all Israel, that are near and that are far off, through all the countries whither thou hast driven them, because of their trespass that they have trespassed against thee."

The other point is that those who gladly received Peter's word were baptized "and that same day there were added unto them about three thousand souls." It should be noted that there is not the slightest intimation that these first ones to be baptized at Pentecost were formed into an entirely new entity, the Body of Christ. They were added to those Jewish Kingdom saints, the ones saved during the earthly ministry of Christ. There was no Gentile as such preached to until Acts 10, which was at least seven or eight years after Pentecost.

These Pentecostal believers constituted the remnant of Israel which is referred to in the Old Testament in numerous places. The word remnant means a small remaining number. The remaining number does not refer to the total number of Jews who remain in the world, but to the number of Jews who have remained faithful to God out of the entire nation. Another name for them would be "the believing remnant." This is the sense in which Paul uses the word in Rom. 11:5. In the days of Elijah the remnant consisted of several thousand Israelites who had not bowed the knee to Baal. This remnant was only a small fraction of the nation. Likewise Paul states: "Even so at the present time also there is a remnant according to the election of grace . . . What then? Israel hath not obtained that which he seeketh for; but the election (remnant) hath obtained it, and the rest were blinded." Jesus called the remnant of His day "the little flock," to whom it was the Father's good pleasure to give the Kingdom (Lk. 12:32). The 144,000 will comprise the remnant during the coming Tribulation, when God again takes up His dealings with Israel (Rev. 7:3-8). After that, when the Kingdom is established "all Israel will be saved" (Rom. 11:26), that is, the whole nation, and not merely a remnant, as in the past. This does not mean that every Israelite then alive or who has ever lived will be saved. It means that after the unbelieving Israelites have been judged and cut off, all who remain to comprise the Millennial nation of Israel will be saved.

6. *All Things Common,* 2:43-47: All of these Jewish believers sold their possessions and shared everything equally with others. This was a true communism, far different from what is called communism in Marxist controlled countries such as Russia and China. These governments are actually dictatorships, and atheistic to the core. Many attempts have been made by Christian groups down through the centuries to duplicate this Acts 2 type of communism, but none of them has succeeded for any length of time, simply because such a system can only succeed if every member is

completely controlled by the Holy Spirit of God, as these Jewish believers were at Pentecost. Verse 4 of this chapter states that they were ALL filled with the Holy Spirit. There does not exist today, nor has there ever existed since that early Pentecostal era a church or a society of which it could be said, "they were or are ALL filled with the Holy Spirit." This miraculous outpouring of the Holy Spirit was a fulfillment of Old Testament prophecies made to Israel. It is a condition which will prevail in the Millennial Kingdom. Many of the Kingdom promises speak of this miraculous outpouring of the Spirit: (cf. Isa. 32:15; 44:3; Ezek. 37:14; 39:29; 36:26,27). The last reference is especially significant, for it states: "And I will put my Spirit within you, and CAUSE YOU to walk in my statutes, and ye shall keep my judgments, and do them." The entire context should be studied carefully, but the important point to understand is that at Pentecost God took complete possession of these Jewish believers and CAUSED them to do God's will. As we shall see later on, this condition broke down when God began turning away from Israel in preparation for bringing in the new dispensation of the Body of Christ.

It should also be noted that these Jewish believers "continued daily with one accord in the TEMPLE." The Holy Spirit did not lead them to forsake the Israelitish temple. Jesus called the temple "My Father's House" (John 2:16). The fact that the Spirit-filled Jewish believers continued daily in the temple is evidence that God had not yet disowned that house. This is just one more evidence that Pentecost was a part and parcel of God's program with Israel in bringing to pass events associated with the earthly, millennial kingdom.

The word "church" appears for the first time in Acts in vs. 47: "And the Lord added to the church daily such as should be saved." (In the Revised Greek Text the word appears for the first time in 5:11.) It is a pity that the translators chose to use this word to render the Greek word "ekklesia," which means "a called out assembly." It is the word used to describe what is called "the congregation, assembly, company, multitude" in the Old Testament. The word "church" comes from a Greek word meaning "belonging to the Lord." Since the cattle on a thousand hills belong to the Lord, the cattle could be called the church. Everything that belongs to the Lord is the church. The English word "church" may mean a building, or a whole denomination, any kind of religious sect, Christian or anti-Christian, a group of people who meet for religious services, or universally, all Christians everywhere. The fact that the word "church" appears here has given some people the impression that the present day church, the Body of Christ, began at Pentecost. There was an Israelitish church at Pentecost but there is no statement that it began there. Christ called His disciples "the church" in Matt. 18:17, and it was to this church believers were added at Pentecost. However, from Paul's epistles we learn that in the present dispensation God is calling out a separate and distinct assembly of believers which He calls the Body of Christ. The facts about this outcalling, he says, were kept secret from men in past generations and are the burden of the special revelation given to the Apostle of the Gentiles. It is not simply a continuation of the Israelitish, Kingdom outcalling with its earthly, millennial destination: it is an outcalling separate from Israel and Israel's covenant, having a heavenly destination.

C. *Events Leading up to Peter's Second Sermon,* 3:1-11. As we have seen the disciples continued daily in the Temple. On the day now before us Peter and John were coming to the temple at the hour of prayer, which was 3:00 o'clock in the afternoon. As they came to the Beautiful Gate of the temple they passed a beggar who had been lame from birth. The beggar asked them for a handout. Peter told the man they didn't have any money, but what they did have they would give him. Then Peter commanded him in the name of Jesus Christ of Nazareth to rise up and walk. Immediately his feet and ankle bones were restored and he leaped up and entered the temple with them, all the while jumping and running and praising God. He aroused so much attention that crowds began to gather around them in Solomon's porch, greatly amazed: since they recognized the beggar as the one who had been laid at the Beautiful Gate for so many years. With the man holding on to Peter and John, Peter saw his opportunity to tell the crowds actually what had happened.

This miracle no doubt has a typical significance. The man who was lame from birth is representative of the nation of Israel. Throughout its fifteen centuries of history we see Israel's inability to measure up to God's standards. And just as the man needed a miraculous restoration, so the nation needed to be made whole, and that, of course, became the topic of Peter's sermon: "the times of the restoration of all things." The condition of mankind under sin is depicted in several ways in Scripture: as being sick, as being without strength, as being in the dark, as being spiritually dead in trespasses and sins.

D. *Peter's Second Sermon,* 3:12-26.

1. *Why the Gospel to Israel First?* We notice first of all that Peter addresses his message to "Ye men of Israel," just as he addressed his Pentecostal sermon (v. 12 cf. 2:14,22,36). Peter also stated that the message of salvation was being sent to the nation of Israel first of all, (3:26). But why, if the nation of Israel had rejected Jesus Christ and had turned Him over to the Romans to crucify, would God choose to send salvation first of all to Israel? And why, if Pentecost marked the beginning of the new "Joint-Body" of Jews and Gentiles, as many suppose, did God restrict the message to Jews only for a number of years? Peter answers these questions in verse 17. He says, "I understand that through ignorance you did it," that is, you rejected and crucified your Messiah. When Jesus prayed for Israel as He hung upon the cross He said, "Father, forgive them; they know not what they are doing," (Lk. 23:34). If they didn't know, they were ignorant, and God took into account their ignorance, and He answered the prayer of Jesus for their forgiveness. In our judgment the Jews were not ignorant of who Jesus was, but God saw that their minds were blinded in unbelief. However, when the Holy Spirit was poured out upon Israel, His convicting power (John 16:8) left them without excuse. Their sin against the Son of man was forgivable, but not their sin against the Holy Spirit (Matt. 12:31,32). While the message of salvation was being sent to the Jew first, it is evident that it was being sent to the Jew only. Wherever we find God's message going to the Jew first, we may safely conclude that the message concerns Israel's earthly Kingdom program. When Paul wrote to the Romans that the gospel of Christ was "the power of God unto salvation to every one that believes: to the Jew first, and also to the Greek," (Rom. 1:16), he did not mean that it was at that time going to the Jew first, for had that been true it could not have been going to the Greeks also. Historically, it did go to the Jew first. Under the Kingdom program the Jews must first be filled before the message can go to the Gentiles, (Mark 7:27). No such rule holds for the present dispensation of the grace of God.

2. *All Now Fulfilled:* Peter began his sermon by explaining it

was not through any power of holiness on their part that this cripple had been healed, but rather it was through the power of Jesus, the Holy and Just One, the Prince of Life, whom they denied and killed. But no miracle could have been performed by a dead man; therefore the healing of this lame man was proof that Jesus was alive, that God had raised Him from the dead.

Peter then established the fact of Israel's sin of ignorance in crucifying their Messiah. But ignorance is not an excuse. Sins of ignorance are sins nevertheless, and must be repented of (Lev. 4:13,22; 5:1-5). People are not automatically forgiven just because they were ignorant of their wrong-doing. Christ died for the sins of the whole world, but that does not mean that everyone is thereby saved. There must be the recognition of sin and the reception of Christ before there is salvation. Just so, Israel must now repent if they are to be forgiven.

Peter then states that everything which the prophets of old had predicted concerning the sufferings of the Messiah had been fulfilled. If all of these prophecies have been fulfilled, what is next on God's program? Is there anything else in prophecy that is yet to be fulfilled? Christ Himself had summed up all prophecy under two heads: the sufferings of the Christ, and the glory that should follow, (Lk. 24:25,26). Peter, in his first epistle, also develops this two-fold theme, (1:11). The sufferings refer to Christ's first coming to earth, and the glory refers to His second coming to earth to establish His Kingdom.

3. *The Kingdom Offered:* Since the prophecies concerning the sufferings of Christ have been fulfilled, Peter goes on to say: "Therefore repent and be converted, so that your sins may be blotted out, so that the times of refreshing may come from the presence of the Lord, so that He may send the Christ appointed for you, even Jesus; whom the heavens must receive, until the times of the restoration of all things, which God hath spoken by the mouth of all his holy prophets since the world began." These words refer to the second coming of Christ, which will usher in the restoration of all things: not all things without exception, including the Devil, but all things spoken of by the prophets. The message to Israel is, "Repent, so that God may send back Jesus to you." This, of course, did not mean that Jesus would instantly return if they repented, for the Scripture teaches that there will be a period of great tribulation before He actually returns (Matt.

24:1-31). Thus, it seems clear that God is here offering to send Jesus back to restore Israel's Kingdom conditioned upon their national repentance.

Many dispensationalists teach that Jesus offered the Kingdom to Israel during His earthly ministry. It is true that the Kingdom was at hand during that time (Matt. 4:17; 10:7), but it could not have been actually offered until after the prophecies concerning Christ's death had been fulfilled. That is why Peter begins vs. 19 with "Therefore." Now the prophecies concerning Messiah's sufferings have been fulfilled. What is next on the prophetic program? The glory of His second coming. Therefore repent, so that God may send Him back. We call this the offer of the Kingdom to Israel.[1]

Of course, God foreknew that Israel would not repent and that Jesus would not return at that time, and He also foreknew that He had planned before the ages began, to inject an entirely new dispensation of His grace through the Apostle Paul as a consequence of Israel's rejection. This fact in no way minimizes the legitimacy of the offer of the Kingdom. Remember what Jesus said about John the Baptist: "And if ye will receive it, this is Elijah which was for to come . . . Elijah truly shall first come, and restore all things. But I say unto you that Elijah is come already, and they knew him not, but have done unto him whatsoever they listed. Likewise shall also the Son of man suffer of them" (Matt. 11:14; 17:11,12). If the rulers of Israel had received John's ministry he would have been the promised Elijah. And in like manner, had the rulers repented and received Jesus Christ as their Messiah-King in Acts 3, Jesus would have returned to restore the Kingdom. But they did not accept John or Jesus. Since Jesus said that Elijah must come before He Himself returns, another Elijah apparently must come before Christ returns. It does not appear that Christ will return to earth in the future as the result of Israel's acceptance of Him, as was offered in Acts 3, although we know there will be a remnant of 144,000 Israelites who will accept Him during the Tribulation and that they will evangelize a great multitude of Gentiles (Rev. 7:4-9). It seems, from such passages as Ezek. 20:33-38, that there will be rebels in Israel when Christ comes back and that they will be purged out of the nation. And Zech. 12:10-14 indicates that when Christ returns they will look upon Him whom they had pierced, and God will pour out the Spirit of grace upon Jerusalem, and there will be genuine repentance on the part of Israel.

He will not return because of Israel's repentance, but Israel will repent when He returns.

When we speak about God's dealings with Israel, it is important to remember that God deals with Israel as a nation. The rulers of the nation are responsible for the actions and decisions which affect the whole nation. Multitudes of Israelites accepted John the Baptist and Jesus, but the rulers did not: therefore Israel as a nation did not. Notice the emphasis which is placed upon the chief priests and rulers in Lk. 24:20; John 7:26,48; Acts 3:17; 4:5,8,26; 13:27. Likewise in early Acts there were multitudes of Jews who believed, (Acts 5:14-16), but the chief priests and rulers did not believe, and therefore Israel as a nation did not believe. And the judgment which fell upon Israel as a result of the ruler's rejection of Christ, fell upon believing as well as unbelieving Jews when Jerusalem was destroyed in 70 A.D. This principle has always been true with national life. The same is true in the United States. Our rulers in Congress decide whether the nation goes to war or not, and who shall bear arms, whether they want to or not.

We may wonder what would have happened had the rulers of Israel received John the Baptist as the Elijah who was to come? And what course would events have taken had these same rulers repented in Acts 3 and had acknowledged Jesus as their Messiah and King? We could only speculate and there would be no value in that. But God knew, just as Jesus knew that the ancient cities of Tyre and Sidon would have repented if His mighty works had been done in them (Matt. 11:21). Thus God foreknows not only every event of human history; He also knows that which would have happened under different circumstances. We believe there is a contrasting parallel to Acts 3 in Jonah's preaching to Nineveh (Matt. 12:41). Jonah was sent to preach that Nineveh would be destroyed in 40 days (Jon. 3:4). In contrast to Israel, the king and all of his subjects believed God; proclaimed a fast; put on sackcloth and sat in ashes. Their genuine repentance caused God to repent, and He spared that great city. Jonah became very angry when God reversed Himself and showed mercy on Nineveh, for it made him feel that he had lost face with the people of Nineveh. Might it not be that God in His sovereignty, although He had pronounced so many predictions of judgment upon Israel, could have likewise spared Israel in His mercy, had they repented as Nineveh had done? But God foreknew, when He pronounced judgment upon Israel, that they would not repent. And He foreknew, when He pronounced judgment upon Nineveh, that they would repent and the judgment would be suspended.

Returning to the last verses of Ch. 3, we see clear evidence that God had not yet cast Israel aside. They are called "children of the covenant," and the Gospel is sent first of all to them. As the multiplied seed of Abraham, these believing Israelites are to be of blessing to all the kindreds of the earth. It was God's announced intention to bless the Gentiles through Abraham's multiplied seed (Gen. 22:17,18; 26:4; 28:3,4). In the present dispensation God is still blessing the Gentiles through Abraham's seed, but now it is not through the multiplied seed, that is, the nation of Israel, but through the One Seed, that is, Christ alone, entirely apart from Israel (Gal. 3:16). In the future Kingdom God will again bless through the multiplied seed, who in turn will be blessed by the One Seed.

E. *The Apostles Testify Before the Sanhedrin,* 4:1-22.

1. *Their Arrest:* The Jewish rulers who had condemned Jesus to death were very naturally much disturbed by the preaching of the Apostles that Jesus had been raised from the dead. They therefore arrested them and since it was evening they kept them in jail until morning. However, as a result of Peter's testimony many more of the Jews became believers. There is a question of whether five thousand men were converted on this day or whether the total number of believers arose to about five thousand. Probably the latter was the case.

2. *The Rulers' Question and the Apostles' Answer:* The Jewish Council convened the next morning and had Peter and John and the man who was healed brought in. They asked: "By what power or by what name have you healed this man?" Apparently they hoped that they could find something in the Apostles' answer by which they could condemn them.

The boldness and courage with which Peter answered the rulers can be attributed to but one fact: he was filled with the Holy Spirit. This is the man who only a few weeks earlier had denied three times that he even knew Jesus. Now we see something of the powerful influence the Spirit of God can have when He takes control of man. Peter came right to the point: "Be it known unto you all, and to all the people of Israel, that by the name of Jesus Christ of Nazareth, whom ye crucified, whom God raised from the dead, even by him doth this man stand here before you whole." This miracle of healing was not due to the beggar's faith, for all he was expecting from the apostles was a few pennies. Christ had given the apostles power to heal all manner of diseases. Modern day healers place the responsibility for healing upon the faith of the afflicted one, and can thereby excuse their failures by lack of faith. It should be noted about the healings performed by the apostles that they were instantaneous and complete. In this man's case, it seems almost as much a miracle, not only that his feet and ankle bones were made new, but that never before having balanced himself in a standing position, he was able to walk, run and jump.

Peter further identifies the One by whom this miracle was done by referring to Ps. 118:22: "This is stone which was set at naught by you builders, which is become the head of the corner." There are numerous references to Christ as a stone. Isaiah saw Him as "a stone of stumbling and a rock of offense" (8:14); as "a foundation stone, a tested stone, a precious corner stone" (28:16). Daniel saw Him as the "stone cut out without hands, which smote the image" (of Gentile world power) and ground it to powder (2:34). Jesus Himself quoted Ps. 118 and applied it unto Himself. He told the apostate rulers of Israel: "Did ye never read in the Scriptures, The stone which the builders rejected, the same is become the Head of the corner: this is the Lord's doing and it is marvelous in our eyes? Therefore I say unto you, The kingdom of God shall be taken from you, and given to a nation bringing forth the fruit thereof. And whosoever shall fall on this stone shall be broken, but on whomsoever it shall fall, it will grind him to powder" (Matt. 21:42-44). When stones were cut out of the quarry and found to have cracks or flaws they were cast aside and marked: "Rejected." Christ was thus rejected by those who were supposed to be the builders of Israel. But now this Stone has been exalted at the right hand of God and has become the "head of the corner," or the cornerstone which supports the two walls of a building. When Christ returns to earth He will come as the "smiting Stone." That smiting Stone will then become a great mountain which will fill the whole earth, which describes His universal rule over the earth.

Finally, Peter sets forth Christ as the only Savior: "Neither is there salvation in any other, for there is none other name under heaven given among men, whereby we must be saved." When we speak of the difference between Peter's Gospel and the Gospel given to Paul (Gal. 2:7) we are not speaking of any difference in salvation. Both Gospels were gospels of salvation. Acts 4:12 is just as true of the Gospel given to Paul as that given to Peter. The main difference is that one has to do with the nation of Israel and the establishment of the messianic Kingdom here on earth, whereas the other has to do with the outcalling from all nations of the heavenly Church, the Body of Christ. Christ is Savior in both, but there are sharp differences in the religious programs of each.

3. *The Consternation of the Rulers,* 4:13-18: When the rulers perceived that Peter and John were "unlettered and common men," (not "unlearned and ignorant men," as stated in the King James) they marvelled at their courage and boldness and they took note that these men had been with Jesus. It would appear from John 18:16 that John was acquainted with the high priest, but we do not know in what way. He was at least able to get into the palace at the trial of Jesus and was able to get Peter in also. This may be how they knew these men had been with Jesus.

The rulers looked at the healed man who was standing before them, whom they had seen many times in his crippled condition begging at the Beautiful gate, and they couldn't deny a great miracle had been done. So they sent the men out of the meeting while they tried to scheme how they could silence these apostles, for they knew that all Jerusalem was aware of this healing miracle. They decided that instead of punishing them they would intimidate and threaten them if they didn't stop preaching in the name of Jesus. So they called them back and informed them they must keep silent about this Jesus and His resurrection.

4. *The Apostles' Reaction,* 4:19-22: The Apostles' answer stopped the mouths of the rulers, for they said, "Whether it be right in the sight of God to hearken unto you more than unto God, judge ye." What reply could the rulers make? Could these rulers who claimed to be governing for God say that man's word was more important than God's word? All they could do was to further threaten them and let them go. But the Apostles made it clear that they could not but speak the things that they had seen and heard. Their example has been an encouragement to the people of

God down through the centuries who have been placed in
similar circumstances. The Scripture clearly teaches that
we should be subject to human rulers (Rom. 13:1-6; 1 Pet.
2:13), but there is a higher law. If believers have to
disobey man in order to obey God, then they must submit
to the penalty of breaking man's law. Peter has a further
word for us: "But and if ye suffer for righteousness' sake,
happy are ye: and be not afraid of their terror, neither be
troubled . . . For it is better, if the will of God be so, that
ye suffer for well doing than for evil doing" (1 Pet.
3:14,17).

5. *The Believers' Prayer for Boldness,* 4:23-31: When
released, Peter and John went back to their own company
and reported what the rulers had said. We might have
supposed that this little company of believers would have
been saddened and discouraged, but instead we read that
they reminded themselves that God was sovereign over
heaven and earth, and that He had predicted in His Word
the things that were coming to pass and then they prayed.
It is well to remind ourselves of God's Word before we
begin to make requests. They prayed: "And now, Lord,
behold their threatenings; and grant unto thy servants, that
with all boldness they may speak the word, by stretching
forth thy hand to heal; and that signs and wonders may be
done by the name of thy holy child Jesus." They did not
ask for their own safety or protection, but that they might
be bold in proclaiming God's word and that God would
demonstrate His power in doing those wonders and signs
which the prophets had predicted would be the credentials
of the Messiah and a foretaste of Millennial blessedness
(Isa. 35:1-10). Again, there was a physical demonstration
of the power of God, for the house was shaken and they
were all filled with the Holy Spirit. As a general rule we
feel that when the Greek text uses "Holy Spirit" without
the definite article it refers to the gift or empowerment of
the Holy Spirit; and when the definite article is used it
refers to the Person of the Holy Spirit. Thus far in Acts
"Holy Spirit" has appeared without the article in 1:2,5; 2:4;
4:8; and with the article in 1:8,16; 2:4 (l.c.), 17,18,33,38;
4:31. No English version, however, makes this distinction.
One would need to refer to the Greek text for such
information. However, the distinction is not too important
at this point since divine power never operates apart from
the Person of the Spirit. In some cases, it does seem that
the reference is primarily to the gift or divine power when

speaking of outward signs and miracles.

Twice in this chapter Jesus is referred to in the King James as God's "holy child." While the Greek word does mean child, it also means servant, and the R.V. so translates it here. The King James translates this word as servant when referring to Jesus in Matt. 12:18. He is the Servant of Jehovah. He is not now a child, but "the Man Christ Jesus."

6. *All Things in Common,* 4:32-37: We have already had a section by this title in Ch. 2:43-47. The story is repeated here as an introduction to the next chapter. Up to this point this selling of possessions and pooling them with all of the believers had worked very well. There was no one among them that lacked. This condition existed as long as they were ALL filled with the Holy Spirit. But in the next chapter we begin to see a breaking down of this program. Not all of the believers are being filled with the Spirit. As we look back on this situation we can perhaps sense that this breakdown was due in part to a change in God's dealing with the nation, due to their rejection of the offer of the Kingdom. Whatever the cause, we do not read again in this book that they were "ALL" filled with the Holy Spirit. And as far as having all things in common and not one lacking in any way, when we come to the latter part of Acts we find great want among these same believers (Rom. 15:26). Paul had to take up a collection from the Gentile churches to help the poor saints at Jerusalem.

F. *The First Failure — Ananias and Sapphira,* 5:1-11. There is no specific command given to these Jewish believers to sell all their possessions and share everything in common, unless it be construed from Lk. 12:33, but since they were all filled with the Holy Spirit and they all had everything in common we must believe that the Holy Spirit led them to do this. In the case of Ananias and Sapphira it appears from v. 4 that each believer had the liberty to sell or not sell his possessions and to give part or all to the common treasury. Hence, these two could have lawfully kept part of the sale price for themselves had they made known the facts. Their sin lay in making believe they were giving the entire sale price to the treasury. There may have been several different sins involved in this, although Peter mentions only one: lying to God. There was also probably the sin of selfishness and a lack of faith that God would supply their needs if they went all the way in giving all. The question arises, when is lying a sin against God and when is it just a sin against man? Or is any sin just a sin against man? Another question is why God dealt so severely with Ananias and Sapphira, while people today can commit the same or worse sins and seem to get off scot-free? A reading of Psalm 73 might answer some of these questions. If the Bible teaches anything it is that no one gets off scot-free. Just because God does not intervene immediately, as in the case before us, we may feel our sin was not too bad, or that God didn't notice it, but the universal principle still holds: "Whatsoever a man soweth, that shall he also reap" (Gal. 6:7,8). But someone may ask, don't we get off scot-free when we are saved by grace? Perhaps, in a sense, but only because Christ suffered and died because of those sins. Just because we are saved from the eternal penalty of sin through the death of Christ does not mean that sin in our lives after we are saved cannot have any consequences. Ananias and Sapphira were no doubt saved people. They did more than nine-tenths of what Christians would do today. They sold their possessions and gave perhaps half, or two-thirds, or more of it to the Lord. Did their lie condemn them to eternal punishment? We think not. If they became lost through this sin then there are few if any Christians today who are saved, for who as a Christian has not committed sins? Let us not make the mistake of saying, "Christians today will not lose their salvation through sinning because they are saved by grace, whereas back there under the Kingdom gospel they were saved by works." If the message preached by the Twelve was salvation by works it could hardly be called gospel or good news, for Scripture is clear that no one can ever be saved by that means. If such were the case Paul says that Christ died in vain (Gal. 2:15-21). It should be noted that Paul spoke these words to Peter and Peter is the spokesman in early Acts.

G. **Signs and Wonders Performed,** 5:12-16. The question naturally arises, if the early Gospel ministry was characterized by miraculous healings, even to the extent that people were healed simply by Peter's shadow falling upon them, why do we not see similar miracles today? This question has been answered in various ways. Some say the reason is lack of faith on the part of the Christians today. Others say that miracles were necessary to get the Gospel planted in the world, but after it has become established they are no longer necessary. Of course, there are those of the modern charismatic movement who claim they have brought the miracles back and claim the gifts of healing and tongues. But the results they claim for themselves do not in any way approximate the mighty works of the Pentecostal era. In Acts EVERY ONE was healed completely. Where do we see such results today? There are still others who explain the lack of such outward, physical miracles today upon what they would call a dispensational basis. Pentecost and the days that followed after were what might be called an opening of the door of the Kingdom. What proof was there that the Apostles were actually opening the door to the long-promised Kingdom? The Old Testament predicted certain signs which would herald the Kingdom's establishment. Tongues was one of these signs, as Paul explains in 1 Cor. 14:20-22. Likewise healing was another sign (Isa. 35:3-6). As long as God was dealing with Israel in regard to the establishment of the Kingdom these Kingdom sign-miracles abounded. But when God began a new dispensation under Paul's ministry, the earthly Kingdom was no longer a part of God's program, and during the latter half of the Acts and in Paul's post-Acts ministry we can see the Kingdom signs passing away and being replaced by the spiritual program for the Body of Christ.[2]

H. *Persecution Increases,* 5:17-42.

1. *The Apostles Arrested and Divinely Released,* 5:17-33: When the rulers of Israel saw that the Apostles had defied them by continuing to preach Jesus and the resurrection they were filled with indignation and arrested and jailed them. But that night an angel of the Lord set them free and the next morning they were at the temple again with their preaching. The rulers in the meantime had sent officers to the prison to bring the Apostles before the council. The prison doors were locked but the jail was empty. While they were trying to figure out what had happened to the Apostles a man ran in with the news that the men they were seeking were in the temple teaching the people. The officers were then sent to the temple to bring the Apostles before the council. They were careful not to use violence, for they feared that the multitudes might stone them. The high priest asked why they had disobeyed his orders and again Peter replied, "We ought to obey God rather than man." Then Peter again accused the rulers of slaying Jesus whom God had raised from the dead and continued, "Him hath God exalted with his right hand to be a Prince and a Savior, for to give repentance to Israel and forgiveness of sins." Here again in these early chapters of Acts we see the emphasis is completely upon the nation of Israel. When the rulers heard Peter's word they were

furious and made plans to put them to death, for Peter had made them guilty of the blood of Jesus. In modern times there has been an attempt to absolve the Jews of all guilt and responsibility for the death of Christ. One who believes the Bible must surely agree that the Jews condemned Him to death, refused to accept the execution of a murderer in His place, and said, "His blood be upon us and upon our children." However, a serious mistake has been made by Christendom in this regard. Persecutions and pogroms have been unleashed against the Jews, which has brought a blot upon the name of the Church. Several things should have been remembered. First of all, not all the Jews conspired to put Jesus to death, but only the rulers and those they controlled politically. Next, God never commissioned the Church to bring vengeance upon Israel: vengeance is God's business (Rom. 12:18-20). Paul said that as far as the Gospel is concerned, the Jews are enemies, but they are beloved for the sake of the fathers of Israel, (Rom. 11:28). Finally, in this dispensation of the grace of God, God is forming a joint-body of believing Jews and Gentiles. The Church should have been showing love to the Jews and evangelizing them, so that the visible church would be a joint-body and not simply a Gentile body. Naturally the Jewish people today do not want to admit the guilt of their nation anymore than did the rulers of old, but it is ridiculous to claim that the Jews had nothing to do with putting Christ to death. The fact that the Roman soldiers drove the nails and thrust in the spear in no way absolves those who demanded this be done. But in a wider sense, the whole world is guilty of the death of Christ, for He died for the sins of the whole world.

2. *The Counsel of Gamaliel,* 5:34-40: Not even every member of the Jewish council or Sanhedrin was guilty of the death of Christ. We remember Nicodemus and Joseph of Aramathaea (John 19:38-40). Now another member of the Sanhedrin stands up and warns the council not to take any rash action against the Apostles. He cited examples of men who had claimed to be the Christ and had gathered a following, but they had all perished. He counselled his fellow-Jews: "Refrain from these men, and let them alone: for if this counsel or this work be of men, it will come to naught: but if it be of God, ye cannot overthrow it; lest haply ye be found even to fight against God." The others agreed with Gamaliel's counsel, and calling the Apostles back, they beat them and warned them again to desist

from their teaching and let them go.

3. *Rejoicing of the Apostles,* 5:41,42: The cause of their rejoicing was not that they were released, although they must have been thankful for that, but they rejoiced that they were counted worthy to suffer shame for the sake of Jesus. These words remind us of what Paul wrote to the Philippians: "And in nothing terrified by your adversaries: which is to them an evident token of perdition, but to you of salvation, and that of God. For unto you it is given in the behalf of Christ, not only to believe on Him, but also to suffer for His sake" (1:28,29). The Apostles, having been released, ceased not to teach and to preach Christ in the temple and from house to house.

I. *Appointment of Deacons,* 6:1-7. As the multitude of the disciples increased in number, problems arose in seeing to it that everyone received the daily allotment of food. A complaint arose that the Grecian widows were not receiving as much as the Hebrew widows. The Grecians and the Hebrews were all Jews. A Grecian or Hellenist was a Greek-speaking Jew who most likely belonged to the dispersion, whereas a Hebrew was a Jew who spoke Hebrew and retained Hebrew customs and most likely was one who was born and reared in the land of Israel. When the Apostles heard of the complaint they said it was not reasonable that they should give their time to supervising the daily administration of food, so they appointed seven men of honest report who were full of the Holy Spirit to oversee this work. These men are sometimes called the first deacons, but such a statement is misleading. The Greek word "diakonos" simply means a servant or minister. The word is used of Christ (Rom. 15:8); of Paul (Eph. 3:7); of civil rulers (Rom. 13:4); of demon spirits (2 Cor. 11:15); of servants (John 2:5); of preachers or teachers of the Word (1 Cor. 3:5); and of what seems to be a special officer in the churches Paul organized (1 Tim. 3:8,12; Phil. 1:1). Of the 29 times the word is used in the N.T., it is translated "deacon" only 5 times, and four of those are in 1 Tim. 3. The seven who were appointed in Acts to serve tables are not to be confused with the deacons in Paul's churches although the spiritual qualifications were similar. Paul's churches did not practise the communism of the early Jerusalem church.

Although the rulers of Israel were plotting to get rid of the Apostles, the number of disciples in Jerusalem continued to multiply greatly, and even a great company of priests became obedient to the faith.

J. *Martyrdom of Stephen*, 6:8-7:60.

1. *The Arrest of Stephen*, 6:8-15: Although Stephen was one who had been chosen to wait on tables, he was also a mighty preacher. He was full of faith and power and performed great wonders and miracles. But there were certain Jews of the synagogue of the Libertines who opposed him. The Libertines were Jews who had been carried captive as slaves and had later regained their freedom. Most modern translations call them the synagogue of the Freedmen. It is not clear whether those of Cyrene, Alexandria, Cilicia and Asia were all of this one synagogue or were all of separate synagogues. Rabbinic tradition speaks of 480 synagogues in Jerusalem. However that may be, it has been supposed that these Jews may have been afraid that Stephen's preaching might bring the wrath of Rome on them and enslave them again. When they were not able to stand up against Stephen's wisdom, they hired false witnesses who testified that Stephen had spoken blasphemous words against the temple and the law. This is almost a repetition of what happened at the trial and condemnation of Jesus (cf. Matt. 26:59-61). As Stephen stood before the Jewish council to be tried they fixed their eyes on him and his face appeared as the face of an angel. There was apparently a divine radiance, somewhat like that which was upon the face of Moses (Ex. 34:29).

2. *Stephen's Defense*, 7:1-53: Stephen makes his defense by relating the highlights in God's dealings with Israel from the call of Abraham to the building of the temple by Solomon (vs. 2-50). It is not at first apparent how this review of history will be used by Stephen to answer the high-priest's question: "Are these charges against you true?" However, contained in this review are two incidents which God no doubt used to strike conviction to the hearts of the rulers. One concerned Joseph and the other Moses. In both cases Israel had rejected these leaders of Israel just as they were now rejecting the Lord Jesus Christ.

Joseph is nowhere called a type of Christ, but the events of his life so parallel those of Christ that it can hardly be doubted that Stephen considered him to be one. Joseph was ordained of God to be the leader of His people, but his brethren conspired against him and figuratively put him to death. In the meantime Joseph, raised up from the pit where his brothers had thrown him, became the savior of the known world and was exalted at the right hand of the King. At the second time, corresponding to the second coming of Christ, Joseph revealed himself to his brothers, forgave them, and established them in the most fruitful place in the land.

Then there was the case of Moses whom God raised up to deliver His people from the bondage of Egypt. It came into his heart to visit his brethren the children of Israel, "for he supposed his brethren would have understood how that God by his hand would deliver them; but they understood not." They said, "Who made thee a ruler and a judge over us?" "This is that Moses, which said unto the children of Israel, A Prophet shall the Lord your God raise up unto you of your brethren, like unto me; him shall ye hear. This is he that was in the church in the wilderness, with the angel which spake to him in the mount Sinai, and with our fathers who received the lively oracles to give unto us: to whom our fathers would not obey, but thrust him from them and in their hearts turned back again into Egypt." These remarks in particular should have struck deep conviction in the hearts of the rulers that they were committing the same kind of sins their fathers committed, but to an infinitely greater degree.

Stephen concluded his address by bringing the accusation directly to his audience: "Ye stiffnecked and uncircumcised in heart and ears, ye do always resist the Holy Spirit; as your fathers did, so do ye." He then accused them of betraying and murdering the Just One.

3. *Stephen Stoned,* 7:54-60: The convicting power of the truth of God either causes men to repent or to rebel, and rebel they did! Enraged by his accusations, they gnashed upon him with their teeth as a pack of wild animals. But Stephen, filled with the Holy Spirit, looked up into heaven and said: "Behold, I see the heavens opened, and the Son of man standing at the right hand of God." This is the only time we read of Jesus in the standing position at God's right hand. Some think this indicates that Jesus was ready to return if Israel would only repent. However, at this point it seems clear as crystal that they have given their final answer that they will not repent. Others think that His standing was to receive Stephen's spirit which would very soon be crushed out of his body.

Putting their hands over their ears to shut out Stephen's voice, and shouting aloud to drown out his words, they rushed upon him, dragged him out of the city, and began stoning him. The executioners laid down their coats at the feet of a young man named Saul. This is the first mention of Saul, and we learn from the first verse of the next chapter that he was consenting to or giving approval to his death. Before being battered into unconsciousness, Stephen prayed, "Lord Jesus, receive my spirit." And then kneeling down he cried with a loud voice, "Lord, lay not this sin to their charge," and then he fell over dead.

The stoning of Stephen is one of the crisis points in the book of Acts. Many see it as Jerusalem's final answer to the claims of Jesus Christ. It would seem that the time had come for the parable of Matt. 22:7 to be fulfilled, when the king would send forth his armies to destroy those murderers and burn up their city. But just as Jesus had prayed for the forgiveness of His murderers, so Stephen prayed for those who were stoning him. Whether or not his prayer was answered, we know that Jerusalem was spared for the time being, and that the other Jews who were dispersed throughout the Roman world were given the opportunity to hear the gospel and to repent.

K. *Saul Persecutes the Church at Jerusalem,* 8:1-3. The church at Jerusalem was not the Body of Christ of which Paul speaks. It was simply the group of Jewish believers who assembled at Jerusalem. It was no more the Church of our present dispensation than was "the church in the wilderness," of which Stephen spoke in the previous chapter. After the stoning of Stephen a great persecution arose against this group who had acknowledged Jesus as Messiah. Saul became the chief leader of this persecution, going from house to house, ferreting out believers and haling them to prison.

Most of the believers fled from the city and were scattered throughout Judea and Samaria. However, the Apostles remained in Jerusalem. Some commentators have mistakenly supposed the Apostles were unwilling to carry out the Great Commission, so God sent a great persecution to scatter them. If this had been His purpose, it failed; for the Apostles were not scattered. But why did they stay in Jerusalem? One answer that has been given is that the Apostles knew that the Kingdom had to be established in Jerusalem and it could not be established until Jerusalem had repented. Therefore they could not carry out the commission to go to the Gentiles until Jerusalem had accepted Jesus, and for this reason they stayed in Jerusalem awaiting the repentance of the Jewish leaders. Now while it is true that in Acts 3 God graciously offered to send Jesus back if the rulers would repent, it is plain from the stoning of Stephen that the rulers have rejected that offer. It appears most unlikely that the Apostles could still have had hopes the rulers would repent. Another explanation, and one that seems to be more in keeping with the facts is to believe that the Apostles who knew that they would form the new nation of Israel in the Kingdom (Lk. 12:32) and would reign as judges over Israel (Matt. 19:28 cf. 21:43), were waiting in Jerusalem for some kind of sign that God had officially recognized them as the leaders of that new nation. As yet they knew nothing about this present dispensation of the secret which was yet to be committed to Paul, who was not yet even saved. They didn't know the "times and seasons" (Acts 1:6,7), but they did know that now Jerusalem had rejected God's offer, the city would be destroyed and the Great Tribulation would come (Matt. 24:2-22; Lk. 21:20-24). They may have thought this was the beginning of it. In the future Christ's return will not be conditioned upon Israel's repentance, but just the opposite (cf. Rev. 11:2-12). They will repent only after they see Him (Zech. 12:10).

III. PHILIP'S MINISTRY IN SAMARIA AND JUDEA, 8:4-40.

A. *Ministry in Samaria,* 8:4-25.

1. *Scattering of Believers,* 8:4: But does not v. 4 state that those who were scattered by the persecution went everywhere preaching the Word? Is not this evidence that God sent the persecution so they would be scattered and begin preaching to the Gentiles? To answer this question one should turn to ch. 11:19, where we read: "Now they which were scattered abroad upon the persecution that arose about Stephen travelled as far as Phenicia, and Cyprus, and Antioch, preaching the Word TO NONE BUT THE JEWS ONLY." This persecution did not result in any preaching to Gentiles until some years later at Antioch. Apparently those who were scattered understood the Lord's plan and commission, as did the Apostles who stayed in Jerusalem.

2. *Identity of the Samaritans:* The story of ch. 8 concerns Philip's preaching in the city of Samaria. But were the Samaritans Jews? Were they not Gentiles? It must be remembered that almost a thousand years earlier after King Solomon's death, the nation of Israel was divided

into two kingdoms, Judah and Israel, or Samaria. The king of Samaria ruled over the northern ten tribes, and the king of Judah ruled over the two southern tribes, Judah and Benjamin. On an unusual occasion Jesus Himself had ministered in Samaria (John 4:1-12). Was the woman at the well an Israelite or a Gentile? The woman asked Jesus, "Art thou greater than our father Jacob which gave us the well?" She was not a Jew (belonging to Judah), but she was an Israelite. It is very important to understand this distinction, for it is closely related to the fulfillment of prophecy in the earthly Kingdom.

We read that when multitudes of the Samaritans believed Philip's preaching they were all baptized with water, but none of them received the Holy Spirit. When the Apostles heard that Samaria had received the Word they sent Peter and John to confirm this ministry. When they arrived and saw that the work was genuine, they prayed for them that they too might receive the Holy Spirit. Then they laid their hands on them and they received the Holy Spirit. It is apparent that in receiving the Holy Spirit there must have been miraculous manifestations as there had been at Pentecost. But why was it necessary for the Apostles to come from Jerusalem before the Samaritans could receive the Holy Spirit?

It must be remembered that Samaria under king Jereboam had rebelled against the Lord and against the worship of Jehovah at the temple in Jerusalem, and had set up all kinds of idol worship. Finally God's anger against Samaria caused the Assyrians to come and carry them into captivity. But God's covenant with Abraham, Issac, and Jacob was not only with the two southern tribes, but with all the tribes of Israel. Therefore the prophets are full of predictions that when Messiah returns to establish the Kingdom here on the earth, all twelve tribes are going to be included (cf. Rev. 21:12). Ezekiel 37 is especially enlightening. The vision of the valley of dry bones is interpreted as representing "the WHOLE House of Israel," that is, all twelve tribes. Then follows the sign of the two sticks. The prophet was to take two sticks and write on one "For Judah," and on the other "For Ephraim" (another name for the northern ten tribes, or Samaria). Then he was to join the two sticks into one stick. This sign was to show that in the coming Kingdom God will reunite the Twelve Tribes into one nation and kingdom with one King over them.

Up to this point in the Book of Acts the message has

been to the Jews only and the message itself was the Gospel of the Kingdom. Before the rebellious ten tribes could be incorporated into that Kingdom, there must be true repentance and turning on their part. That is why, we believe, it was necessary for Peter and John to go to Samaria and with their apostolic authority receive the Samaritans into the one fold. We find no other occasion in the Apostles' preaching where the Holy Spirit was withheld from believers who had been duly kingdom-baptized until they had come and laid hands on them and prayed that they might receive the Holy Spirit. It should be noted that in the Greek text Holy Spirit appears without the definite article. We have suggested before that "Pneuma Hagion" (Holy Spirit) refers to the miracle-working gifts of the Spirit, rather than to the Person of the Spirit. The question naturally arises concerning the Samaritans who believed and were water-baptized but did not receive "Holy Spirit," were they saved? What was their spiritual condition during the interval between their believing and the sending of Peter and John to impart to them "Pneuma Hagion?" It must have required considerable time for news of the conversion of Samaritans to get to Jerusalem and for the Apostles to make the trip to Samaria. If they were saved during this interval, did they have the Person of the Spirit? It is difficult to see how they could have been born again by the Spirit without possessing the Person of the Spirit. If they were saved and had the Person of the Spirit, then the "Pneuma Hagion" they later received by the laying on of the Apostles' hands must have been a special enduement of power which manifested itself in physical ways which could be observed.

3. *Simon Magus,* 8:9-25: Among those who heard and believed and were water-baptized was a man named Simon, a sorcerer. For a long time he had deceived the Samaritans with his practise of the art of magic into believing that he was the great power of God. But he was amazed when he saw the miracles which Philip performed in the name of Jesus. And then when Peter and John came and laid their hands on the believers and they received Pneuma Hagion, he was really amazed. He offered the Apostles money if they would give him this power to convey Pneuma Hagion upon whomsoever he laid his hands. From this offer to buy religious power and prestige has come our English word "simony," the sale of ecclesiastical offices, a practise prevalent in the medieval church.

The Scripture says that Simon believed and was baptized. But was he saved? Did he actually become a child of God? From Peter's response to Simon it is evident Simon had no part or share in the matter; his heart was not right with God; he was full of bitter envy and captivated by sin. It is also evident that his believing contained no element of repentance, for Peter told him to repent of his wickedness and pray to the Lord and the Lord might forgive him for having such a thought in his heart. Simon then asked Peter to pray for him that none of the things Peter had spoken would come upon him. From Simon's response we might suppose that he did repent and get saved. It is possible that he did become a true child of God, but from what we learn of him from the early church fathers, this seems very unlikely.

According to such writers as Justin Martyr, Jerome, Irenaeus, Epiphan, and Hippolytus, Simon Magus withdrew from early Christianity and initiated a movement of his own which was a mixture of Christianity and pagan gnostic ideas. According to Jerome he made this claim for himself: "I am the Word of God, I am the Comforter, I am Almighty, I am all there is of God."[3] There is much of legend and myth associated with the history of Simon, but many scholars believe there is sufficient evidence to link the Simon of Acts 8 with the heretic referred to by the early Christian writers. If we are to believe these early writers, it is evident that Simon's conversion was due, not to a change of heart and faith in Christ, but to the belief that the Apostles possessed magical powers superior to his own, and he therefore became a disciple with the idea of improving his practise of magic.

B. *Ministry to the Ethiopian Eunuch,* 8:26-40.

1. *Identity of the Eunuch:* It may appear exceedingly strange that an Ethiopian eunuch, treasurer for Queen Candace, would go to Jerusalem to worship the Lord in the temple and that he would be carrying with him in his chariot a scroll of the Prophet Isaiah, or that he would be engaged in studying this portion of Scripture as he traveled back to Ethiopia. But according to Abyssinian legend the Queen of Sheba who visited King Solomon was from Ethiopia (2 Chron. 9). She learned a great deal about Jehovah from her visit and the legend has it that she had a son by Solomon. It is altogether possible that the knowledge of the one true God remained alive in Ethiopia over the centuries.

However that may be, it is certain that this eunuch was either a proselyte to Judaism, or actually a Jew. Prof. W. Max Mueller states that this Ethiopian was no black proselyte, but a Jew who had placed the business ability of his race at the disposal of this Nubian queen.[4] Ethiopia is mentioned nineteen times in the Old Testament, and seven more times as Cush. Ethiopians are mentioned twenty-one times. Moses married an Ethiopian woman (Num. 12:1). An Ethiopian by the name of Ebed-melech saved Jeremiah from death (Jer. 38:7-13). And it is evident from Zeph. 3:10 that some of the Jews were dispersed in Ethiopia: "From beyond the rivers of Ethiopia my suppliants, even the daughter of my dispersed, shall bring mine offering." So it is altogether possible that this eunuch from Ethiopia whom Philip met was a Jew.

2. *Angelic Visitations:* Then notice how it happened that Philip met this eunuch. An angel appeared to Philip and told him to go down into the southern desert to Gaza. This is the area we call the Gaza Strip, which was given back to Egypt in the 1979 treaty between Israel and Egypt. Angelic visitations are very common in the Old Testament, in the Gospels, and in the Acts. It was one of God's characteristic means of communicating with the people of Israel. Since God has completed His revelation in the written Word of God we do not believe He communicates in this manner in this present dispensation. Paul says that some day we are going to judge the angels (1 Cor. 6:3). And instead of the angels ministering unto us, we are actually ministering unto the angels, for he states, "this grace was given to me: to preach to the Gentiles the unsearchable riches of Christ, and to make plain to everyone my administration of this mystery, which for ages past was kept hidden in God, who created all things. His intent was that now, through the church, the manifold wisdom of God should be made known to the rulers and authorities in the heavenly realms, according to his eternal purpose which he accomplished in Christ Jesus our Lord." (Eph. 3:8-11, N.I.V.). God's angels are no doubt still active in His service, but not in visible visitations as in our present story.

3. *Exposition of Isaiah 53:* When Philip arrived in the desert he saw a man sitting in his chariot reading from a scroll. The Spirit told Philip to go near the chariot. When he approached he discovered the man was reading from the

prophet Isaiah. Philip asked the man if he understood what he was reading. "How can I," he replied, "unless someone explains it to me?" At that, he invited Philip into the chariot to sit with him. He had just read ch. 53:7,8: "He was led as a sheep to the slaughter; and like a lamb dumb before his shearer, so opened he not his mouth. In his humiliation his judgment was taken away; and who shall declare his generation? for his life is taken from the earth." The eunuch asked, "Of whom speaketh the prophet this? of himself, or of some other man?" Beginning at that very Scripture, Philip preached Jesus unto him. Thus there can be no doubt that the suffering servant of Isa. 53 is none other than our Lord Jesus Christ.

We may ask, "How much theological understanding did the Eunuch have of the redemptive work of Christ in His death, burial and resurrection?" No doubt he did not understand all that was later revealed to the Apostle Paul about the gospel of salvation, but he surely knew that the death of Christ was substitutionary: for "He was wounded for our transgressions and bruised for our iniquities, and the Lord hath laid on Him the iniquity of us all." He knew that Christ's soul had been made an offering for sin. He knew it was for the transgression of "my people" (Israel) He was stricken. Does this mean that at that time the value of the death of Christ was limited to the people of Israel? Hardly, for John the Baptist preached, "Behold the Lamb of God, which taketh away the sin of the world" (John 1:29). And the prophets are full of such statements as Isa. 45:22: "Look unto me, and be ye saved, all the ends of the earth: for I am God, and there is none else." It is true that in the Old Testament God promised to channel His salvation for the Gentiles through Israel, but that did not mean that Christ's death was viewed as only for Israel. It should be pointed out too, that there were differences in emphasis in the way the death of Christ was preached. In the early Acts period where the preaching was to the very people who had put Him to death, the emphasis was upon their guilt and their need to repent of their wicked deed. But when Paul went to the Gentiles he could not accuse them of murdering the Son of God; for they had not even heard of Him before Paul preached to them. He simply told them that Christ had died for their sins in accordance with Old Testament prediction and that He was buried and raised again the third day from the dead.

There seems to be confusion in the minds of many over what was brand new truth, never before revealed until it was made known to Paul and that which was old truth, previously revealed in the Old Testament and Gospels. It is just as much a mistake to suppose that everything in Paul's epistles was brand new as to think that everything Paul received was merely further enlightenment on some old truth. The fact that Christ died for the sins of the world is not new truth with Paul, although his revelation concerning the truth goes much deeper and into more detail, as well as showing its special relationship of the Body of Christ in this present dispensation.

4. *Conversion and Baptism of the Eunuch:* It is evident that Philip, in preaching the gospel to the Eunuch, mentioned water baptism for the remission of sins (Acts 2:38). As they traveled through the desert they came past some water, and the Ethiopian asked: "Look, here is some water. What can hinder me from being baptized?" (Verse 37 is not found in the better Greek manuscripts. Perhaps the scribe who added these words thought there was need to make sure this man's belief was genuine in contrast to that of Simon, of whom we have just read.) At that the chariot was stopped and both of the men went down out of the chariot into the water, and Philip baptized him. The fact that they both went down into the water and both came up out of the water does not in any way prove immersion. It would be very unusual to find a pool in the desert deep enough for immersion. Neither was the baptism done as a witness to the world, for they were alone in the desert, far from other people. As we shall see in the case of Saul's conversion in the next chapter, baptism was a ceremonial washing away of sins. In the development of doctrine for the new Body of Christ under Paul's later ministry, the Gospel of the grace of God was freed from all ceremonialism, so that the baptism and the circumcision for the believer are completely spiritual in nature, "made without hands" (Col. 2:11,12).

It should be noted that God always dealt with Israel through signs and miracles. Baptism was one of the ceremonial signs. There were many such baptisms or washings in the Jewish religion as given through Moses (Heb. 9:10), where the Greek word is baptismois. It is our understanding that all such signs ceased when God suspended His covenant dealings with the nation of Israel. That is why we believe baptism was not a specific part of Paul's commission (1 Cor. 1:17), as it was for the commission of the Twelve for Israel (Matt. 28:19; Mk.

16:16).

The narrative ends with a miraculous snatching away of Philip by the Spirit of God, so that the Eunuch saw him no more. Philip was found at Azotus (Ashdod of the Old Testament), a town about 18 miles N.E. of Gaza. He continued north along the coast, preaching in all the cities until he came to Caesarea, where the story ends.

IV. SAUL'S CONVERSION AND MINISTRY IN DAMASCUS AND JERUSALEM, 9:1-31.

A. *Saul's Conversion.* The resurrection of Jesus Christ and the conversion of Saul of Tarsus have long been considered two of the strongest evidences for the truthfulness of Christianity. Two English unbelievers by the name of Gilbert West and Lord Lyttleton, recognizing this fact, undertook the task of writing books to disprove the historicity of these two events. After years of study and research both of these men became converts to Christianity and wrote books proving the very opposite of their original theses. Lord Lyttleton's conclusion in his book, *Observations on Saul's Conversion,* was that the conversion and Apostleship of St. Paul, alone duly considered, is of itself a demonstration sufficient to prove Christianity to be a divine revelation.[5] No doubt the conversion of Saul, the leading persecutor of the early followers of "the way," is one of the most important events in the Book of Acts. The expression in v. 2, "this way," should be translated "the way." Christ had said, "I am THE Way," and this expression is used in Acts to describe faith in Christ (cf. Acts 19:9; 22:4).

The story of Saul's conversion is related three times in the Acts. Luke relates the actual conversion in ch. 9, and Paul makes reference to it in ch. 22:1-16 and ch. 26:9-18. All three accounts should be read together to get all of the details of what happened on the Damascus road. Some have thought there is a contradiction between 9:7: "And the men which journeyed with him stood speechless, hearing a voice but seeing no man," and 22:9: "And they that were with me saw indeed the light, and were afraid; but they heard not the voice of him that spake to me." However, the verb "they heard not" should be understood in the sense "they understood not." The same Greek verb is used in 1 Cor. 14:2 where it is translated, "for no man *understandeth* him." The men with Saul heard a sound but they did not understand what the sound was saying.

It should be noted that Saul thought he was serving God by persecuting those of "the way." Paul stated: "I verily thought with myself that I ought to do many things contrary to the name of Jesus of Nazareth" (Acts 26:9). Moreover he stated: "I have lived in all good conscience before God until this day" (Acts 23:1). Conscience is not always a safe guide. Saul had a good conscience about killing Christians. He did it ignorantly in unbelief (1 Tim. 1:13). Christ had told His disciples, "They shall put you out of the synagogues: yea, the time cometh, that whosoever killeth you will think that he doeth God service." Conscience is an accurate guide if it has the Word of God as its standard by which it judges, but if our standard is simply what we think is right it can lead us far astray.

Saul's conversion is an example of God's sovereign election. Many people reject this doctrine because they cannot reconcile it with justice or with man's freedom of will. It seems quite evident that Saul the persecutor would never have become Paul the Apostle unless God had taken the initiative and struck him down at the height of his opposition to Christ. If we are thinking about justice, we may ask, "Is He unjust in not striking down every unbeliever and making a believer out of him? Paul says that God separated him from his mother's womb and called him (Gal. 1:15). Paul was a chosen or elected vessel (Acts 9:15). This was not a case of simply choosing one who was already saved to a particular type of ministry. He was chosen at a time when he was the chief persecutor of Christ and His people. Some may reason that Paul was an exception to the rule: that in the usual course of events God does not use force or means to save people. He leaves them on their own, to believe or not believe, as they see fit. It is my belief that no one would ever be saved unless God first of all brought various influences to bear to convince people of their need of Christ and to bring forth faith in Christ.

When these early Jewish believers heard that their chief persecutor had been converted and that the churches through-out Judea, Galilee, and Samaria had rest and were edified (v. 31), they must have been encouraged to believe that the prospects for the establishment of the Kingdom had greatly improved. They could surely have had no intimation that this man would ultimately be the one under the Lord to pronounce blindness upon the nation of Israel and unfold a completely new dispensation which concerned the Gentile world. However, when the Lord sent Ananias to lay hands upon Saul that he might receive sight after the blinding light had left him sightless, He told Ananias that Saul was a chosen vessel to bear His name before the Gentiles, and kings, as well as the children of Israel, and that He would show Saul how great things he must suffer for the name of Christ. As we look back now from our vantage point, we can see that the conversion of Saul was the first step in preparing for the new dispensation.

As soon as Ananias had laid his hands on Saul, scales or incrustations fell from his eyes and he received his sight. Saul was then baptized. Although Saul's conversion was not the result of human preaching, but of divine intervention, it is evident that he was saved under the prevailing Kingdom program of baptism for the remission of sins. Ananias told him, "Arise, and be baptized, and wash away thy sins, calling on the name of the Lord" (Acts 22:16). He told Saul what he would have told any other Jew. Baptism under the Kingdom gospel was a washing or cleansing ceremony, the same as the many baptisms of the Old Testament (Heb. 9:10). But we never read of Paul telling his Gentile converts to be baptized in order to wash away their sins, even while he was practising baptism during the Transition period. Baptism was not a part of his commission (1 Cor. 1:17). After the Transition, Paul recognized only one baptism, that done by the Spirit (Eph. 4:5; 1 Cor. 12:13).

Although Saul's sight was restored, it appears from Gal. 4:15 and 6:11 that he was afflicted with poor eyesight. This may have been a lasting result of the blinding flash of the light of Christ's presence, or it may have been the thorn in the flesh given to keep him from becoming overly exalted (2 Cor. 12:7).

B. **Saul Preaches at Damascus,** 9:20-22. Luke does not mention the fact that Saul went to Arabia after his conversion. We learn this fact from Gal. 1:17. It is therefore difficult to be sure of the exact order of events. Luke tells us that Saul stayed certain days with the disciples at Damascus, and straightway he preached Christ in the synagogues. Then after many days the Jews took counsel to kill him and the disciples let him down by the wall in a basket to escape from the city. From Damascus he went to Jerusalem. Where, in this series of events, should we place his trip to Arabia? And how long did he stay there? We know from Gal. 1 that Paul went to Jerusalem three years after his conversion. How much of that time was spent in Arabia and how much in Damascus is not known. From Luke's account it appears that immediately after his conversion Saul preached in the synagogues of Damascus, but Paul uses the same Greek word for immediately when he says: "Immediately I conferred not with flesh and blood: neither went I up to Jerusalem to them which were apostles before me; but I went into Arabia, and returned again unto Damascus" (Gal. 1:16,17). According to Paul's account, it would seem that he went to Arabia immediately after his conversion. I would tend to adopt this latter view, since I believe that there had come such a complete revolution in Saul's life that he needed a period of isolation and reflection and meditation, and perhaps further revelation before he was ready to start a public preaching ministry.

Verse 20 should read, "straightway he preached *Jesus* in the synagogues, that he is the Son of God." The word "Christ" is a title, meaning "the Anointed One." The Hebrew word is Messiah. Many people do not get the significance of these terms. The human name of the Son of God is Jesus. We learn from ch. 17:2,3 that Paul's custom was to go into the synagogues and reason with the Jews from the O.T. Scriptures that the Messiah must needs suffer and arise from the dead, and having proved this he then declared that this Jesus whom he preached is the Messiah, the Son of God. The Greek name "Jesus" is the same as the Hebrew "Joshua." There were no doubt numerous Jews who were named Jesus. Paul mentions one of his fellow-workers who was named Jesus (Col. 4:11). Therefore Jesus the Messiah is identified as "Jesus of Nazareth." He is thus identified 14 times in the Gospels and 7 times in the Acts. His full title as used by Paul in his epistles is "the Lord Jesus Christ."

C. **Saul Escapes to Jerusalem**, 9:23-29. It didn't take long for Saul to discover in reality what the Lord had told Ananias to tell him, how great things he must suffer for the sake of Jesus Christ. He found out that the Jews of Damascus had set a trap for him in order to kill him. They were lying in wait for him at the city gates. Therefore the disciples put Saul in a basket and let him down at night through a window in the city wall. This is not the first time God's servants were saved in this manner. The harlot Rahab saved the lives of the two spies from death by letting them down through a window in the wall of Jericho (Josh. 2:15). And Michal saved David from King Saul by the same means (1 Sam. 19:12).

Saul probably thought that he would be received with open arms by the disciples at Jerusalem, but instead they could not believe that their chief persecutor had actually become a believer in Jesus. They were sure he was laying a trap for them. But Joses, whom the apostles surnamed Barnabas (son of consolation), a Levite from the island of

Cyprus (Acts 4:36,37), took Saul to the Apostles and explained how he had been converted and had preached boldly the Name of Jesus in Damascus. He was then accepted into the fellowship. It is very difficult to harmonize the account of this visit as recorded in Acts with that given by Paul in Gal. 1:18,19. For this reason some have supposed Acts does not record the Gal. 1:18 visit. However, they both end with Paul going from Jerusalem to Syria and Cilicia. Paul says he went up to see Peter and abode with him 15 days and that he saw none of the other apostles, save James the Lord's brother. Acts states that Barnabas presented him to the Apostles, and that he was with them coming in and going out of Jerusalem, and that he spoke boldly in the name of Jesus and disputed with the Grecian Jews, who went about to slay him. Paul speaks of this visit again in Acts 22:17-21. Here he says nothing about his visit with Peter or of his preaching. He gives his reason for leaving Jerusalem in these words: "And it came to pass, that, when I was come again to Jerusalem, even while I prayed in the temple, I was in a trance; and saw Him saying unto me, Make haste, and get thee quickly out of Jerusalem: for they will not receive thy testimony concerning me. And I said, Lord, they know that I imprisoned and beat in every synagogue them that believed on thee; and when the blood of thy martyr Stephen was shed, I also was standing by, and consenting unto his death, and kept the raiment of them that slew him. And He said unto me, Depart: for I will send thee far hence unto the Gentiles." The Twelve Apostles were also commissioned to preach to the Gentiles. But Paul calls himself THE Apostle of the Gentiles (Rom. 11:13). What then is the distinction between the Gentile ministries of Paul and of the Twelve?

Some make the mistake of supposing that wherever Gentile salvation is found, we are necessarily involved with the Church of this dispensation. But there was Gentile salvation in the Old Testament times, but the Gentile had to conform to the rules laid down in Ex. 12:48,49. There was Gentile salvation while Jesus was on earth. There is certainly the plain inference that the Syro-phoenician woman and the Roman centurion were forgiven their sins and therefore saved. And there were Gentiles in the audience on the first Pentecost in Acts, for we read that there were Jews and proselytes (2:10), and proselytes were Gentiles who had turned to Judaism. In the Jewish synagogues throughout the Gentile world there were Gentiles who attended the services and some became proselytes, just as we find in the synagogue at Antioch in Pisidia (Acts 13:42). And, of course, there is to be worldwide

Gentile salvation in the coming Kingdom after the Great Tribulation has taken place. What then is unique about Gentile salvation today? The uniqueness as I see it, is that Gentiles are being saved entirely apart from any association with Israel; in fact, Israel, nationally, has been cast aside and has become an enemy of the Gospel (Rom. 11:28), while salvation is being sent to the Gentiles. When Paul returned from his first missionary journey he announced that the door of faith had been opened to the Gentiles. This surely did not mean that on this missionary trip, Gentiles for the first time had been saved, for there were Gentiles in the church which commissioned him. But never before this trip do we read of Paul turning away from the Jews and turning to the Gentiles. This "casting away of Israel" (Rom. 11:15) and "turning to the Gentiles" (Acts 13:46; 18:6; 28:28) was one of the chief characteristics of Paul's ministry. This is a distinctive characteristic of the present dispensation, that through the fall of Israel salvation has come to the Gentiles (Rom. 11:11). In the prophetic Scriptures referring to the Kingdom it is always through the rise of Israel that salvation would come to the Gentiles.

D. **Saul Returns to Tarsus,** 9:30-31. Returning to our text in Acts 9, Paul left Jerusalem and returned to his home city of Tarsus in Cilicia, where he remained for perhaps seven years before being brought to Antioch by Barnabas. During this time he no doubt preached in the synagogues and doubtless reached Gentiles also through the synagogue ministry. There is no record of Paul establishing churches in Syria and Cilicia on his first missionary journey, but there were churches in those regions, for he visited them on his second journey (Acts 15:41). Whether Paul established these assemblies or Jews who were scattered abroad after the stoning of Stephen (Acts 8:4; 11:19) were responsible is not clear. But what seems to be clear is that in these years of Paul's ministry in Cilicia before God separated him unto his special ministry in Acts 13 he was not engaging in a ministry of pronouncing blindness upon Israel, so that through Israel's fall salvation was being sent to the Gentiles. His ministry up to Acts 13 seems to have been in and through the synagogue in reaching the Gentiles. But on his first missionary journey after his separation to the ministry for which God had called him, the first recorded event was that of pronouncing blindness upon a Jew, Bar-Jesus, a false prophet, and turning to a Gentile, Sergius Paulus, with salvation. This was a chief characteristic of Paul's ministry from this point on. At Antioch in Pisidia, after the

Jews had blasphemed Paul's message, he declared: "It was necessary that the word of God should first have been spoken to you; but seeing ye put it from you, and judge yourselves unworthy of everlasting life, lo, we turn to the Gentiles" (Acts 13:46). Again, at Corinth, when the Jews blasphemed, he shook his raiment, and said unto them, "Your blood be upon your own heads; I am clean: from henceforth I will go to the Gentiles" (Acts 18:6). And finally, when we come to the end of the Transition Period, we hear Paul's final pronouncement of blindness upon Israel as he applies Isaiah's prophecy against them and declares, "Be it known therefore unto you, that the salvation of God has been sent unto the Gentiles, and that they will listen" (Acts 28:28). This third recorded turning away from Israel and a turning to the Gentiles marks the end of the Transition Period and the emergence of the full-blown dispensation of the grace of God.

E. *The Significance of Saul's Conversion.* The most evident significance of Saul's conversion was the effect it had on the persecution of the Jewish saints. The effect was, when the chief persecutor was converted, "Then had the churches rest throughout Judea and Galilee and Samaria and were edified." But there was also a great dispensational significance.

Saul was to become the Apostle of a completely new and hitherto unrevealed dispensation of the grace of God. He was to become the Apostle of the Gentiles. He was to become the greatest missionary of all time. He was to become the great theologian of the Church, dealing systematically with the great doctrines of soteriology, ecclesiology and eschatology.

Chiefly we think of Paul as the man who, under Christ, was used as the founder of the Church, which is called the Body of Christ. There is no statement in Scripture to tell us exactly at what time the Holy Spirit did His first baptizing work in forming the Body of Christ. Many, of course, believe that Christ baptizing with the Holy Spirit is identical with the Holy Spirit baptizing into Christ, and thus they place the beginning on the day of Pentecost in Acts 2. In our exposition we have shown why we believe these are two distinct baptisms, and have given a number of reasons why we do not believe the Body of Christ can be fitted into the period before the conversion of Saul. We believe members of the Body are addressed in all of Paul's epistles, so that we can say with much assurance that the Body of Christ began with Paul before he wrote any of his epistles. To say anything beyond that is to speculate.

SECTION ONE

Note Page

   1   30. – Baxter, op. cit., See Vol. VI., pp. 17-20 for an exposition of this truth.

   2   38. – Anderson, op. cit., has very helpful explanations of why miracles, tongues, and healings have ceased in the present dispensation.

   3   47. – See the entire article on Simon Magus in the International Standard Bible Encyclopedia, or that in the Encyclopedia Britannica for further details and the tenets of the Simoniani.

   4   48. – *International Standard Bible Encyclopedia* (Chicago, The Howard Severence Co., 1915), Vol. II, p. 1033.

   5   51. – Ibid., Vol. IV, p. 2568.

The Gospel to the Gentiles Through Peter and Others

Chapters 9:31-12:25

I. PETER'S MINISTRY IN LYDDA AND JOPPA, 9:32-43.

Peter apparently made a tour throughout Judea, at least we see him on this trip travelling about 40 miles northwest to Lydda, another ten miles to Joppa on the sea coast, and thence to Caesarea, about forty-five miles north. His purpose was to visit his fellow-Jewish believers. In Lydda he found a man by the name of Aeneas, a paralytic, who had been bedridden for eight years. Peter said to him, "Jesus Christ heals you." And instantly he was completely restored to health. Peter then told him to get up and make his bed. It might have seemed too much to ask this man who had spent eight years in bed to make his own bed, but apparently Peter wanted people to see that he was indeed completely healed and able to do this chore. Peter was continuing the "sign ministry" of the commission of Mark 16. As a result of this miracle all who dwelt in Lydda and Sharon turned to the Lord.

While Peter was at Lydda two men came from Joppa asking him to come with them immediately, for a certain woman named Tabitha, or Dorcas, had died. She was a highly respected believer in Joppa who spent her time in doing good and helping the poor. Her name is given in Aramaic and Greek and means "gazelle," which in the east was a favorite type of beauty. The Song of Solomon uses this terminology (2:9,17; 4:5; 7:3). It was customary for Jews in a seaport town, such as Joppa, to have both a Jewish and a Gentile name. When Peter arrived he was taken to an upper chamber where the body was laid out. All of the widows stood around him, crying and showing him the garments Dorcas had made while she was yet alive. Peter sent them all out of the room and then he kneeled and prayed and said, "Tabitha, arise!" She opened her eyes and seeing Peter, she sat up. Peter took her by the hand and helped her to her feet. Then he called in the widows and other believers and presented her alive. This miracle, as the one at Lydda had done, caused many in Joppa to believe. Peter spent several days in Joppa, staying with a tanner by the name of Simon. We would have thought that the believers could have found a better smelling place than a tannery for Peter, but perhaps Simon's home was dissociated from his place of business. We have no idea how many such miracles took place throughout the land by the hands of Peter and the other apostles.

II. THE CONVERSION OF CORNELIUS, 10:1-48.

Up to this point the scattered Jews had preached the word to none but the Jews only (Acts 11:19). We know that this preaching did include Gentiles by birth who had become proselytes to Judaism. A true proselyte, called a "proselyte of righteousness," or a "proselyte of the covenant," was a Gentile who had become circumcised and lived according to the customs and commands of the Mosaic Law. There was another type of proselyte who was known as a "proselyte of the gate." This was a Gentile who attended the synagogue services and worshipped the God of Israel, but did not submit to circumcision and did not therefore enjoy the full privileges of the Jewish religion.

It seems evident that Cornelius must have been a proselyte of the gate. We know he was uncircumcised. We know that he feared the God of the Bible with all of his family. We know that he gave alms to the Jewish people and that he prayed to God always. And we further know that he observed the Jewish hour of prayer, for he prayed at the ninth hour (3:00 P.M.), which was the Jewish hour of prayer according to Acts 3:1. It appears from Peter's words that Cornelius was somewhat familiar with the Old Testament prophets, as well as with the story of Jesus, for he says to Cornelius: "That word, I say, ye know, which was published throughout all Judea, and began from Galilee, after the baptism which John preached; how that God anointed Jesus of Nazareth with the Holy Spirit and with power, who went about doing good, and healing all who were oppressed of the devil; for God was with him." No doubt some of the Jews who had been scattered from Jerusalem had testified in the synagogue at Caesarea where Cornelius lived.

There is nothing new about an uncircumcised Gentile attending synagogue service: what seems to be new is that a Jewish believer is sent into the home of an uncircumcised Gentile to have fellowship and to eat Gentile food, all of which was considered unclean and unlawful by the Jews. At least, this was the objection raised by the Jerusalem believers in Acts 11:3. This appears to be the first time an apostle was sent to an uncircumcised Gentile. This long delay of eight to ten years in going to the Gentiles since the commission was given was not due to Jewish bigotry, as some commentators contend. It was simply not God's time until now. The fact that the Jewish disciples rejoiced and glorified God when they learned of Gentile salvation is proof they were not prejudiced against Gentiles.

A. *Cornelius' Vision*, 10:1-8. Cornelius is one of two Roman centurions mentioned in the New Testament who were godly men. The first, strangely enough, loved the Jewish nation and had built a synagogue for the Jews (Lk. 7:1-10). Jesus said of this Gentile: "I have not found so great faith, no, not in Israel." The centurion in our present story is described as "a devout man, and one that feared God with all his house, who gave much alms to the people (of Israel), and prayed to God always." Surely Cornelius was an exceptional man, especially when we think of Roman soldiers as ruthless and brutal. According to human standards, he was a saved man, if anyone was. But as yet, he was not, for we are told in 11:14 that Peter was sent to him to tell him words whereby he and his family would be saved. Good works have never in any dispensation produced spiritual salvation.

Cornelius is exceptional in another way. God did take account of his good deeds and for that reason sent an angel to tell him that his prayers and alms had been remembered by God, and that he should send messengers to Joppa to find a certain man by the name of Simon Peter who would tell him what he ought to do. This is the only recorded case in the New Testament where God took account of an unsaved man's good deeds and as a result sent an angel to tell him to send for a certain evangelist who would tell him how to be saved. How shall we explain this exceptional case? This Gentile was far different from the Gentiles described by Paul in Rom. 1:21-32, among whom not even one was to be found who did good.

It is the writer's personal opinion that Cornelius stands as an example of Gentile salvation in the coming Tribulation period. According to the Abrahamic Covenant, God had promised to bless those who blessed the descendants of Abraham (Gen. 12:1,2). At the judgment of the nations at the end of the Great Tribulation, the Gentiles are going to be judged on the basis of their treatment of the Lord's brethren, the Jewish people (Matt. 25:40). Those who had treated Israel well would be allowed to enter the Kingdom: the others would be destroyed. It should be remembered that during our Lord's earthly ministry and up to this time, God was dealing exclusively with the nation of Israel in regard to the establishment of their Messianic Kingdom. Both the centurion of Luke 7 and Cornelius loved the Jewish people and gave alms to them, and as a result God recognized them for what they had done and sent salvation to them. One thing is certain: God is not duplicating the Cornelius event in this present dispensation.

It was the ninth hour, or 3:00 p.m., when the angel appeared to Cornelius. As soon as the angel departed he called two of his household servants and a soldier who was a religious man and after he had told them about the vision he had received from God he sent them to Joppa to find Peter.

B. **Peter's Vision,** 10:9-22. The servants of Cornelius arrived in Joppa the next day about noon. At the same time Peter went up on the housetop to pray. He became very hungry and wanted to eat, but while the meal was being prepared he fell into a trance. He saw heaven opened and something that looked like a large sheet being lowered by its four corners. It was full of all kinds of four-footed animals, reptiles, and birds. Then he heard a voice: "Arise, Peter; kill and eat." Peter replied, "I certainly will not, Lord. I have never eaten anything defiled or unclean." And the Voice answered him, "Do not call anything impure that God has made clean." This happened three times and then the sheet was taken back into heaven.

While Peter was wondering what could be the meaning of this vision, the messengers from Cornelius arrived at the gate and inquired whether Simon, who was known as Peter, was staying there. While Peter was still thinking about the vision, the Spirit said to him, "Three men are looking for you. Get up and go down stairs. Don't hesitate to go with them, because I have sent them." Peter went down and met the men and asked, "Why have you come?" The men then told him about the experience of Cornelius and that he was a righteous and God-fearing man who was highly respected by all the Jews. Peter invited the men in for the night and prepared to leave with them the next morning.

C. **Peter's Meeting with Cornelius,** 10:23-33. Peter left Joppa with the messengers and a number of Jewish brethren and on the second day arrived in Caesarea, a distance of about 30 miles. Cornelius had assembled all of his family and near friends and was anxiously awaiting their arrival. As Peter came in, Cornelius fell down at his feet and worshipped him. But Peter lifted him up and said, "I myself am also a man." [It is interesting to see the parallels in the ministries of Peter and Paul. Paul was also worshipped (14:11-15). Both healed a lame man (3:2-7 and 14:8-10). Both had dealings with a sorcerer (8:9-24 and 13:6-11). Both imparted the Holy Spirit by the laying on of their hands (8:17 and 19:6). Both raised a person from the dead (9:36-41 and 20:9,10). Both healed people by what might be called remote control (5:15 and

19:12). Both suffered imprisonment (12:3 and 16:23).]

Peter began by explaining to Cornelius that it was unlawful for a Jew to keep company or to come unto one of another nation, but that he now understood from the "sheet-vision" that he should not call any man common or unclean. Actually, there is no specific command in the Law of Moses forbidding Jews to associate with Gentiles, but the Law did place many restrictions on the Jew. A Gentile could not take part in Israel's worship unless he was circumcised (Ex. 12:43-49). The uncircumcised man was considered unclean (Isa. 52:1). Jews were forbidden to eat many of the foods which Gentiles ate, and especially so when the meat had been sacrificed to idols, as practically all Gentile meat was (Lev. 11; Acts 15:20). The slightest infraction of the Law defiled the Jew (Lev. 5:2; 7:19,21; Num. 19:16; Ezek. 44:23). With these many restrictions it is easy to see why a Jew would feel that he was breaking God's Law in associating and eating with Gentiles. But, we may ask, had not Christ commanded His Apostles to go into all the world and preach the gospel to every creature? Why would Peter need a special revelation at this late date to show him that he could and should go to the Gentiles?

In answer we might ask, did not Jesus know that the Gentiles were to be incorporated into the Kingdom? Why then did He say, "I am not sent but to the lost sheep of the house of Israel?" (Matt. 15:24). And why did He command His apostles not to go to the Gentiles? (Matt. 10:5). He referred to the Gentiles as dogs (Matt. 15:26). Dogs were classified as unclean animals (Prov. 26:11; Matt. 7:6; Phil. 3:2; Rev. 22:15). Jesus answered this question by stating that the children of Israel had to first receive their blessing and be filled before the Gentiles could receive their blessing. This statement is based upon the Abrahamic promise that all nations would be blessed through the multiplied seed of Abraham (Mk. 7:27 cf. Gen. 22:17,18). Just as Jesus knew that the Gentiles would be incorporated into the Kingdom in due time, so the apostles knew the same truth, but the due time was not at Pentecost, even as it was not while Christ was on earth. However we interpret the conversion of Cornelius, it would appear that it was God's time to bring about Gentile salvation by the fact that He gave a special revelation to Peter to go to Cornelius.

After Peter had explained his new relation with the Gentiles, he asked why Cornelius had sent for him. Cornelius then rehearsed his vision of how the angel had bidden him send for Peter with explicit directions where he would be found. Therefore he said, "We are all here present before God, to hear all things that are commanded thee of God."

D. *Peter's Sermon*, 10:34-43. Peter's opening words are the conclusion he reached from his vision and subsequent events. "I perceive that God is no respecter of persons; but in every nation he that feareth God and worketh righteousness is accepted with Him." This statement raises two important questions. The first is, if God is no respecter of persons, how do we explain the fact that for two thousand years He dealt almost exclusively with one little nation, Israel? Here it must be remembered that the Bible shows that the whole human race apostasied from God and that God in justice could have destroyed them all. However, in sovereign grace He chose this one small nation through which to work His redemptive program, so that in the end He might provide salvation for all. The other problem with Peter's statement is that it sounds like salvation by character or works, plain and simple. Does the gospel preacher tell people if they fear God and work righteousness God will accept them? Or does he tell the sinner, "There is none righteous, and it is not by works of righteousness which we have done, but according to His mercy He saves us?" The problem seems to lie in the connotation of the word "accepted." It is evident that we are not to equate this word with "salvation" in this context, for it is clear that although Cornelius was acceptable to God, he was not as yet saved, for Peter was sent to him to tell him words whereby he could be saved (Acts 11:14). God was pleased with the way Cornelius had responded to the sanctifying influences which God had brought into his life, and which finally led up to his salvation.

Next, Peter preaches exactly the same word which God had sent to the children of Israel. He was given nothing new or different to preach to the Gentiles. His message, of course, exalted Jesus Christ as Lord of all. Strangely enough he says that Cornelius knew this story of Jesus from the baptism of John down to His death and resurrection. He knew all about the history of Jesus Christ, but that knowledge had not saved him. Peter goes on to tell him and his friends that he and the other apostles were eye-witnesses of Christ's resurrection and that all of the prophets give witness that through His Name whosoever believes in Him shall receive remission of sins.

E. *Cornelius' Salvation*, 10:44-48. While Peter was speaking these words the Holy Spirit fell on all who heard the word. Peter and the Jews who had come with him were all amazed, because that on the Gentiles also was poured out the gift of the Holy Spirit. How did they know the gift of the Spirit had been given? They knew, for they heard them speak with tongues and magnify God. At Pentecost Peter had told the people to be baptized and they would receive the Holy Spirit. But these Gentiles had received the Holy Spirit upon believing. Peter therefore hastens to ask: "Can any one keep these people from being baptized with water?" Then he commanded them to be baptized. Cornelius and his friends requested Peter to stay with them certain days, during which Peter no doubt gave them further instructions concerning the Kingdom.

F. *The Significance of Cornelius.* Cornelius was a Gentile, and we have referred numerous times to the statement of Christ that the children must be filled before the Gentiles were to be blessed. Some dispensationalists have taken this statement to mean that the nation of Israel must be blessed or converted before the Gentiles could have the gospel of the Kingdom preached to them. Thus it is argued that Peter's being sent to a Gentile before Israel had been converted is a departure from this kingdom principle and is evidence that a new dispensation had begun with the conversion of Saul. We feel, however, that there are serious objections to this view.

First of all, we believe "the children," of whom Christ spoke comprise the believing remnant in Israel and not the whole nation including its rulers. In Matt. 13:38 Christ said, "The good seed are the children of the kingdom, but the tares are the children of the wicked one." The tares represented the rulers of Israel. Christ told these rulers: "Ye are of your father, the devil" (John 8:44). He also told those rulers, "The kingdom of God shall be taken from you, and given to a nation bringing forth the fruit thereof" (Matt. 21:43). He did not say it would be given to the Church, or to the Gentile nations, but to a nation. It is evident that "the nation" of which Christ spoke consisted of His followers, the believing remnant in Israel, for He said to them, "Fear not, little flock; for it is your Father's good pleasure to give you the kingdom" (Lk. 12:32). Whole chapters in the Gospels could be quoted to show that the rulers of Israel would never be converted or enter into the Kingdom. Therefore, we believe it is a mistake to teach that under the kingdom commission the disciples could not go to the Gentiles until the nation of Israel had been converted.

Next, there is the plain teaching in the Gospels that the Gentiles would have the gospel of the Kingdom preached to them before Israel as a nation had turned to the Lord. Christ warned His disciples that they would be persecuted by the leaders of Israel, "for they will deliver you up to the councils, and they will scourge you in their synagogues" (Matt. 10:17; Lk. 21:12). Then He told them that in the Tribulation period, "This gospel of the Kingdom shall be preached in all the world for a witness to all nations; and then shall the end (of the age) come" (Matt. 24:14). And this dovetails perfectly with Rev. 7:9,14, where we are shown a great multitude "of all nations, and people, and tongues," who are saved "out of the great tribulation," as a result of the witness of the Jewish remnant. This great harvest among the Gentiles takes place while Israel nationally is under the reign of the Anti-christ, when Jerusalem is referred to as "Sodom and Egypt, where our Lord was crucified" (Rev. 11:8). Thus it is evident that the Great Commission of the Gospel of the Kingdom was to be carried out before the whole nation of Israel is saved.

An important passage which reveals the sequence of events in the preaching of the Gospel of the Kingdom is Matt. 22:1-14. The Lord here likened the kingdom of heaven to a king who prepared a wedding feast for his son. He sent his servants to tell those who were invited to come to the feast, but they refused to come. This call to Israel to come no doubt refers to the earthly ministry of our Lord. Then a second call went forth. He sent other servants to tell the invited guests, "Behold, I have prepared my dinner; my oxen and fatlings are killed, and all things are ready; come unto the feast." But the invited guests paid no attention. One went off to his field, another to his business, and the rest seized the king's servants and mistreated and killed them. This second call to Israel must refer to the preaching in Acts 2 and 3, where Peter states that all things have been fulfilled, all things are ready; God will send Jesus back if they will only come. We have seen the reaction of those who were invited. They have thrown Christ's servants into prison, beaten them, and have stoned Stephen to death. Then what does the king do? He becomes angry and sends his armies and destroys those murderers and burns up their city. This doubtless refers to the destruction of Jerusalem. Then after the destruction of Jerusalem a third call goes forth. The servants are told to go into the streets and invite as many people of all kinds as they can find. This they do and the feast is finally furnished with guests. If the originally invited guests represented Israel, then those from off the streets must represent non-Israelites, or Gentiles. Therefore this parable seems to teach clearly that the Gentiles were to receive the Gospel of the Kingdom after Israel had been judged and Jerusalem had been destroyed. But this order of events poses a problem. Actually, we know, Cornelius, the Gentile, received the Kingdom message twenty-five or thirty years before the destruction of Jerusalem. How can we explain this seeming inconsistency?

We know from Paul's epistles that God had a secret eternal purpose to form the Church which is the Body of Christ, and that it was through the fall and the casting away of Israel that He brought this new order or dispensation into being (Rom. 11:11,15). God, therefore, interrupted His dealings with Israel for the time being, to bring this new program into being, and His first step in preparation for this new program was to save the man whom He had chosen to administer this new dispensation, Saul of Tarsus. Then, in order to prepare the way for Paul's coming Gentile ministry, He gave a special revelation to Peter to go to an uncircumcised Gentile so that the Jewish Apostles would be convinced that Paul's ministry to Gentiles was according to the will of God.

We can not find any Scriptural evidence that the new dispensation as such began with the conversion of either Saul or Cornelius, but that these events were only to prepare for it. Saul was saved under the Kingdom order and received water baptism for the remission of sins (Acts 22:16). Cornelius did receive the Holy Spirit and spoke with tongues before he was baptized with water, but perhaps God reversed the order of baptizing and receiving the Spirit to convince Peter that a true work of salvation had occurred. From Peter's amazement at Gentiles receiving the Spirit, it is doubtful whether Peter would have baptized him unless God had given evidence Cornelius was saved. But notice that Peter preached exactly the same message to Cornelius as he had been preaching to the Jews. He was given no new revelation such as was given later to Paul. And we are plainly told that the Holy Spirit did exactly the same work on Cornelius as He had done on the Jews at Pentecost. Read carefully Acts 11:15-17. If Christ baptizing Cornelius with the Spirit placed him in the new Body of Christ, why did not the same baptizing work at Pentecost place those Jews in the Body? If we do not distinguish between Christ baptizing with the Spirit and the Spirit baptizing into Christ, we must agree that both Cornelius and those at Pentecost were baptized into the Body. But we do not read of the latter baptism or of the Body of Christ until we come some years later to Paul's epistles. It is the writer's personal belief that the dispensing of this new order under Paul began when God separated him unto the work for which He had called him (Acts 13:2). It is here that he is first called "an apostle." It is here that he performs for the first time "the signs of an apostle." And it is here that "the door of faith" is opened to the Gentiles.

Thus it would seem that Peter, having been filled with the Holy Spirit, and having had the ministry of that Spirit operating in his life of "being guided into all truth," and "shown things to come" (John 16:13), now understood the meaning of the Lord's teaching while He was on the earth, and therefore understood the order in which the Great Commission was to be carried out. And since it was not yet time in the prophetic order to go to the Gentiles, we can understand why Peter had not been disobedient in not going to them, and why God had to give Peter a special revelation to go contrary to that prophetic order, as He was preparing to bring in His hitherto secret dispensation of the mystery (Eph. 3:1-11; Col. 1:24-27).

III. PETER EXPLAINS GENTILE SALVATION TO THE OTHER APOSTLES, 11:1-18.

When Peter returned to Jerusalem, "they that were of the circumcision" contended with him because he had gone in unto uncircumcised Gentiles. On the surface this sounds as though there were two groups of believers in Jerusalem, the circumcised and the uncircumcised. However, this could not be, for at least two reasons. Peter was the first to go to the uncircumcised, so there could not have been uncircumcised believers in Jerusalem. Next, had there been uncircumcised believers in Jerusalem, there would have been no point in criticizing Peter's action. Further, the six Jewish believers who accompanied Peter to Cornelius are called, "they of the circumcision" (10:45). "They of the circumcision," is an expression which came to be used later on when Luke wrote the Acts to distinguish between Jewish and Gentile believers. On the question of who are the true circumcision compare Paul's statements in Phil. 3:3 and Col. 2:10-15.

Peter rehearsed the story of chapter 10 almost word for word. He concluded by saying: "As I began to speak the Holy Spirit fell on them, as on us in the beginning. Then remembered I the word of the Lord, how that he said, John indeed baptized with water, but ye shall be baptized with the Holy Spirit. Forasmuch then as God gave them the like gift as he did unto us, who believed on the Lord Jesus Christ, what was I, that I could withstand God?" Peter thus states as clearly as could be expressed that the same thing happened to Cornelius and his household as happened to the Jewish believers at Pentecost. If "Christ baptizing with the Spirit" is identical with "the

Holy Spirit baptizing believers into the Body of Christ," then the Jews at Pentecost and Cornelius were all made members of the Body of Christ, for they all had the same experience. But if these two baptisms are separate and distinct, then neither Cornelius or those at Pentecost were baptized into the Body of Christ, for neither is said to have been baptized by the Spirit into the Body. We do not believe that the baptism which bestows the miraculous gifts of tongues, healing, and prophecy is that which unites believers today as members of the Body. The one is outward, observed, and experiential. The other is inward, unobserved, and not experienced by the senses. Much confusion among Christians over Spirit Baptism would be cleared away if these distinctions were observed. It may be claimed that Peter supposed that God was doing the same thing for Cornelius that He did for the Jews at Pentecost, but secretly He was doing something entirely new and different. But of course, the same thing may be said of what happened at Pentecost: that is, the apostles supposed that Joel's prophecy was being fulfilled, but secretly God was beginning an entirely new dispensation. This seems to us to be reading something into the Scripture and to be throwing discredit upon the words of men who were filled with the Holy Spirit.

Peter's explanation of his mission to Cornelius completely satisfied those who had contended with him, and they glorified God, saying, "Then hath God also to the Gentiles granted repentance unto life."

IV. GENTILES RECEIVED INTO THE CHURCH AT ANTIOCH, 11:19-26.

We are told in Acts 8:4 that those who were scattered abroad after the stoning of Stephen "went everywhere preaching the word." Here we are told that they "were preaching the word to none but unto the Jews only." This scattering took place approximately ten years before the events of this chapter. All during this period none but Jews were evangelized. As far as the record given in Acts is concerned, Peter is the first to have preached to a Gentile, apart from a Jewish setting. Gentiles who had become Jewish proselytes may have been saved before Cornelius, but there is no statement to this effect in Acts. Now, and probably with the knowledge of the Cornelius event, certain of those who were scattered came to Antioch and began preaching to the Greeks, and a large number turned to the Lord. The Authorized Version calls them Grecians (Greek-speaking Jews), but the Revised Text reads, "Greeks."

Since this preaching to the Greeks at Antioch was done by Jews who were scattered abroad after the martyrdom of Stephen which took place approximately ten years earlier, the question arises, Did it take all of those years for these men to get to Antioch? This seems unlikely. Vs. 19 plainly states that some of these men came to Antioch, preaching to none but the Jews only. Thus this Jewish church may have been established quite soon after the dispersion of Acts 7. Then verse 20 states that there were some from Cyprus and Cyrene, which, when they were come to Antioch, spake unto the Greeks. It was not necessarily the founding of a group of believers at Antioch which took place some ten years after Stephen's death, but the beginning of preaching to Gentiles at Antioch.

This contact with the Gentiles at Antioch took place shortly after Peter had preached to Cornelius; so when the Jerusalem church got word of it they sent Barnabas to Antioch to investigate this new development. We cannot agree with Henry Alford that the Jerusalem church sent Barnabas to force circumcision on these Gentiles.[1] We believe they had already agreed to the salvation of Gentile Cornelius apart from circumcision. Rather he was sent to help and encourage these Gentile converts. When he arrived he saw that there was a genuine work of the grace of God taking place and he exhorted them with purpose of heart to cleave to the Lord. Having gotten acquainted with Saul on his first visit to Jerusalem and perhaps having learned of God's purpose to use Saul among the Gentiles, he departed for Tarsus, and having found him, brought him back to Antioch, where the two of them ministered for a whole year and taught much people.

It was here that the disciples were first given the name of Christians. This name is mentioned in only two other places in the Bible (Acts 26:28 and 1 Pet. 4:16). The Biblical name for Christians is believers, or saints, or brethren. There is much speculation concerning the origin of the name Christian. Many think the name originated with unbelievers who coined this word to describe the followers of Christ. The word is used today in such a broad and loose sense that it has little definitive meaning.

V. ANTIOCH SENDS FAMINE-RELIEF TO JERUSALEM, 11:27-30, 12:25.

Agabus, one of the prophets who came to Antioch from Jerusalem foretold the famine which came to pass in the days of Claudius Caesar. Actually a number of famines occurred during the reign of Claudius in different parts of the empire. Ogg dates the one in Judea in 45 or 46 A.D.[2] The church at Antioch took up an offering for the saints in Judea and sent it by the hand of Barnabas and Saul. This was Saul's second visit to Jerusalem after his conversion. Agabus is mentioned again in Acts 21:10. One thing that characterized Paul's ministry was his care for the poor. He spent a great deal of his time on his third missionary journey taking up a collection for the poor saints at Jerusalem. In his report on the Jerusalem Council he states that the Jewish apostles requested that he should be careful to remember the poor, "which," he says, "I was also forward to do" (Gal. 2:10).

VI. PERSECUTION BY HEROD, 12:1-25.

A. *James Beheaded,* 12:1-4. This Herod was called Agrippa and was the grandson of Herod the Great who had tried to kill the infant Jesus. We don't know what precipitated his act of laying hands on certain of the church to afflict them, but when he did and had James killed with the sword and saw that it pleased the Jews, he had Peter arrested, thinking to do the same thing to him. But it was the days of unleavened bread, that is, the feast of Passover, and he decided to wait until after the feast to kill Peter. "Easter" in the King James Version, should be translated "passover." This is the only occurrence of the word "Easter" in the King James Version. Luke says that this took place about the time of the famine. It would be that the disciples were accused of somehow being responsible for the famine. The James who was killed was the apostle, brother of John. James, the Lord's brother, the writer of the Epistle of James and the one who became leader in the Jerusalem church, appears in chapters 15 and 21. Peter was placed under a guard of sixteen soldiers, that is, four quaternions. There were four soldiers guarding him at a time during the four watches of the day and night. The King James states that prayer was made *"without ceasing"* for Peter by the church, but the Greek word means earnestly or fervently. They were praying earnestly for him.

B. *Peter Miraculously Delivered,* 12:5-19. Peter was miraculously delivered from prison by an angel of God. Paul, on the other hand, was allowed to remain in prison for two years in Caesarea (Acts 24:27) and for two years in Rome (Acts 28:30). Why the difference? Was Peter more faithful or spiritual than Paul? And was it that James was less faithful than Peter that God allowed him to be killed while Peter was set free? People often try to explain why calamities befall certain Christians and not others on the basis of their faithfulness or spirituality. One is reminded of the question the disciples asked the Lord concerning the man born blind: "Who did sin, this man or his parents, that he was born blind?" (John 9:2). It is very dangerous for us to try to answer such questions. God is sovereign and He does whatever brings Him the most glory. Paul would never have had the privilege of testifying before kings had he not been arrested and held a prisoner. The man was born blind that the works of God should be made manifest in him.

But while Peter's deliverance was accomplished entirely apart from human intervention or power, there was a human element which entered into it. Many believers were gathered at the home of Mary, praying for Peter. We don't know just what they were asking for, but from their reaction when Peter knocked at the door, it would seem they were not asking for a miraculous deliverance, for they told the servant girl she was out of her mind when she said Peter was at the door. If they were praying for his deliverance they apparently didn't expect their prayer to be answered. But even Peter could not believe what was happening at first. He thought he was dreaming, but he finally came to himself and realized that he was out of prison and on the streets of Jerusalem. After Peter had explained his release to those gathered for prayer he told them to go and tell James and the other brethren. Peter then departed to another place, probably outside Jerusalem, until things quieted down. It is here for the first time that we get an intimation that James, the Lord's brother according to the flesh, was becoming the leader of the church at Jerusalem. We see him officiating in Acts 15 and 21.

It might seem unfair that the guards were put to death for allowing Peter to escape, when they were apparently struck unconscious by divine power and were powerless to act. However, in this world which has rebelled against God, many seemingly innocent people have been tortured and put to death. In this case, we feel sure God will hold Herod accountable for this deed. He was fighting against God and God's people and was playing God himself, as we shall see in the next section. Every sin and wrong will be brought to light in the day of God's judgment and all accounts will be settled in justice and righteousness.

C. **Death of Herod,** 12:20-25. Herod apparently gave up on his campaign of persecution of the believers after Peter escaped his plot. He must have sensed that he was grappling with a power superior to his own. So he left Judea and went down to Caesarea. While there emissaries from Tyre and Sidon came seeking terms of peace, for they knew Herod was angry with them. Then on a certain day Herod gathered the people together and made an oration. He sat on his throne arrayed in royal apparel. Josephus says he wore a robe made entirely of silver. As he spoke the people shouted, "It is the voice of a god and not of a man."

The entire Herodian clan was a wicked lot. The family history over a period of more than a hundred years was one of intrigue, murder, immorality, incest, cunning, craftiness and insufferable egotism. A number of the Herods appear in New Testament history. Herod the Great is mentioned in Matt. 2:1-22 and Lk. 1:5. He ordered the slaughter of the infants in an attempt to kill the child Jesus. He died in 4 B.C., shortly after the birth of Christ. Herod Antipas is mentioned in Lk. 3:1,19; 9:7,9; 13:31; 23:7; Matt. 14:1,2; Mk. 6:14. His mother was Malthace and his brother was Archelaus, Matt. 2:22. Herod the Great also had a son by his wife Mariamne I, Aristobulus, who in turn had two sons and a daughter. One son was Herod, King of Chalcis, who married his niece, Bernice, Acts 25:13. The other son was Herod Agrippa I, the Herod of our present story in Acts 12:1-23. He had a son, Herod Agrippa II, Acts 25:13, and two daughters, Bernice, Acts 25:13, and Drusilla, who married Felix, Acts 24:24. Herod the Great also had a son by his wife Mariamne II, Herod Phillip I (Matt. 14:3; Mk. 6:17; Lk. 3:19). Herod the Great also had a son by his wife Cleopatra, Philip II, who was tetrarch of E. Jordan territory. The Herods were not Jews, but Idumaeans, who were at that time nominal Jews, since they were subdued by John Hyreanus in 125 B.C. and made a part of the Asmonean kingdom through enforced circumcision. The Idumaeans were Edomites, the descendants of Esau, and the old antagonism seen in Gen. 27:41 still remained between them and the Jews.

Returning now to the story of Herod Agrippa, we see him accepting the worship of the people and making himself a god, and immediately an angel of the Lord smote him because he gave not God the glory, and he was eaten of worms and died a horrible death. God's judgments are not always so swiftly carried out. But in his dealings with the Jews God manifested Himself in open signs and wonders and interventions. The death of Agrippa is reminiscent of that of Antiochus, that arch-enemy of the Jews and desecrator of the temple. His death is described in 2 Maccabees 9:8-10.

"And thus he that a little afore thought he might command the waves of the sea, (so proud was he beyond the condition of men), and weigh the high mountains in a balance, was now cast on the ground, and carried in a horselitter, showing forth unto all the manifest power of God. So that the worms rose up out of the body of this wicked man, and whiles he lived in sorrow and pain, his flesh fell away and the filthiness of his smell was noisome to all his army. And the man, that thought a little afore, he could reach to the stars of heaven, no man could endure to carry for his intolerable stink!"[3]

The present dispensation of the grace of God has been characterized by what Sir Robert Anderson has called, "The Silence of God."[4] Instead of judging the world for the murder of His Son, God has in grace declared an amnesty. He has extended His offer of reconciliation instead of judgment. The throne of justice has been transformed into a throne of grace. God has not spoken openly from heaven since He revealed this message of reconciliation through the Apostle Paul. The next time He speaks from heaven will be in judgment. Man today thinks that God is dead, or He doesn't care. Why doesn't He do something about the crimes and wars and injustice in the world? But man does not realize that God has spoken His last word in grace and mankind has rejected it. The day of grace will end and then God will again speak from heaven. "He that sitteth in the heavens shall laugh: the Lord shall have them in derision. Then shall he speak unto them in his wrath, and vex them in his sore displeasure" (Ps. 2:4,5).

Thus Agrippa, just as Lucifer of old, would have exalted his throne above that of God, was cast down to the ground (Isa. 14:9-17). Herod's wicked plot against the church was defeated, "but the word of God grew and multiplied."

The last verse of the chapter tells of the return of Saul and Barnabas from Jerusalem to Antioch, giving the impression that they were in Jerusalem during Herod's persecution. However, Herod died in 44 A.D., and the famine did not start until at least a year later. It would seem then that Herod was already dead when they left on their relief mission. This last verse of the chapter returns the narrative to Antioch.

SECTION TWO

Note Page

1   70. – Henry Alford, *The Greek Testament* (Cambridge, Deighton, Bell and Co., 1877), Vol. II, p. 127.

2   70. – Ogg, op. cit., p. 53.

3   74. – *The Septuagint Version* (London, S. Bagster and Sons Limited, n.d.).

4   74. – Anderson, op. cit., Chapter I.

SECTION THREE

The Gospel to the Gentiles Through Paul

Chapters 13-28

I. THE FIRST MISSIONARY JOURNEY, 13:1-14:28.

A. *Paul and Barnabas Separated unto the Gentile Ministry,*
13:1-3. Acts 13 marks the beginning of what we have called
the Transition Period. A transition is a change from one order
or program to another, covering a period of time during which
a dual program exists. The first half of Acts is a continuation
of the same Israelitish Kingdom program which was carried on
by our Lord in His earthly ministry. There were developments
in that program, but not what we would call a transition.
During the latter part of the first half of Acts we can see
certain events which were preparatory to the transition. By a
transition we do not mean that the Jewish Pentecostal Church
gradually changed into the Church which is the Body of
Christ. The Body of Christ is a new creation, and as such had a
distinct historical beginning. The Transition Period may better
be described as an overlapping period, a period during which
the religious program which accompanied the Israelitish
Kingdom ministry overlapped into the beginning of the new
dispensation of the Body of Christ. During this period the
Jews who believed continued in their Mosaic customs, whereas
the Gentiles who believed were to observe no such things
(Acts 21:25).

It must be remembered that there is a historical continuity
in God's redemptive program. When God began the new
dispensation He did not go to Rome or Athens and begin an
entirely new undertaking separate and distinct from Israel. He
chose a Jew, and while He gave him a distinctly new revelation
of truth, this Jew was saved under the Kingdom program.
Most of his fellow-workers were Jews and he ministered to the
Jews first. From the Book of Acts alone we might have
difficulty in discerning the beginning of a new and separate
Body distinct from Israel. It is only from Paul's epistles that
we learn the truth of the Mystery, and it is from 1
Corinthians, written during the transition, that we see clearly
the character of this period. Paul likens it to the period of
childhood, the development from infancy to maturity

(chapters 13 and 14). Many childhood things pass away with adulthood. Just so, the sign gifts which were a part of the Pentecostal kingdom program overlapped into the infancy of the new dispensation. But when the adult stage of the new dispensation arrived, after God had concluded his dealings with Israel and had completed His revelation of truth for the Body, the childhood characteristics passed away. The transition or period of overlapping was over. No longer was there a different outward program for Jews and Gentiles. No longer was there a place for sign-gifts. No longer was there need for the gift of prophecy, for God's revelation for the Body was now complete. The "one New Man" had come to adulthood.

(For a more detailed treatment of the Transition see the author's book, *A Dispensational Theology,* pp. 506-515, published by Grace Bible College Publications, Grand Rapids.)

It may seem strange that God should wait some ten years after saving Saul before He separated him unto his special ministry. But it may be no more strange than when God calls a man today to the ministry. There may be ten years or more of preparation before the man is fitted to really begin his ministry. We are prone to think that God with one thunderbolt struck Saul down, saved him, gave him a completed revelation and completely outfitted him in an instant of time. It is plain from scripture that God did no such thing. A violent revolution took place in Saul's life. He needed much time for reflection and getting adjusted to his new life. He isolated himself in Arabia for this purpose. God gradually revealed more and more truth to Paul, as is evident from Acts 26:16. Moses spent forty years in the backside of the desert before God used him to deliver Israel (Acts 7:23-30). And Christ spent about four years teaching and preparing the Twelve Apostles before they really began their ministry at Pentecost. God does some things instantaneously and other things progressively. It seems that in the case of preparing His servants for His ministry, He always works progressively. That, of course, does not mean that a believer can render no service for Christ until he has spent some years in preparation. Every Christian can start serving Christ the moment he is saved. That is the way it was with Saul. Immediately he began to testify that Jesus was the Christ, the Son of God. But if a Christian is called of God into some special service, he must go through a course of training, formal or informal, before he is ready to do the job. This principle holds true in every vocation in life, whether it be lawyer, barber, or candlestick maker.

There is a natural division of the Book of Acts at chapter

13. Up to that point Jerusalem has been the center and Peter has been the chief actor. After Acts 13 Antioch is the center and Paul is the chief actor. Almost all commentators recognize this division. But we may ask, What is the significance of this division? Is the second half of the book simply a continuation of what was going on in the first half, or is there something new and different happening in the second half?

There can be no doubt that Paul was a special apostle, separate and distinct from the Twelve. We know that special revelation was given to him concerning God's secret purpose in this present dispensation. Although he began testifying in the synagogues immediately after his conversion, it is not until Acts 13 that he is separated unto his distinctive ministry. Since this distinctive Gentile ministry began in Acts 13, there are those who believe that the subject of that ministry, the Body of Christ, began at the same time. Others think that the Body began with Paul's conversion, while still others speculate it began after the final casting away of Israel at the end of Acts. Others, because they confuse Christ baptizing with the Holy Spirit with the Holy Spirit baptizing believers into Christ, hold that the Body began at Pentecost. And finally there are those who see nothing distinctive about the Body of Christ and thus make it the same church as has always existed since Adam or Abraham. While Scripture does not state specifically when the Body began, it does state when Paul's special ministry for which he was called began.

Notice now the means whereby Barnabas and Saul were separated unto this special ministry. There were certain prophets and teachers in the church, and the Holy Spirit told them to separate these two men for this work. It must be remembered that at this point in time none of the New Testament Scripture was in existence. For that reason God gave a special gift of prophecy to certain men in each local church through whom He communicated His message for the people. This is one of the gifts which Paul said would pass away. God does not communicate directly to individuals today in this manner. His revelation has become permanently embodied in the written Word. God speaks today through His written Word.

Fasting, prayer, and the laying on of hands are mentioned in connection with what we might call their ordination. There is no command in the Bible to fast. The first time it is mentioned in the Bible is in Judges 20:26. A terrible crime had been committed in Israel by the Benjamites, resulting in a war in which the guilty parties seemed to be winning the victory. "Then all the children of Israel, and all the people, went up, and came into the house of God, and wept, and sat there before the Lord, and fasted that day until evening, and offered burnt offerings and peace offerings before the Lord." The people were so overcome with grief and perplexity that they forgot about their physical hunger. Many people who are devoted to their business often miss meals because they are so taken up with their work. Scientists often stick at an experiment in the laboratory to the extent that they may go all day and night without eating. When one's dearest loved one is critically ill, who would think about leaving the bedside and going out to a feast? Fasting becomes legalism when it is made a ritual and when it is believed to be a special work of merit. No doubt the leaders at Antioch realized what an important decision was before them. They were so concerned that they continued in prayer without thought of taking time to satisfy their own appetites. There is nothing wrong with fasting in any dispensation if it is thus motivated.

Then there was the laying on of hands. This practice originated with the offering of animal sacrifices, as recorded in Lev. 1:4; 16:21. The offerer laid his hands on the head of the animal which was to be sacrificed as his substitute, thus identifying himself with the sacrifice. See Gen. 48:14; Lev. 24:14; Num. 8:10; 27:18,23 for other Old Testament examples of laying on of hands. In the New Testament Jesus laid His hands on little children (Matt. 19:13,15) and on the sick (Matt. 9:18). The Apostles laid hands on those they baptized that they might receive the Holy Spirit (Acts 8:17,19; 19:6) and in healing (Acts 28:8). And as in the case now before us laying on of hands was used in setting apart of persons to a specific office or ministry (cf. 1 Tim. 4:14; 5:22; 2 Tim. 1:6). While the prophetic gift was yet in operation, those possessed of that gift had the ability under God of conferring the Spirit by laying on of hands. In the case of Timothy, for example, Paul states: "Do not neglect your gift, which was given you through a prophetic message when the body of elders laid their hands on you" (1 Tim. 4:14, N.I.V.) Although the special gifts have passed away, the hand is still recognized to have a very special meaning in various ways. Why, in a court of law, does one raise his right hand to swear that he is telling the truth, or why does one lay his hand on the open Bible to take an oath of office, or what is the meaning of the shaking of hands? Ordination by man is no proof of God's ordination of a man to the ministry. But when a group of Christian leaders thoroughly examine a man's manner of life, his knowledge and ability to preach the Word of God, and his motivation in going into the ministry, and then identify themselves with him by the laying on of their hands, they have done as much as they can to recommend him to the Christian community as a minister of the Gospel.

B. *The Journey*, 13:4-14:28.

1. *Ministry on Cyprus*, 13:4-12: Saul and Barnabas departed from Antioch to Seleucia, the seaport, located 16 miles from Antioch, where they took a boat for the island of Cyprus a trip of about one hundred miles. They landed on the east end of the island at Salamis, where they preached the Word in the synagogue, with what results we are not told. But we are told that they had brought John Mark with them as a helper. You will remember that Mark returned with Barnabas and Saul when they came back from Jerusalem to Antioch. They traveled the length of the island, about eighty miles until they came to Paphos. There they had a most interesting encounter with two men, one a Jewish sorcerer and the other a Roman proconsul. The Jew had two names. One was Bar-Jesus, which means Son of the Savior. That is what the Jew was intended to be. But his other name was Elymas, an Arabic word meaning "the wise." He was a sorcerer, the Greek word being the same as used for the wise men who came to Jesus at His birth. It is the word "magos" or magician. He is also called a false prophet. As a magi he practised astrology, fortune-telling, and predicted future events. He apparently exercised great influence over Sergius Paulus, even as our modern politicians in Washington are said to consult astrologers and others who claim to forecast the future. Sergius Paulus sent for Barnabas and Saul because he wanted to hear the word of God but Elymas tried to turn the proconsul from the faith. Then Paul, filled with the Holy Spirit, looked the false prophet in the eye and said: "You are a child of the devil and an enemy of everything that is right. You are full of all kinds of deceit and trickery. Will you never stop perverting the right ways of the Lord? Now the hand of the Lord is against you. You are going to be blind, and for a time you will be unable to see the light of the sun." And immediately this apostate Jew was stricken with blindness and began groping about, seeking some one to lead him by the hand. As a result of this miraculous judgment, Sergius was amazed and became a believer.

There are several things to be noted here. The first is the extent of the miraculous powers which were committed to the Apostles. There was such a thing as the gift of miracles which was given to certain believers, but Saul was an apostle, and he tells us that powers given to the Apostles were to be classified as "signs of an apostle" (2 Cor. 12:12). Next is the fact that Saul's name changes to Paul. This is the first recorded Gentile convert after he was separated to his special ministry. He takes for himself the name of this Gentile convert. Never again is he called Saul, although Paul later on in rehearsing his own conversion, relates the Lord's word from heaven, "Saul, Saul, why persecutest thou me?" (Acts 22:7,13; 26:14). Finally, we believe that Paul's acts of pronouncing blindness upon this Jew is symbolic of his ministry to Israel nationally from this point on. Whereas the Twelve were sent to offer the Kingdom to Israel, Paul's ministry is to pronounce blindness upon Israel. Paul had great love for his own people of Israel and his heart's desire and prayer to God was that they might be saved (Rom. 10:1). But in spite of this, Paul knew that Israel had become enemies of the Gospel and that judicial blindness had been pronounced upon them (Rom. 11:7,25). But this blindness did not include every Israelite, for there was a remnant according to the election of grace, and Paul along with others, was among that number. And the blindness was not to last for ever, for God had made an unconditional covenant that He would finally save Israel, and so Paul says that after this present Gentile dispensation, "All Israel shall be saved." It seems most significant, therefore, that this first recorded event after his separation, the Apostle of the Gentiles takes on a Gentile name, converts a Gentile, and pronounces blindness upon the Jew.

2. *On to Antioch in Pisidia,* 13:13-52: Having finished their ministry in Paphos, they sailed north to the mainland and landed at Perga. John Mark, however, deserted them and returned to his home in Jerusalem. Mark was a cousin of Barnabas and he later became the cause of a break between Barnabas and Paul. There is no record of any preaching in Perga. Perhaps they were too upset over Mark's defection to engage in a preaching campaign. However, on their return trip they did preach the word to that city also. From Perga they went on to Antioch. This whole region of Asia Minor to which they ministered on this expedition is now southern Turkey, a region which is now almost one hundred percent Moslem. History shows us that nations which were once the bastions of the faith are now in

heathen darkness. When Israel finally apostastized from Christ, God broke their branches out of the tree (Rom. 11:19-22). And God warns the Gentiles if they abide not in the truth He will break them off also. If moral and spiritual declension continue at the present rate, the United States, which has been such a stronghold for the faith, could well become as godless as the Soviet Union.

Here we have the first recorded sermon of Paul. Paul and his companion went to the Jewish synagogue on the sabbath day and after the reading of the law and the prophets they were invited to speak a word of exhortation if they so desired. That gave Paul the opportunity to preach, and that day the synagogue audience got more than they expected. Before giving a word of exhortation, he reviewed the history of God's gracious dealings with Israel from the time God exalted and delivered them from Egypt under Moses. When he got down to the time of King David, a man after God's own heart, he got to the heart of his message. He proclaimed that according to His promise, God had raised up from David's seed a Savior for Israel, even Jesus. He told of John the Baptist's introduction of Jesus to Israel and of his testimony concerning the Messiahship of Jesus. He addressed his message primarily to the descendants of Abraham but included everyone who feared God. He explained that the rulers and those that dwell at Jerusalem really didn't know who Jesus was, nor did they understand the message of the prophets which they read every sabbath day, and yet they had fulfilled the prophets in condemning Him. This reminds us of Paul's words in 1 Cor. 2:8: "For had they known it, they would not have crucified the Lord of glory." But they did crucify Him and when they had fulfilled all that had been predicted concerning Him in the writings of the prophets, they took Him down from the cross and laid His body in a sepulchre, "BUT God raised Him from the dead." The fact of His resurrection was attested, not on the basis of a rumor, or even upon the word of one or two witnesses, but there were many witnesses who saw Him in His resurrection body. Paul states that on one occasion over five hundred brethren saw Him at once (1 Cor. 15:6). Paul then shows that the resurrection of the Messiah was predicted in the Old Testament by quoting from the Psalms and Isaiah. The first quotation is from Ps. 2:7: "I will declare the decree: the Lord hath said unto me, Thou art my Son, this day have I begotten thee." Since God has always been the Father, He must always have had a Son.

Theologians speak of Christ having been eternally begotten. However, this reference speaks of a day when the Son was begotten, and Paul shows this begetting refers to being begotten from the dead. This same truth is stated in Heb. 1:5 and 6. And Rev. 1:5 speaks of Christ as the first begotten, or first born, from the dead. The next quotation is from Isa. 55:3 concerning the sure mercies of David. Isaiah 55 is the proto-evangel. It speaks of salvation without money and without price and shows that it is based upon an everlasting covenant, even the sure mercies of David. This promise was made to David back in 2 Sam. 7:8-17. Psalm 89:27-29 reads: "Also I will make Him my firstborn, higher than the kings of the earth. My mercy will I keep for Him for evermore, and my covenant shall stand fast with him. His seed will I also make to endure forever, and His throne as the days of heaven." Thus it was necessary for Christ to be raised from the dead for these promises to be realized. The third quotation is from Ps. 16:10: "For thou wilt not leave my soul in sheol; neither wilt thou suffer thine Holy One to see corruption." Peter, as we have seen earlier, also quoted this Psalm concerning the Resurrection of Christ (Acts 2:25-28). Both Peter and Paul point out the fact that David, to whom this promise was made, died and his body did see corruption. Therefore the promise must have referred to David's greater Son, whom God raised from the dead before corruption of His body occurred.

Having established the Messiahship of Jesus, His death and His resurrection, Paul declares that through this Man is preached forgiveness of sins, and by Him all that believe are justified from all things, from which they could not be justified by the law of Moses. Although Habakkuk 2:4 had said that the just shall live by his faith, this is the first time we read about justification by faith apart from the law. The Jews had lived many centuries under the law and had come to believe that they could be justified by the keeping of the law. This message of Paul must have come to them with a shock. Many found great difficulty in giving up their law righteousness for the free gift of God's righteousness, even as Paul describes in Rom. 10:1-13. From the reaction of the crowd in the synagogue, it would seem that the Gentiles who were present were more receptive of this truth than were the Jews.

But along with the good news of the gospel, Paul sounded a warning. Significantly Paul addresses these Jews of the dispersion in Antioch by quoting a prophecy which was addressed to the dispersion: "Behold, ye among the heathen and regard, and wonder marvellously: for I will work a work in your days, which ye will not believe, though it be told you" (Hab. 1:5). Apparently Paul quoted from the Septuagint, for he adds after "wonder marvellously" the words, "and perish." Although the Jews were told the message, the majority did not believe it. However there were many of the Jews and devout converts to Judaism who followed Paul and requested that he tell them more of this message the next sabbath. There is a difference in the reading of the Greek manuscripts in verse 42. The King James reads: "And when the Jews were gone out of the synagogue, the Gentiles besought that these words might be preached to them the next sabbath." The A.S.V. reads: "And as they went out, they besought that these words might be spoken to them the next sabbath." Verse 43 makes it clear that both Jews and Gentiles followed Paul and wanted him back the following week. When practically the whole city turned out to hear Paul the following sabbath, the Jewish leaders were filled with jealousy and contradicted what Paul was saying and spoke abusively against him. They not only didn't believe Paul's message, they could not endure anyone who drew greater crowds than they did. This reaction was an example of what Paul relates in Rom. 10:19-21: "But I say, Did not Israel know? First Moses saith, I will provoke you to jealousy by them that are no people, and by a foolish nation will I anger you. But Esaias is very bold, and saith, I was found of them that sought me not; I was made manifest unto them that asked not after me. But to Israel he saith, All day long have I stretched forth my hands to a disobedient and gainsaying people." Again, Paul states concerning Israel's fall: "I say then, Have they stumbled that they should fall? God forbid; but rather through their fall salvation is come to the Gentiles, for to provoke them to jealousy." (Rom. 11:11).

When the Jewish leaders began blaspheming, Paul and Barnabas spoke back very boldly, "It was necessary that the word of God should first have been spoken to you, but seeing ye put it from you, lo, we turn to the Gentiles." The gospel was to the Jew first (cf. Rom. 1:16; also Acts 3:26). It was necessary for Paul to go to the Jew first, for that was God's order. However, when they rejected and blasphemed, the Jew was set aside and Paul turned to the Gentiles. Now, the gospel is no longer to the Jew first. Neither Jew nor Gentile has the priority now. There are those who interpret Rom. 1:16 to mean that we should go to all of the Jews first before we go to the Gentiles with the gospel. Rather, we should go to both without distinction.

This is the first official turning away from Israel and turning to the Gentiles. This principle characterized Paul's ministry. It should be evident that from this point onward, God is no longer carrying out His Kingdom program with Israel. If national Israel is committing the unpardonable sin by blaspheming the Holy Spirit and God is turning away from them, how could any one imagine that God was still offering the Kingdom to Israel? There can be no doubt but that the new dispensation which is not based upon Israel's covenant priority has begun. And since this new dispensation concerns the outcalling of the Church which is Christ's Body, there can be no doubt but that Body has also begun.

We have just stated that God has begun a new dispensation, which Paul elsewhere calls "the mystery," or secret, because God is doing something that He had never before revealed to the sons of men (Col. 1:24-27). But it might appear that verse 47 contradicts this fact: "For so hath the Lord commanded us, saying, I have set thee to be a light of the Gentiles, that thou shouldest be for salvation unto the ends of the earth." This sounds like God is doing exactly what He predicted in the Old Testament. However, Paul does not say that Isa. 42:6,7 is being fulfilled by His ministry, in the sense that it will be fulfilled when God again resumes His dealings with Israel and brings light to the Gentiles through the instrumentality of Israel. It is apparent on the surface he could not mean this. Also, of whom is He speaking when He says: "I have set thee to be a light of the Gentiles?" The "thee" does not refer to Paul, but to Christ. Christ is the Light of the world: not Paul. God had predicted that Christ would enlighten the Gentiles, and in the Kingdom order of things, that He would do this through the instrumentality of Israel's Kingdom. But Israel has now fallen and refused to be God's instrument. Will Israel, then, defeat God's purpose to bless the Gentiles? By no means! Under the new dispensation committed to Paul, Christ is going to bless the Gentiles in spite of Israel and entirely apart from Israel. This is the key to the understanding of Paul's use of the Old Testament. For example, see Rom. 15:9-12. Paul is not saying that he is fulfilling Old Testament prophecy, but that God in sovereign grace is now blessing Gentiles, It is as though a very wealthy man had set up a corporation through which he had promised to help a certain minority group. But the heads of the corporation proved to be dishonest and absconded with the profits of the business. Now, what will the rich man do? Will he say, The corporation has failed, therefore I cannot carry out my promise? He could, of course, but in the case before us he says, "Hang the corporation! Out of my own riches, apart from that corporation, I am going to carry out my purpose to help that minority group." No wonder then, that the Gentiles represented by this minority group, when they heard this, were glad and glorified the word of the Lord, and as many as were ordained to eternal life believed. It should be remembered that when God instituted this new plan, He did not do it because Israel's action had taken Him by surprise and forced Him to change His plan. Paul makes it plain that this new plan was formulated before the world began, but it was never announced by God beforehand.

No doubt a great work of salvation was accomplished at Antioch, for we read that the word of the Lord was published throughout the whole region. But the Jews stirred up persecution against Paul and Barnabas. It was evidently quite severe, for Paul in writing later to Timothy makes special mention of it: "Persecutions, afflictions, which came unto me at Antioch, at Iconium, at Lystra: what persecutions I endured; but out of them all the Lord delivered me" (2 Tim. 3:11). The Jews stirred up devout and honorable women and chief men of the city to persecute Paul and Barnabas and to expel them from the city. One would not think that people guity of such actions could be called devout and honorable. But it has ever been true that the most devout people are capable of being incited to persecution of those they suppose are the least bit heretical. Think of Paul himself before he was saved. Read of his devotion in Phil. 3:4-6. He thought he was serving God by putting the early believers to death (Acts 26:9-12). Sincere fundamentalists can be stirred up to persecute severely fellow-believers who may differ over a very minor matter more than over the blatant apostasy of liberal theologians. When people come to believe they are the final authority on the Word of God, they feel duty bound to put down any one who dares disagree with them. The people of Antioch, the devout and honorable people, drove the apostles out of their city, but Paul and Barnabas shook off the dust of their feet against them (cf. Matt.

10:14), and went on to Iconium. The believers they left behind were filled with joy and the Holy Spirit (cf. 1 Pet. 4:12-14).

3. *The Ministry at Iconium,* 14:1-7: As Paul's custom was at this time, he went first to the Jewish synagogue. There he and Barnabas preached so effectively and convincingly that a great multitude of both Jews and Greeks believed. But the unbelieving Jews poisoned the minds of the Gentiles by speaking evil against the brethren. They remained at Iconium for a long time, preaching the message boldly, and the Lord gave testimony to the word of His grace by enabling them to perform miraculous signs and wonders. The city became so divided over the preaching that both the unbelieving Jews and Gentiles plotted to kill the apostles, and when they discovered the plot they fled to the Lycaonian cities of Lystra and Derbe and the surrounding regions, where they continued to preach the gospel.

It should be remembered that the Jews require a sign (1 Cor. 1:22) and that the sign gifts were active as long as God was dealing with the Jews. God did not cut off His dealings with the Jews all at once: the-cut off was progressive. The first we read of God turning away from Israel was at the end of the last chapter. Then progressively as we trace Paul's ministry throughout the latter half of the Acts we find the turning away becoming more complete. Finally, when we come to the end of the Acts it seems that the turning away from Israel becomes final, and no doubt God ceased giving these sign gifts. We find no references in Paul's epistles written after the Acts period of these sign gifts: instead, we discover just the opposite. The gift of healing, for example, was prominent during the Acts period, but after the end of Acts Paul had to leave Trophimus, one of his faithful fellow-workers, at Miletum sick (2 Tim. 4:20), and another fellow-worker, Epaphroditus, came near dying and it was just the mercy of God that he recovered, not an act of instantaneous, miraculous healing (Phil. 2:26,27).

4. *Paul Stoned at Lystra,* 14:8-20: It is interesting to note that Paul duplicated practically all of the apostolic miracles performed by Peter. Peter had healed a man lame from his mother's womb at the Beautiful Gate of the temple, and here Paul heals a man with crippled feet from his mother's womb who had never walked in his whole life.

As Paul was preaching at Lystra this cripple attracted his special attention, and perceiving that he had faith to be healed he shouted to the man: "Stand up on your feet!" Immediately the man jumped up and began to walk. This was a sort of double miracle. The man's leg and feet bones which were malformed were instantly restored to normalcy, and the atrophied muscles which had never been utilized were made strong. And then there was the further miracle that the man could balance himself and walk without practise or help.

When the townspeople beheld this supernatural act, they said: "The gods have come down to us in the likeness of men." Because Paul was the chief speaker they called him Mercurius, and probably because Barnabas had a more imposing personal appearance than Paul (cf. 2 Cor. 10:1,10), they called him Jupiter. Actually in the Greek text the names are Hermes and Dia or Zeus. The King James gives the Latin names of these gods. Hermes or Mercury was the messenger of the gods, and Zeus or Jupiter was the father of the gods. The priest of Jupiter brought oxen and garlands to the temple which was before the city and was getting ready to make sacrifices to Paul and Barnabas. Since the people were expressing their worship of Paul and Barnabas in the Lycaonian language, which the apostles apparently did not understand, they did not realize what was going on until they saw the preparations for making sacrifices. When they realized that the people wanted to worship them as gods, they tore their clothes and rushed into the crowd shouting: "Why are you doing this? We are just ordinary human beings like yourselves. We have come to bring you good news (the Gospel), that you should turn away from these worthless things to the living God, who made heaven and earth and the sea and all that is in them. In the past He let all nations go their own way, but He has always given proof of Himself by the good things He does. He gives you rain from heaven and crops in their seasons; He provides you with food and fills your hearts with joy." After having said all of this to the people they had difficulty in keeping the crowd from offering sacrifices to them. We can only imagine what some of the modern so-called faith healers would have done under similar circumstances. What an opportunity for popularity and to cash in on the situation. The world is filled with religious charlatans, but here is proof that Paul was not in the ministry for personal gain or self-aggrandizement.

Miraculous signs produce only a superstitious kind of faith. One day the people were ready to offer sacrifices to Paul as a god and the next day they picked up stones to kill him. The Jews in Antioch and Iconium who had successfully turned the populace against the apostles, when they heard of Paul's success in Lystra, they came to Lystra and won over the crowd, claiming Paul was a fraud, and incited the mob to stone Paul and to drag his body out of the city. It is not certain whether Paul was actually dead or only unconscious. The Scripture says they "supposed" he was dead. Some think that Paul refers to this experience in 2 Cor. 12:2, where he was caught up to the third heaven and knew not whether he was in or out of the body. However, Paul said that this happened fourteen years prior to his writing to the Corinthians. It is thought that 2 Corinthians was written around 57 A.D., and 14 years earlier would be about 43 A.D. Paul was apparently in Cilicia in 43 A.D., two or three years before Barnabas brought him to first minister at Antioch. Paul's stoning at Lystra took place around 48 A.D., some five years after his vision of paradise. We do not know what precipitated his experience of being caught up into the third heaven and seeing things which it was not lawful for man to utter. We know only that after this exalted vision God had to give Paul a thorn in the flesh to keep him from exalting himself or of becoming conceited.

We can only imagine how Barnabas and the other believers felt as they stood around gazing on Paul's battered and seemingly lifeless body. They must have felt somewhat like the two on the road to Emmaus who had trusted that Jesus was the one who was to redeem Israel but had been brutally put to death and his dead body was in a tomb guarded by Roman soldiers. Their hopes were crushed to the ground. But just as Jesus arose victoriously from the grave, so Paul to their wonderment stood up and walked back into the city from whence he had been dragged as a dead man. All who saw him must have been greatly impressed, not only with the truthfulness of his message, but with his courage in coming back into the city which had just tried to kill him.

5. *The Return Trip to Antioch in Syria,* 14:21-28: The very next day Paul and Barnabas left Lystra and went on to Derbe where they preached to many people. There is no record of further persecution. Perhaps the unusual event at Lystra discouraged the Jews from dogging his steps

further. This was the furtherest penetration of this missionary journey. Leaving Derbe they retraced their steps through Lystra, Iconium, and Antioch. In each city they strengthened the believers and encouraged them to remain true to the faith. They reminded them of a truth that is mentioned numerous times in the New Testament: we must go through many tribulations to enter into the kingdom of God. There are those who suppose that since Paul mentions the kingdom of God here and elsewhere throughout the latter half of the Acts, he must be preaching what we have called "the kingdom message of the Twelve Apostles," and not the message of the Mystery. However, when we turn to those epistles which all agree specifically set forth the truth of the Mystery, we find Paul still talking about the kingdom of God. See Eph. 5:5; Col. 4:11. The Kingdom of God, according to O.T. prophecies and the accounts in the Gospels and early Acts, refers specifically to the earthly phase of that kingdom which will be established when Christ returns to earth, or to the extension of that kingdom beyond the millennium. Paul's references to the kingdom of Christ and of God refer mainly to the spiritual outcalling of believers to form the Church which is also called the Body of Christ. Paul tells us what the kingdom of God is not and what it is in his usage: "For the kingdom of God is not meat and drink (that is, it does not consist of the meat and drink ordinances associated with the O.T. concept of the kingdom), but righteousness, and peace, and joy in the Holy Spirit" (Rom. 14:17). Actually, the Kingdom of God includes everything which is under God's sovereignty, and that includes things good and bad (cf. Matt. 13:41,47,48), but when the kingdom is actually established on earth all of the bad will be cast out. It is important to understand that the kingdom of God is a broad, general term and that there are a number of specific phases or parts to that kingdom.

It is noteworthy how quickly churches were formed under Paul's ministry. After a few weeks or months at the most, Paul returned to the converts and organized them into churches or assemblies, ordaining certain men as elders to oversee the spiritual welfare of the churches.

Leaving Antioch they came to the region of Pamphilia, and, as noted earlier, they preached the Word in Perga, but no results of the preaching are given. Then they went to the nearby seaport of Attalia, from whence they took passage on a boat to Seleucia and Antioch, thus bypassing the island of Cyprus. Upon arriving at Antioch they assembled the church and gave a full report of all that God had done through them, "and how He had opened the door of faith to the Gentiles." The last statement we believe to be significant. What does it mean? That for the first time Gentiles had heard and believed? No, for the Antioch church had many Gentile members, and even earlier, Peter had preached to a Gentile household. Does the statement mean simply that some more Gentiles had been saved? It surely means that, but it must mean more than that. Not only is it that Gentiles are being saved, but they are being saved entirely apart from Israel's covenants and promises. In fact, the main significance of this open door is that for the first time Israel has been turned away from. From now on the Jew must come in on the same basis as the Gentile, entirely apart from his covenant priority.

II. THE JERUSALEM COUNCIL, 15:1-35.

A. *Reason for the Council,* 15:1-6. Paul and Barnabas remained at Antioch for a long time ministering to the saints, but trouble arose when certain men came down from Judea who began teaching the Gentile believers that unless they had been circumcised according to the law of Moses they could not be saved. It is understandable how the Jews could take such a stand, considering the fact that for fifteen hundred years the nation had lived under the covenant of circumcision. Under this covenant made with Abraham an uncircumcised man was to be cut off from the congregation: "he must needs be circumcised" (Gen. 17:11-14). God had commanded Israel concerning the passover: "And when a stranger shall sojourn with thee, and will keep the passover to the Lord, let all his males be circumcised, and then let him come near and keep it; and he shall be as one born in the land: for no uncircumcised person shall eat thereof" (Ex. 12:48). Then Ezekiel, in a passage which seems to apply to the coming millennial kingdom age, states: "Thus saith the Lord God, no stranger. uncircumcised in heart, nor uncircumcised in flesh, shall enter into my sanctuary, or any stranger that is among the children of Israel" (Ezek. 44:9). Jesus said that Moses had given Israel circumcision (John 7:22), and He Himself was circumcised according to the law of Moses (Lk. 2:21,22), and no where is there the slightest hint in all of the recorded teachings of Jesus that circumcision was to be done away. And, of course, in the early chapters of Acts the Jewish believers in Jesus continued in the temple worship which would have excluded any uncircumcised person (Acts 2:46; 3:1; 5:19,20,42). What a shock it must have been for those Jewish believers to hear that circumcision was no longer necessary and that uncircumcised Gentiles could enter into all of the spiritual blessings in Christ. And, of course, for the unbelieving Jews there was not only the matter of circumcision, but that of the preaching of Jesus as the Messiah. To them, Paul and his message was a double insult.

It is felt that few modern Christians realize what a great change of dispensation came under Paul's message. It is almost akin to telling Soviet citizens they are now to enjoy all of the freedoms and liberties of the American government.

When these Jewish believers in Jesus came to Antioch to try to convince the Gentile believers they must submit to circumcision, Paul and Barnabas defended their "uncircumcision" message and as a result there was a great deal of argument and dissension. The church decided to send Paul and Barnabas and others up to Jerusalem to the apostles and elders to have this matter settled. Their visit to Jerusalem was not for the purpose of finding out whether Paul was right or not, for Paul tells us in Gal. 2:2 that the Lord gave him a special revelation to go to Jerusalem and communicate or make plain to the Jewish believers there exactly what was the content of the gospel which God had given him to preach to the Gentiles. He calls that message "the gospel of uncircumcision," to distinguish it from Peter's message, "the gospel of the circumcision" (Gal. 2:7). Most Christians suppose there was no difference in the content of these gospels, the only difference being that the Twelve were carrying the same message to the Jews as Paul was carrying to the Gentiles. But if there was no difference in content, what was all of the argument about? If it be argued that the Jerusalem apostles' agreement with Paul is proof there was no difference, it should be pointed out that they did not agree there was no difference between the circumcision and uncircumcision gospels, but they agreed that Paul had received a new dispensation from the ascended Christ. Paul says that when they saw that, they extended to him and Barnabas the right hands of fellowship.

The church sent Paul and his party on their way to Jerusalem, which seems to indicate that they provided for them financially. To get to Jerusalem they had to travel through Phoenicia and Samaria, where they reported the conversion of the Gentiles. The assemblies in these regions were apparently mainly Jewish. It should be remembered that Jesus had ministered as far north as Tyre and Sidon, which were chief cities of Phoenicia, and it is apparent from the story of the Syrophoenician woman that He was ministering to the lost sheep of the house of Israel in that region (Matt. 15:21-28). It is significant that these Jewish believers rejoiced when they heard that the door of faith had been opened to the Gentiles. It seems that in general the Jewish believers in Jesus were glad to hear the news that God was now saving Gentiles, as well as Jews, although, as we have seen, not all of them agreed that the Gentiles could be saved without first becoming Jews through circumcision. When they finally arrived at Jerusalem they were welcomed by the church there and by the apostles and elders, and, as they had been doing along the way, they reported all that God had done through them in evangelizing the Gentiles.

We are not told how long Paul and his party stayed at Jerusalem or how many meetings they had with the apostles and leaders of the church. However, it was not long before certain believers who belonged to the sect of the Pharisees expressed their views that it was necessary for the Gentiles to be circumcised and observe the law of Moses. This matter apparently came up in a public meeting, for we read that as a result the apostles and elders then had a meeting to consider this matter. It seems that some of these Jews held that Gentiles must be circumcised in order to be saved, while others believed that after they were saved it was necessary for them to be circumcised in order to belong to the congregation. The problem is similar to that which exists today regarding the subject of water baptism. There are those who contend that one must be baptized in order to be saved. Others contend that one must be baptized only after he has been saved by grace alone. And still others say that baptism is unnecessary either before or after salvation, just as it was decided concerning circumcision.

In order to understand more fully all that was going on we must refer to Paul's account in Gal. 2:2. There Paul tells us that he went first of all privately to those who seemed to be leaders and explained to them the gospel which he preached among the Gentiles. He did this, he says, "lest by any means I should run, or had run, in vain." What does he mean by this? Some take it to mean that Paul had misgivings about the soundness of his own teaching and was seeking the approval of the Jerusalem apostles. But such an interpretation is contrary to the facts. Paul had received his gospel by direct revelation from Jesus Christ and he had seen this gospel doing its work in the conversion of the Gentiles. There was no doubt in Paul's mind about the correctness of his preaching. What Paul wanted was the formal endorsement of his Gentile ministry by the apostles and leaders of the church at Jerusalem, that he had not run or was running in vain. Such a declaration would aid him materially in his ministry, as it would help stop the mouths of the Judaizers who were dogging his steps and upsetting his Gentile converts. And Paul says that they accepted his position to the extent that there was no suggestion even that his Gentile companion, Titus, should be circumcised. The question about Titus would never have come up, except that certain "false brethren," who had slipped into the meeting unawares to spy out the freedom enjoyed under Paul's gospel, brought up the matter. Acts speaks of certain of the Pharisees "who believed," demanding the circumcision of the Gentiles, but Paul calls them "false brethren," which seems to indicate they were not true believers. At Pentecost all in the church at Jerusalem were miraculously filled with the Holy Spirit. Now, some sixteen to nineteen years later, there were false brethren, unsaved ones, who were part of the church. Such unsaved ones can often influence those who are true believers. Their purpose here was to make the believers slaves to religious rules and regulations, to bring them into religious bondage. But Paul says that he did not give in to them for one moment, in order to keep the truth of the gospel safe for generations to come.

B. *Peter's Speech*, 15:7-11. Acts tells us that after there had been much disputing, the first of the leaders to speak up was Peter. It is to be expected that he would be the main one of the Twelve to speak to this point, for God had chosen Peter to be the one through whom a Gentile was first to hear the gospel. So Peter reminds them that a good while ago God had saved Cornelius and his household entirely apart from circumcision, putting no difference between the Jews and the Gentiles, purifying their hearts by faith alone. This being the case, he continues, "Why tempt ye God, to put a yoke upon the neck of the disciples, which neither our fathers nor we were able to bear?" The yoke of which Peter speaks is not merely circumcision, but all of the ceremonial observances inseparably connected with that rite. The Judaizers were saying that the Gentiles *must* be circumcised and keep the law of Moses. There were literally hundreds of restrictions and observances in the law system which Peter calls a yoke of bondage, a heavy burden which neither our fathers nor we were able to bear. But the burden of the law went much deeper than the observance of a multitude of ceremonies. There was the burden of legal death of which Paul speaks in Rom. 7:24 which caused Paul to cry out, "O wretched man that I am." Paul makes it plain that every one who is circumcised as a legal, religious requirement is thereby made a debtor to observe the whole law (Gal. 5:3).

Peter then makes a rather remarkable statement. He says, "We believe that through the grace of the Lord Jesus Christ we shall be saved even as they (the Gentiles) are." We might have expected him to say, "They shall be saved even as we are." It seems that Peter must have realized that God had begun a new dispensation under Paul, and that now the Jews had to come in under the same conditions as the Gentiles. He surely recognized the fact that Gentiles were not coming in as required under the law of Moses, through circumcision and the keeping of the law. And instead, he says that we Jews are being saved solely through the grace of the Lord Jesus Christ, just as the Gentiles are.

C. **Testimony of Paul and Barnabas,** 15:12. These remarks from Peter, the chief spokesman for the Twelve, quieted the multitude and they listened attentively to the words of Barnabas and Paul as they declared how God had wrought miracles and wonders through them among the Gentiles, which attested to their claims of apostleship (cf. 2 Cor. 12:12 – "the signs of an apostle").

D. **James Gives His Judgment,** 15:13-21. When they had finished speaking, James arose. This James was the son of Mary, the mother of Jesus. He is the human author of the inspired epistle which bears his name. He is mentioned by name only twice in the Gospels (Matt. 13:55 and Mk. 6:3). However, he is no doubt to be included among the brethren of Jesus, and as such is mentioned in Matt. 12:46; John 2:12; 7:3,5,10. In the next to last of these references we learn "neither did his brethren (which would include James) believe in Him." But in Acts 1:14 we see James with the Apostles and others in the upper room continuing in prayer and supplication with one accord. Paul tells us of a special appearance of Christ after His resurrection to James (1 Cor. 15:7), which apparently resulted in his conversion, just as Christ's appearance to Saul resulted in his conversion. This special appearance apparently set James forth for a special place of ministry, as we see him in our present context as the overseer of the church at Jerusalem. Paul first met James on his first visit to Jerusalem after his conversion (Acts 9:26, cf. Gal. 1:18,19). He met him again here, and at his last visit to Jerusalem (Acts 21:18).

There is one other incident which concerns James, mentioned in Gal. 2:12. Most commentators take the position that this incident took place shortly after the Jerusalem Council and before Paul started his second missionary journey. Their reason for believing this is that Paul records it right after telling of the meeting in Jerusalem. Others think it took place sometime shortly before the Jerusalem Council. It seems almost unbelievable that after Peter's and James' speeches upholding the equality of Jewish and Gentile believers, and the letter which they wrote to the Gentiles at Antioch, and the presence of the two prophets sent to Antioch to confirm personally the action of the Council, that Peter could have denied everything that took place at the Council by separating himself from the Gentiles. It likewise seems impossible that Barnabas, who just a few days earlier had fought along with Paul at the Council for Gentile equality could have been likewise carried away by Peter's hypocrisy. It seems much more likely to me that this event happened before the Council, and was, in fact, the cause for the Council.

Since Peter's visit to Antioch is not recorded in Acts, we have to draw our conclusions from Paul's reference to it in Gal. 2:11. Paul tells us that before Peter's dissembling, James sent certain men to Antioch, much as he had sent Barnabas there at the first (Acts 11:22). These men apparently belonged to the same group of Pharisee believers in Jerusalem who argued at the Council that Gentiles had to be circumcised and keep the law of Moses. So when they came to Antioch they began teaching this in the church, or they may have worked privately with individual Gentiles. About this time Peter dropped in for a visit, and at first he had full fellowship with the Gentile believers, eating and visiting with them. But then he came in contact with the men James had sent, and he became fearful of what kind of report they might take back to James and the trouble it might cause in the church at Jerusalem, so he withdrew and no longer ate with the Gentiles. The other Jewish believers, noticing Peter's action, felt that they too should withdraw. And even Barnabas, who was instrumental in getting Saul to come to Antioch to minister to the Gentiles, was carried away with Peter's hypocrisy. Paul saw that if this situation were allowed to continue it would wreck the church and destroy Gentile liberty. He, therefore, was forced to rebuke Peter publicly. This controversy and contention over circumcision caused the church leaders at Antioch to send Paul and Barnabas to

Jerusalem to settle this matter once and for all. If this event with Peter had happened right after the Jerusalem Council, it would have been most logical for Paul to at least make reference to the conclusions of the Council contained in the letter when he rebuked Peter. If the church at Antioch had this letter in their files, they would certainly have brought it out, which would have settled the question once and for all. Therefore it seems more reasonable to suppose that Paul's rebuke of Peter occurred before the Jerusalem Council.

We have run ahead of our story in discussing at length the person of James. To return to our text in Acts, James arises to speak and refers to the fact that Simeon, that is, Peter had declared how God at the first visited the Gentiles to take out of them a people for His name. Then James says that this outcalling of Gentiles is in agreement with the prophecy of Amos 9:11,12. James does not say that this is that which was spoken by Amos, or that the prophecy of Amos has been fulfilled in the salvation of Gentiles at the present time. James surely knew that Christ had not returned and rebuilt the tabernacle of David. The salvation of Gentiles in the prophecy of Amos was to occur after the second coming of Christ and the restoration of the house of David. God had predicted a future outcalling of Gentiles; God is now calling out Gentiles, and thus there is agreement between these two facts. But what has that to do with the question before the Council? The Council was called, not to decide whether Gentiles could be saved, but to decide whether they had to be circumcised in order to be saved. It is evident from Amos and the other prophets that the Gentiles in the coming Kingdom are not going to become Jews by being circumcised. Circumcised Israel will remain separate and distinct from uncircumcised Gentiles in the Kingdom. Circumcision is the thing that distinguishes Jews from Gentiles in the Bible. Gentiles could become Jews by submitting to circumcision (Esth. 8:17). But in the Kingdom the Gentiles are to remain Gentiles. Therefore if Gentiles are to be saved in the Kingdom apart from circumcision, surely they can be saved today without circumcision. The quotation from Amos settled the matter, as far as James was concerned and he therefore gives his judgment: don't impose any Jewish restrictions on the Gentiles who are turning to God, but ask them to abstain from pollutions of idols, from fornication, from things strangled, and from blood. While James recognized that Gentiles were not to be placed under the law of Moses, there is no intimation that the Jewish believers were to be absolved from obedience to the law. He states concerning the Jews:

"For Moses of old time hath in every city them that preach him, being read in the synagogues every sabbath day." Christ had instructed His disciples saying, "The scribes and the Pharisees sit in Moses' seat: all therefore whatsoever they bid you observe, that observe and do." And up to this point not the slightest hint can be found that this order of Christ had been rescinded.

E. **_Letter Sent Freeing Gentiles from Law Observance,_** 15:22-35.
The apostles and elders and the whole church then agreed to send chosen men, Judas Barsabbas and Silas, to Antioch to personally confirm the action of the Council, and also to write a letter to the Gentile believers setting forth the decision of the Council. The letter made it clear that the church at Jerusalem had no part in sending out these Jews who had troubled the Gentiles with words, subverting their souls by teaching that they must be circumcised and keep the law. They then showed their high esteem for Paul and Barnabas by calling them "our beloved Paul and Barnabas, men that have hazarded their lives for the name of our Lord Jesus Christ." Finally they stated the decision of the Council: "For it seemed good to the Holy Spirit, and to us, to lay upon you no greater burden than these necessary things; that ye abstain from meats sacrificed to idols, and from blood, and from things strangled, and from fornication: from which if ye keep yourselves, you shall do well."

It is interesting to read what Paul has to say about meats sacrificed to idols (see 1 Cor. 8:1-13; 10:23-33). Meat purchased in the public market in Gentile cities was usually sacrificed to an idol. However, Paul said that the believer ought to know that an idol is not really a god and therefore the meat itself had not been contaminated, and therefore could be eaten with a clear conscience. But if one believed the idol was a god and ate such meat he would be sinning against his own conscience. Likewise, one with Paul's knowledge about idols who ate such meat in the presence of one without that knowledge was sinning against the conscience of the weaker person and therefore was doing wrong. His advice to Christians who were invited out to eat was to ask no questions about the food. But if some one remarked, "This meat has been sacrificed to idols," then the believer would do well to abstain. Paul was willing to sacrifice his own personal liberty. If his eating of such meat caused a brother to be offended, he would eat no meat as long as the world endured.

This is the only reference to things strangled and to blood in the N.T. Paul never mentions it. When an animal was killed by choking it, all of the blood remained in the flesh. So when the meat was eaten the blood was also eaten. The command to abstain from eating blood actually antedated the law of Moses by some 800 years. When Noah came out of the Ark God changed man's dietary regulations and for the first time placed His approval upon the eating of animal flesh. He said: "Every moving thing that liveth shall be meat for you; even as the green herb have I given you all things. But flesh with the life thereof, which is the blood thereof, shall ye not eat. And surely your blood of your lives will I require; at the hand of every beast will I require it, and at the hand of man; at the hand of every man's brother will I require the life of man" (Gen. 9:3-5). While the law of Moses forbad the eating of blood (Lev. 7:26-27; 17:10-14), it was a command which was carried over from an earlier dispensation.

It is important to see that this agreement was not simply a human act of mediation. It is plainly stated: "It seemed good to the Holy Spirit, and to us." James and the other Jewish leaders who composed this letter were directed by the Holy Spirit. Therefore there could be no argument whether their action was right or wrong. In those days when the prophetic gift was still in operation, God made His will known in unmistakable ways. It is evident that many church councils since that time have not been so certain or correct.

When Paul and Barnabas, along with those from Jerusalem, arrived at Antioch, the letter was read to the church, and, as could be expected, there was great rejoicing for its encouraging message. Judas and Silas, who were prophets, confirmed and exhorted the Gentile believers. Soon after, Judas and others returned to Jerusalem, but Silas decided to remain and minister at Antioch. Paul and Barnabas also continued there in teaching and preaching. The truth of the gospel of the grace of God had been established and the threat of a Judaizing mixture had been thwarted, for the present, at least.

III. THE SECOND MISSIONARY JOURNEY, 15:36-18:22.

A. *Paul Separates From Barnabas,* 15:36-41. Paul felt a burden for each of the churches he had established. In speaking of all of his persecutions and burdens he said, "Beside those things that are without, that which cometh upon me daily, the care of all the churches" (2 Cor. 11:28). How Paul longed to hear that his new converts were growing and standing fast, in spite of the persecutions which many were enduring. He wrote to the Thessalonians, "For now we live, if ye stand fast in the

Lord" (1 Thes. 3:8), as though it would have killed him to hear the opposite. It was with such concern that Paul in our present story said to Barnabas, "Let us go again and visit our brethren in every city where we have preached the word of the Lord, and see how they do." Barnabas was agreeable, but he was determined to take along with them John Mark. Paul thought it unwise to take this young man who started out with them on their first journey but deserted them when the going got rough. The contention became so strong that the two split up and Barnabas took his nephew and sailed for Cyprus. Paul then chose Silas as his new companion, and they departed, being recommended by the brethren unto the grace of God.

It might seem that Paul was ungracious in demanding that Mark not go with them, but that depends upon the reason Mark left them on the former trip. Some commentators think that Mark was not in favor of granting Gentiles full freedom in the gospel, and that even Barnabas might have had some lingering doubts, in view of his being influenced by Peter's defection at a later date. If there was anything in Mark's mind about Gentile salvation, it is understandable that Paul would take such an adamant stand against his going with them again. Whatever the problem was we know that Paul finally found Mark to be profitable for the ministry (2 Tim. 4:11). The church at Antioch apparently sided with Paul for they recommended Paul and Silas, whereas nothing is said about such action toward Barnabas and Mark.

B. **Timothy Joins Paul's Party,** 16:1-5. The fact that Barnabas had gone to Cyprus probably caused Paul to take a different route on this journey. He headed north and then west through Syria and Cilicia, confirming the churches. We have no record of the establishing of churches in Cilicia, but Paul may have been responsible for this sometime between his conversion and his moving to Antioch. Going still further west they came to Lystra and Derbe, where he found a young man by the name of Timothy who was well reported of by all the believers in Lystra and Iconium. His mother was a Jewess and his father was a Greek. Paul saw that Timothy would make a valuable addition to his party, and in order to overcome Jewish prejudice in the community, he had Timothy circumcised. In sharp contrast to this action, Paul would not listen for a moment to the demands to have Titus circumcised while attending the Jerusalem Council. Titus was a full-blooded Greek. Timothy was half Jew and half Greek. (In Jewish custom the son of a mixed marriage took the religion of the mother.) We do not believe Paul was inconsistent in circumcising Timothy. First of all, this took place during the period of transition from the Jewish to the Gentile order, during which there was a divinely recognized difference of order for the Jews who believed and the Gentiles who believed. This was the decision of the Jerusalem Council. It was perfectly legal for Jewish believers to practice circumcision, but illegal for Gentile believers to do so. This is most plainly stated in Acts 21:24,25. The Jewish believers were still taking part in the ceremonies at the temple, and even Paul joined in, but "As touching the Gentiles which believe, we have written and concluded that they observe no such thing." Timothy, being a half-Jew could be circumcised without violating any Scriptural principle in force at that time. Next, Timothy was not forced to be circumcised. He did it voluntarily. Had the Jews demanded it or made it a requirement for salvation, Paul would surely have objected. And further there was a principle involved. As an uncircumcised man, Timothy would have had no access to the synagogues to witness to the unsaved Jews. All the Jews in that area knew Timothy's father was a Greek and that Timothy was uncircumcised. Therefore to have Timothy circumcised was to open a wider door of testimony to the Jews.

As we learn from Paul's epistles, Timothy became one of Paul's most faithful and trusted fellow-workers. He could say of Timothy: "I have no man likeminded, who will naturally care for your state" (Phil. 2:20). And, of course, Paul addressed two of his epistles to Timothy which have become a part of the inspired Scripture.

As they went through the cities they delivered to the believers the decisions reached at the Jerusalem Council and the churches were established and increased in number daily.

C. *Vision of the Man of Macedonia,* 16:6-12. Having visited the churches he had established on his first journey throughout Phrygia and the region of Galatia, Paul tried to enter a new territory, the province of Asia. We today think of Asia as that great land mass to the east, the largest continent in the world occupied mainly by Russia and China. Asia Minor, on the other hand, is the southwest peninsula of Asia, occupied by modern Turkey. The Province of Asia referred to in our text was a small region in what is now western Turkey, containing such cities as Ephesus, Colosse, and Smyrna. The seven churches of Rev. 2 & 3 were in this province. Paul tried to enter this province, but strange to say, he was forbidden to do so by the Holy Spirit. Then after they came to Mysia they decided to go north into Bithynia, but again the Spirit (of Jesus) would not permit them to go there either. We do not know why the Spirit of God passed by these regions without giving the people a gospel witness. As far as we know Paul never had a ministry in Bithynia, but later on he had a very effective ministry in Asia, so that he could say: "all they which dwelt in Asia heard the word of the Lord Jesus, both Jews and Greeks" (Acts 19:10). However, Peter addresses his first epistle "to the strangers scattered throughout Pontus, Galatia, Cappadocia, Asia, and Bithynia. These scattered strangers were Jews of the dispersion. Whether Peter actually visited Bithynia we do not know, but at least we know that the good news about Jesus Christ reached that area.

Paul continued to journey westward for some three hundred miles from Iconium until he came to Troas, the westernmost point of the continent of Asia. Troas was the site of ancient Troy, the scene of Homer's Iliad, and the Trojan Horse. There is no record in the text of Paul preaching at Troas, but he must have established a church there before his trip into Greece, for when he returned to Troas in Acts 20:5-11, he had a church service with the disciples there. This was the occasion when Paul preached late into the night, and Eutychus, sitting in a third story window dozed off and fell to his death. It seems that wherever Paul went he established a testimony to the grace of God.

One night at Troas Paul had a vision. He saw a man of Macedonia beseeching him to come over to Macedonia to help them. We know, as it is stated in Heb. 1:1, that in the past God spoke to man in various ways. One way was by visions. This word occurs about 80 times in the Bible. It occurs 11 times in the Acts (9:10,12; 10:3,17,19; 11:5; 12:9,10; 18:8; 26:19). God is still able to speak to man by means of visions, but we believe that since He has completed His revelation in the completed Bible, He no longer speaks in visions. Much spiritual harm has come to the Church through people who have claimed to have received visions from the Lord. God has said all He is going to say in His revealed Word. The canon of Scripture is closed. But in the period of transition God was still speaking through visions, and Paul was able to discern that he was not just having a dream, but that God was speaking to him to go over into Macedonia.

Up to this point (verse 10), Luke has been saying, "They," in referring to Paul and his party. Now he says, "We." It is evident that Luke joined Paul's party here at Troas. The sign gifts, miraculous healings, etc., were beginning to pass away, and Paul would have need of "the beloved physician" (Col. 4:14). Luke proved to be one of Paul's most faithful companions. At the very last, while in a Roman prison, shortly before his death, Paul wrote to Timothy: "Only Luke is with me" (2 Tim. 4:11).

Being assured that the vision was from the Lord, Paul immediately went to the dock and booked passage on the first ship sailing to Macedonia. We are told that the ship took a straight course, indicating that the winds were favorable, and after two days arrived at Neapolis. Later on, the return trip took five days (Acts 20:6), showing what a difference the wind could make on a sailing ship. Paul apparently went on directly to Philippi, just a few miles inland. Philippi was an ancient town which had been rebuilt and enlarged by Philip, the father of Alexander the Great. Luke notes that it was the chief city in that part of Macedonia, and a colony, that is, it was a branch of Rome itself and enjoyed certain privileges of self-government.

D. *First Convert in Europe,* 16:13-15. Paul spent several days in Philippi and apparently heard there was a place by the river outside the city gate where some Jews met for prayer. Going out on the sabbath day he found some women gathered there and began speaking to them about the Scripture. The Lord opened the heart of one of them to Paul's words, for she was a worshipper of the Lord. Her name was Lydia. She was from the city of Thyatira and was a merchant selling purple cloth. Thyatira was a wealthy town in the northern part of Lydia of the Roman province of Asia. The city was noted for its trade guilds, one of which was the dyers guild. Instead of getting their purple dye from shell-fish, they used an extract from the root of the Madder Plant *(Rubia tinctorum).* It is not certain whether Lydia was selling the purple dye or purple cloth. From ancient times purple was the sign of royalty (cf. Judges 8:26). When the soldiers mocked Jesus before they crucified Him they put a purple robe on Him (Mk. 15:17). The rich man of Lk. 16:19 was clothed in purple. And finally the Mother of Harlots, Mystery Babylon the Great is depicted as "clothed in fine linen, and purple, and scarlet" (Rev. 17:4; 18:16). No doubt Lydia did business with the wealthy citizens.

When Lydia believed she and her household were baptized. This is the first mention of baptism under Paul's ministry. Paul himself was baptized (Acts 9:18) and the Lord speaking through Ananias gives the reason for the baptism: "Arise, and be baptized, and wash away thy sins, calling on the name of the Lord" (Acts 22:16). Many different meanings have been attached to this ceremony, but this and other Scriptures make it plain that baptism was a washing or cleansing ceremony. We do not believe that baptismal water or the blood of animal sacrifices ever had the power in themselves to wash away or cleanse from sin. Hebrews 10:4 and 9:8-14 make this fact unmistakably plain. Only the blood of Christ can do that work. But the ceremonies, while they were in force, were not optional. They were required. During the transition period circumcision, baptism, miraculous healings, angelic appearances, supernatural jail deliveries, visions, tongues, and other outward, physical manifestations of the Holy Spirit were in evidence. Although Paul practised circumcision during this time, circumcision was surely not a part of his commission for this age. Although he spoke in tongues more than others, he made it clear that this gift was to pass away. And while he practised baptism during this time, he made it plain that baptism was not a part of his commission. And while he experiences miraculous jail delivery in this chapter, after the transition to the full age of grace there was no longer such miraculous deliverances: he remained in prison until his martyrdom. And although he performed miracles of healing during the transition, he later had to leave behind sick some of his most faithful workers.

Lydia showed evidence of a real work of grace in her heart, for she invited and even constrained Paul and his party to make their headquarters at her house. She must have been a successful business woman of means to have a house large enough to care for so many extra people. Lydia's experience was real, for the Lord had opened her heart. We do not understand why some believe and some do not, or just how and why God works in the way He does, but we do know that the Lord must open a person's heart, otherwise he would never believe.

E. *Paul and Silas Arrested, Beaten and Jailed,* 16:16-29. Satan is always active wherever the gospel is being preached, and on this occasion he used a young woman who was under the control of one of his demons. The evil spirit which possessed her is called in the Greek, "Python." In Greek mythology Python was a large serpent which guarded Delphi, and which Apollo killed in order to establish his shrine and oracle at that spot. Python came to be used to denote a prophetic demon, and was also used to describe soothsayers who practised ventriloquism (speaking from the belly). This slave girl brought much gain to her masters by fortune-telling and was regarded by the inhabitants of Philippi as inspired by Apollo. Satan's trick apparently was to identify Paul's preaching with that of this Pythian priestess by having her follow Paul and crying out, "These men are the servants of the most high God, which show unto us the way of salvation." What she said was true, and at first Paul may have been pleased to have this kind of publicity. But she kept this up for many days, and apparently Paul found out more about her and perceived that she was demon possessed, and understood that this was a trick of the devil to compromise his ministry. So he commanded the Python spirit to come out of the woman in the Name of the Lord Jesus and the demon left her. She was no longer able to practise her soothsaying and fortune telling, and when her masters saw that their source of income had been destroyed they laid hold of Paul and Silas and dragged them before the magistrates, saying, "These men, being Jews, do exceedingly trouble our city, and teach customs, which are not lawful for us to receive, neither to observe, being Romans." The crowd joined in the attack and the magistrates ordered them to be stripped and flogged and then thrown into prison. The jailer was ordered to keep them securely, so he placed them in the inner cell and placed their feet in stocks.

These two prisoners must have been in severe pain, for their backs had been laid open by the beating they had received. But at midnight Paul and Silas prayed and sang praises to God and the other prisoners heard them. One should read Paul's letter to the Philippians in connection with this story. He tells them, "And in nothing terrified by your adversaries; which to them is an evident token of perdition, but to you of salvation, and that of God. For unto you it is given in the behalf of Christ, not only to believe in Him, but also to suffer for His sake; having the same conflict which ye saw in me, and now hear to be in me" (Phil. 1:28-30). This reminds us of Peter's words: "If ye be reproached for the name of Christ, happy are ye; for the spirit of glory and of God resteth upon you: on their part He is evil spoken of, but on your part He is glorified. . . Yet if any man suffer as a Christian, let him not be ashamed; but let him glorify God on this behalf" (1 Pet. 4:14,16). We read that when Paul and Silas began praying and praising God in song, something that had never before been heard in that Roman prison, all of the other prisoners were listening intently, as the verb used indicates. Suddenly the earth began to quake violently and the doors of the prison sprung open and all of the bonds of the prisoners were loosed. The prisoners were so impressed and amazed by what they had been hearing and by the earthquake which broke their shackles, they stood transfixed, frozen, as it were, not even giving thought to making their escape. The jailer, awakened by the quake and seeing the prison doors open, was about to take his own life, thinking the prisoners had escaped. We don't know how Paul could have sensed this in the stygian darkness of the inner prison. Perhaps the jailer uttered a cry which told Paul what was going on in his mind. In any case, Paul cried out with a loud voice, "Do thyself no harm; for we are all here." Then the jailer called for some torches, apparently to have the whole prison searched, and then he sprang in and fell down trembling before Paul and Silas.

F. *Conversion of the Jailer*, 16:30-34. The first words of the jailer, after bringing Paul and Silas up out of the prison were: "Sirs, what must I do to be saved?" Probably everyone in Philippi had heard about the salvation these two Jews were preaching. Perhaps Paul had even witnessed to the jailer while he was binding their feet in the stocks. A few hours earlier this jailer probably scoffed and laughed at the message Paul was preaching, but now he was under such deep conviction that the most important thing was to get the question of his soul salvation settled. Everything else could wait. And how simple was the answer: "Believe on the Lord Jesus Christ, and thou shalt be saved and thy house." This answer was followed by an exposition from the Word, not only to the jailer, but to all in his house. This Scripture does not teach that when the head of the house is saved, the rest of the household are automatically saved, or that they become children of the covenant. We do not know who was in his house, whether it was his wife, or his children, or his servants, or all of them together. Paul expounded the Word to all that were in his house, so they must have been old enough to understand and to believe.

Salvation involves a regeneration and we surely see it in this jailer: one moment a hardened jailer accustomed to deal harshly with violent men, robbers, murderers, criminals; the next a compassionate, gentle nurse, bathing the torn flesh on the backs of the apostles, and binding up their wounds. And in doing this he was probably risking his own standing with the authorities who would look with displeasure upon such acts of favoritism to prisoners.

Then we read that straightway he, and all his household were baptized. Churches have developed strange practises about baptism. Some teach that one must be baptized in order to be saved. Others teach that one must be totally immersed in water to be baptized. Others make the new converts wait for a period of probation to prove that they are worthy of being baptized. If one would stop and try to reconstruct this scene in his own mind of what happened between midnight and the break of day, he would see the falsity of such ideas. To begin with, Paul said nothing about being baptized in order to be saved. And how much time intervened before these people were baptized? The Scripture says it was immediately, straightway. And a reference to all of the baptisms recorded in the book of Acts will bear out the same rule. People were baptized as soon as they believed. And then, how were they baptized? Did the jailer have a tank of water large enough for both him and Paul to get into, and deep enough for Paul to completely submerge the jailer? Did Paul have a rubber baptismal suit to wear as many modern preachers have for this ceremony? Could all of these arrangements have been made in the brief span of not more than six hours, which included bringing Paul and Silas out of jail, securing the jail as far as the other prisoners were concerned, of bathing and bandaging the wounds of Paul and Silas, of listening to Paul and Silas expound the Scriptures, of baptizing the jailer and all those gathered in his house, and finally of preparing a meal for them to eat? It would surely seem that the time element and the local circumstances would completely rule out any idea of making arrangements for completely immersing each of these converts in baptism. This is not to say that a baptism could not have been performed by immersion, for baptism signified a washing or cleansing. When Paul himself was baptized he was told, "Arise, and be baptized, washing away thy sins" (Acts 22:16). There are other ways of bathing the body besides completely immersing the body. And as far as the baptisms of the Old Testament are concerned, none of them called for complete immersion.

G. **Paul and Silas Released,** 16:35-40. We don't know why the magistrates decided to release Paul and Silas. No doubt they had been awakened by the earthquake and perhaps had heard what had happened at the prison. They may have been moved by a superstitious fear that the sooner they got rid of these two preachers the better it would be for them. At least, they thought they had taught them a lesson not to trouble Philippi again with their teaching, and had discouraged any of the local populace from turning against the worship of Apollo to this new religion. Whatever their motivation, as soon as it was day, they sent officers to tell the jailer to release these men. So the jailer told Paul and Silas the good news and bid them depart in peace.

However, Paul had other ideas. He told the jailer, "They beat us publicly without a trial, we who are free-born Roman citizens, and threw us into prison. Now, do they want to get rid of us secretly? No! Let them come and escort us out publicly." It is difficult to know why Paul did not tell the authorities at the first that they were Roman citizens. Perhaps Paul was willing to sacrifice himself in order to place these magistrates in a position where they would be afraid to persecute his new converts. For when the magistrates heard that these men were Roman citizens they knew they had committed a grievous error and that they might be punished severely if news of their actions leaked out to those in higher authority. Vincent quotes Cicero: "It is *a dreadful deed to bind* a Roman citizen; *it is a crime to scourge him;* it is almost *parricide (murder of a parent) to put him to death.*"[1] Now Paul had forced these magistrates to come and publicly release them from prison, thus, admitting they had been in the wrong in beating them with rods and throwing them into prison.

The magistrates came and released them and requested them to leave the city. This is the way other cities responded to the good works of the Lord (cf. Lk. 8:37). Paul was in no hurry to leave. He entered into the house of Lydia, probably to pick up his belongings, and then after meeting with the believers and comforting them, he and Silas left the city.

H. *In Synagogue at Thessalonica,* 17:1-9. Leaving Philippi, Paul and Silas headed west through the cities of Amphipolis and Apollonia until they came to Thessalonica, which was the residence of the provincial proconsul and where Paul found a Jewish synagogue. It is interesting to note that Luke resumes the narrative in the third person, perhaps indicating that he had for some reason left Paul while they were at Philippi. Luke does not return to the first person until chapter 20, verse 5. Paul followed his usual custom wherever he found a synagogue. He went in and for three sabbath days he reasoned with them from the Old Testament, explaining and proving that the promised Messiah had to suffer and then rise from the dead. Then after he had established those facts from Scripture, he declared that this Jesus whom I preach is the Messiah. He did not begin by preaching Jesus, but by persuading the Jews that their Messiah, when He came, must die and rise from the dead. Then he was able to show them that Jesus had fulfilled all of these predictions, thus proving that He is the Messiah or Christ.

It has been said that wherever Paul went there was a riot or a revival or both. And so it happened at Thessalonica. Some of the Jews were persuaded and joined Paul and Silas, as well as a great number of God-fearing Greeks and a number of influential women. The unbelieving Jews, as they had done elsewhere, were filled with jealousy and resentment, and gathered a mob of bad characters from the marketplace and started a riot in the city. They attacked the house of Jason in an effort to mob Paul and Silas, but not finding them there, they dragged Jason and some of the other brothers before the city magistrates, shouting: "These are the men who have turned the world upside down, whom Jason has received and they are all acting against the decrees of Caesar, saying that there is another king, Jesus." The Jews succeeded in alarming both the citizens and the authorities, who made Jason and the others post bond before releasing them.

The fact that they were charged with teaching that Jesus was a king has been understood by some to mean that Paul was still preaching the gospel of the Kingdom, and had not yet begun to reveal the truth about the Church, the Body of Christ. The fact that Paul spoke about Jesus as a king is no proof that the new dispensation of the Body of Christ had not begun. Paul's method in dealing with the Jews was to go to the Old Testament to prove that Jesus was their Messiah. He would necessarily have to deal with the kingly aspect of the messianic prophecies, even as we ourselves do when teaching the Old Testament. It is agreed by all that the prison epistles of Paul contain the truth about the new dispensation and the Body of Christ. One of these was written to the Philippians, whom Paul had left prior to coming to Thessalonica. In that letter he states: "I thank my God . . . for your fellowship in the gospel from the first day until now; being confident of this very thing, that he which hath begun a good work in you will perform it until the day of Jesus Christ (1:3-6). This shows that there was a unity in Paul's ministry at least from Acts 16 to Acts 28.

I. *The Noble Bereans,* 17:10-15. As soon as night fell, the brethren at Thessalonica spirited Paul out of town and started him on his way to Berea, a trip of about 40 miles. As soon as he arrived he went to the synagogue of the Jews. The Jews here, we are told, were more noble than those at Thessalonica. The reason given is that they received the Word with all readiness of mind, and searched the Scriptures daily to see if what Paul was preaching was in agreement with Scripture. The word "more noble" is the comparative degree of the Greek word "eugenes," which means "well-born." We get our word eugenics from it. Here the word means more noble-minded, that is, more fair-minded or open-minded. They were less prejudiced, less bigoted, than the Jews at Thessalonica. Many non-denominational and even some denominational churches have taken this name to themselves, indicating they are trying to emulate these Jews in being open-minded and at the same time careful to test everything by Scripture.

It should be remembered that the only Scripture these Jews had by which they could test Paul's preaching was the Old Testament. This raises the question of whether Paul was preaching what he calls in several of his epistles "the mystery." Paul states that this mystery was not made known to the sons of men in past generations, so it could not have been found in the Old Testament. It would seem apparent that Paul did not preach about the Mystery when he began his ministry in a Jewish synagogue. His purpose was to convince the Jews from the Old Testament that Jesus was their Messiah. Besides, Paul speaks of "this mystery among the Gentiles" (Col. 1:27). Thus it would have been out of place when addressing the Jews as such in their synagogue, to preach about the Mystery. This he would doubtless do later when addressing the Gentiles. It must always be remembered that Paul had a two-fold ministry during the transition period: one to the Jews who believed and another to the Gentiles who believed. In fact, if one had only the book of Acts he could never discover there was such a thing as the Mystery. It is through reading Paul's letters to the churches written during this time that we begin to learn of this Mystery truth, and which is completed in the epistles written after the transition.

Because of the open-mindedness of the Jews at Berea we read that "many of them believed," as did also a number of prominent Greek women, as well as many Greek men. But when the Jews of Thessalonica heard that Paul was in Berea they came and stirred up the populace against him. Before there was a chance for a riot, the brethren sent Paul to the coast, but Silas and Timothy stayed at Berea. The men who accompanied Paul took him on to Athens and were told to dispatch Silas and Timothy to Athens as soon as possible.

J. *Paul's Sermon on Mars Hill,* 17:16-34. While Paul was waiting for Silas and Timothy he was greatly distressed to see that the whole city was given over to idolatry. Idolatry had been the chief sin of Israel in Old Testament times and was the cause for God's judgments in dispersing them and putting them in subjection to the Gentile nations. It is no wonder then that Paul was so deeply grieved when he saw idols everywhere he looked. This grief spurred him on to begin witnessing without the support of his fellow-workers. He reasoned with the Jews and others in the synagogue on the sabbath and daily with those he met on the streets. Then he encountered some Epicurean and Stoic philosophers. Epicurian philosophy taught that pleasure is the chief good for man. Epicurus himself, who lived a couple of centuries earlier, may have had the higher forms of pleasure in mind, such as the enjoyment of art and literature, but in Paul's day his followers were given to gross sensualism. They were materialists, basically atheistic, believing that the soul was permanently destroyed by death Their philosophy is summed up in the words: "Eat, drink, and be merry, for tomorrow we die" (1 Cor. 15:32). This saying, however, is much older than Epicurus. It is what the inhabitants of Jerusalem were saying during the seige of their city (Isa. 22:13). The doctrine that pleasure is the chief end man should strive for is known as hedonism, from the Greek word for pleasure. It is a doctrine which pervades much of American society today. One of the marks of the last days is that men shall be lovers of pleasure more than lovers of God (2 Tim. 3:4).

The Stoics, on the other hand, were indifferent to pleasure and pain. Virtue was its own reward; vice its own punishment. They were pantheists and fatalists. Our word stoical means indifferent to pain or pleasure, impassive, uncomplaining. This philosophy got its name from the fact that its founder, Zeno, held his school in the Stoa Poikile, or painted porch, at Athens. One writer has said that it is fair to describe Stoicism as the most influential ethical doctrine of the ancient Western world before Christianity. Its basic tenet for achieving personal salvation was to learn to be indifferent to external influences.

When these philosophers encountered Paul they said such things as, "What is this babbler (lit., "seed-picker" — one who picks up scraps of information and retails them second-handed) trying to tell us?" and, "He seems to be advocating the worship of foreign gods." They said the latter because they mistakenly identified "anastasis" (resurrection) as another god along with Jesus. So they took him up to Areopagus. It was the hill on which the highest court of ancient Athens held its sessions. The name is derived from "Ares" the Greek god of war plus "pagus" hill. Since the name of the Roman god of war is Mars, the place is often called "Mars Hill." The philosophers wanted to hear what this new strange doctrine was that Paul was preaching. Luke tells us that everyone in Athens spent all of his time in listening to or talking about novelties. We are afraid there are some church-goers who possess the same bad habit, as well as some teachers. Unless they can come up with a new interpretation of Scripture that had never been concocted before, they feel they have missed the truth. There is surely a place for finding deeper, and sometimes, new meanings of Scripture, but one should not spend all of his time in this endeavor. The Lord spoke of bringing things old and new out of his treasure (Matt. 13:52), and Peter says: "I will not be negligent to put you always in remembrance of these things, though ye know them, and be established in the present truth" (2 Pet. 1:12).

Paul did not antagonize his audience in his opening sentence by calling these philosophers "too superstitious." The Greek word means "reverent to the deity." He actually told them: "You are more religious, or more respectful of what is divine, than other people." Their reverence for the higher powers was a good thing, but it was misdirected, for he says, "As I passed by and observed the objects of your worship, I found an altar with this inscription: TO AN UNKNOWN GOD. Him therefore whom you ignorantly worship, Him I declare unto you." The word for unknown is "agnosto," and the word translated ignorantly is "agnoountes." Both words mean unknown. Compare our word "agnostic," one who says we can't know anything for sure. But if we can't know anything for sure, how can we know for sure we can't know anything for sure?

It is interesting to note the difference between the method Paul used in addressing the Jews in the synagogue and the way he addressed these raw Gentiles on Mars' Hill. These philosophers knew nothing about the Jewish Scriptures, or covenants of promise. He begins with God as the sovereign Creator and Provider. This God who made all things is Lord of heaven and earth. He does not reside in shrines built by man, neither does He stand in need of anything that man can supply Him. Instead, He is the one who gives to all life, and breath and all other things. (There is a difference in the manuscripts in the next statement. The Received Text reads: "And hath made of one blood all nations of men to dwell on all the face of the earth." The Revised Text reads: "From one man He made every nation of men that they should inhabit the whole earth.") He not only created the whole human race from one common stock; He determined how long each nation should exist and what their boundaries should be. He did this so that man might seek Him and perhaps reach out for Him and find Him, even though He is not far from any one of us. For in Him we live, and move, and have our being. Paul quotes one of the Greek poets who uttered the same thought:

"For we are also His offspring." Since we are the offspring of God, we should not think that the divine Being is like gold,or silver, or stone: images made by man's art and skill. God overlooked or tolerated the times past when men were ignorant of these things, but now He commands all men everywhere to repent; for He has set a day when He will judge the world by the man He has appointed. And He has given proof of this by raising Him from the dead.

The mention of the resurrection brought his sermon to an end, for the crowd began to mock and ridicule, while some said, "We will hear you again on this subject."

There are several points in Paul's sermon deserving of special comment. Paul had a liberal education. He was familiar with the Greek poets. He could not only quote them, but he was able to use them when they uttered what was true. We find today an ultra-conservative spirit which opposes vehemently any idea that any truth can be found outside the Bible, and that everything outside the Bible is either the devil's lie or man's depraved wisdom which is foolishness with God. Was Aratus expressing truth or error when he wrote: "For we are also His offspring?" Or was Epimenides right or wrong when he wrote some six centuries before Christ: "The Cretians are always liars, evil beasts, slow bellies" (Tit. 1:12)? Paul says, "This witness is true." Paul knew what were the tenets of Epicurean and Stoic philosophy and was able to fit his words to answer their mistaken ideas. It is true that we do not need to go outside the Bible to find the way of salvation or God's will for the Christian life, but that does not mean that the believer should not have as broad a knowledge of the universe as is possible.

Another point is found not only in Paul's knowledge and use of Greek philosophy and poetry, but in the particular truth he quoted, namely, that man is the offspring of God. We recognize the fact that man is a sinful, fallen, depraved being in his natural state, but it is still true he is the offspring of God. Again there are those who believe they are upholding the teaching of the depravity of man by denying that man is God's offspring, or is the image of God. But Paul told these Athenian unsaved philosophers that they were the offspring of God. And he wrote to the Corinthians: "For a man indeed ought not to cover his head, forasmuch as he is the image and glory of God" (1 Cor. 11:7). The image has been marred, but man is still the image of God, and that is what makes human life sacred and capable of salvation. Man is the only creature made in the image of God.

Another statement of Paul may seem to contradict what he

says elsewhere. Here he states that God did this so that man might seek after God and perhaps find him. But in Rom. 3:11: "There is none that understandeth, there is none that seeketh after God." However, in our Acts text there is a statement rendered in the King James, "if haply they might feel after Him." This expression means, "if by any chance," or, "if perhaps," and indicates a contingency not very likely to happen. We do find commands in the Bible to seek the Lord, such as Isa. 55:6: "Seek ye the Lord while He may be found, call ye upon Him while He is near;" Jer. 29:13: "And ye shall seek me, and find me, when ye shall search for me with all your heart." In considering these and many similar statements one must keep in mind that such words are addressed mainly to God's covenant people Israel who had gone away from God as the prodigal son had left his father's house and later came to his senses and sought his father's face again. All men should seek God, but the fact is, they don't.

One further thing should be said about being the offspring of God. Paul shows there is a universal brotherhood of man, but he does not teach the universal Fatherhood of God. We are all children of God only in the sense that He created the first man from whom the whole human race has sprung. One enters the family of God only by the new birth. Jesus spoke of another fatherhood: "Ye are of your father the Devil" (John 8:44). There are only two men in the Bible who are called "a son of God" by nature: Adam, the first man in his unfallen state (Lk. 3:38) and Jesus Christ. All other men are sons of men. Sons of men may become sons of God by faith in the Son of God.

Marvin Vincent has given an excellent critique of Paul's sermon. "In this remarkable speech of Paul are to be noted: his prudence and tact in not needlessly offending his hearers; his courtesy and spirit of conciliation in recognizing their piety toward their gods; his wisdom and readiness in the use of the inscription 'to the unknown God,' and in citing their own poets; his meeting the radical errors of every class of his hearers, while seeming to dwell only on points of agreement; his lofty views of the nature of God and the great principle of the unity of the human race; his boldness in proclaiming Jesus and the resurrection among those to whom these truths were foolishness; the wonderful terseness and condensation of the whole, and the rapid but powerful and assured movement of the thought."[2]

Some have criticized Paul's sermon because it seemingly produced such little results. Apparently only a few accepted Paul's message. One was Dionysius, the Areopagite. He was one of the judges of the court of Areopagus, a very prominent man of Athens. Then there was a woman, named Damaris, and several others. Generally speaking, the most difficult class to reach with the Gospel are the wiseacres of the world, those steeped in intellectualism and worldly wisdom. Such people usually feel themselves to be so above the common strata of society, they find it difficult to humble themselves and admit their own unworthiness and their need of the grace of God. Godly wisdom is the principal thing in life (Prov. 4:7), but Paul tells us that "not many wise men after the flesh are called by God" (1 Cor. 1:26). It is no wonder, then, that Paul found such little response to the Gospel in Athens.

K. ***Year and a Half Ministry at Corinth***, 18:1-18 a. Corinth is 40 miles west of Athens on the Isthmus between Hellas and Peloponnesus. It was the commercial and political metropolis of Greece, being the residence of the Roman proconsul. Corinth was a by-word for moral corruption and licentiousness. Upon arriving in Corinth Paul met a Jewish couple, Aquila and Priscilla, who had recently come from Italy because Emperor Claudius had expelled all Jews from Rome. Paul went to visit them and discovered that they were tentmakers by trade, as he himself was; so he lodged with them and worked with them. On the sabbaths he would go to the synagogue and reason with the Jews as he was accustomed to doing. Then when Silas and Timothy arrived from Macedonia he was pressed in the spirit, or as the best Greek texts read, he was pressed or engrossed in the Word. This is taken to mean that he gave up his tentmaking and gave his whole time to preaching the Word, He now testified boldly that Jesus was the Messiah, and when the Jews opposed him and blasphemed, Paul shook the dust from his clothes at them and said: "Your blood be upon your own heads: I am clean; I have discharged my responsibility; from now on I will go to the Gentiles."

It should be remembered that Jesus had said that sin against the Son of Man would be forgiven, but blasphemy against the Holy Spirit would not be forgiven. The Jews at Jerusalem had blasphemed, and God had raised up Paul to go first to the Jews of the dispersion. The Jews in Pisidia had blasphemed (Acts 13:45), and Paul had turned away from them to the Gentiles. Now the Jews of Greece have blasphemed and for the second time Paul turns to the Gentiles. And, as we shall see, when Paul reached Rome the Jews again blasphemed (Acts 28:25-28) and for the third and final time Paul pronounced blindness upon them and declared that the salvation of God had been sent to the Gentiles. This brought the Transition Period to an end, as well as the book of Acts, the purpose of which was to explain the fall of Israel and the transition to the gospel of the grace of God among the Gentiles.

Leaving the Jewish synagogue, he went next door to the house of a man named Titus Justus. He was no doubt a Roman citizen, for Paul was turning from the Jews to the Gentiles. He had apparently been a god-fearing proselyte, who now turned his house over to Paul for a meeting place. Crispus, the chief ruler of the synagogue believed, along with all his family, and was apparently put out of the synagogue, for a little later we learn that Sosthenes had become chief ruler (v. 17). Others also believed and were baptized. In this connection we should read 1 Cor. 1:13-17, where Paul states that he baptized none of them except Crispus and Gaius, and the household of Stephanas. He didn't remember whether he had baptized any others, for he says that Christ did not commission him to practise baptism, but to preach the gospel. Baptism, being a part of Jewish ceremonialism and one of those things that continued temporarily during the transition, was not a part of Paul's commission.

Paul may have been fearful of what the unbelieving Jews might do to him. He may have thought of moving on to another city. For that reason the Lord appeared to him in a vision at night and told him not to be afraid but to speak out boldly. The Lord promised to be with him and protect him, for He said: "I have much people in this city." Knowing this fact, Paul continued his preaching in Corinth for eighteen months.

When Gallio was made proconsul of Achaia, the Jews banded together and seized Paul and took him to court, charging that he was persuading people to worship God in a way that was contrary to law. The fact that Gallio became proconsul while Paul was at Corinth fixes the date of this event quite accurately. George Ogg in his book, *The Chronology of the Life of Paul,* has devoted a whole chapter on Gallio's proconsulship of Achaia. He refers to inscriptions found at Delphi, which translated read: "Tiberius Claudius Caesar Augustus Germanicus, pontifex maximus, in the 12th year of his tribunicial power, acclaimed emperor for the twenty-sixth time, father of his country, consul for the 5th time, censor, sends greetings to the city of Delphi. I have for long been zealous for the city of Delphi and well-disposed to it from the beginning, and always I have observed the worship of the Pythian Apollo; but with regard to the present stories and those disputes of the citizens of which a report has been made by Lucius Junius Gallio, my friend and proconsul of Achaia ... will still maintain the boundaries as formerly marked out."[3]

Other inscriptions concerning Claudius are given showing that he wrote this letter to Delphi in the first half of A.D. 52. Governors of senatorial provinces continued in office for only one year. Since Gallio had investigated the boundary dispute and sent his report to Caesar before he wrote this letter in 52 A.D., Ogg concludes that he was proconsul in Corinth from May 51 to May 52 A.D. These historical and archeological facts not only help us in fixing the date of Paul's ministry in Corinth, they also attest to the historical accuracy of the Bible.

Having been charged by the Jews of unlawful activities, Paul was about to reply to the charges when Gallio addressed the Jews: "If you Jews were making a complaint about some misdemeanor or serious crime, it would be reasonable for me to listen to you. But since it involves questions about words and names and your own law — settle the matter yourselves. I will not be a judge of such things" (N.I.V.). Then Gallio had them ejected from the court. Then the Greeks grabbed Sosthenes, the chief ruler of the synagogue and beat him in front of the court. But Gallio paid no attention to what they were doing.

It would thus seem that the Jewish attack on Paul backfired. Sosthenes had replaced Crispus as the chief ruler of the synagogue and was probably the one who had lodged the charges against Paul before Gallio. Instead of Paul being punished, the Jewish leader himself was mauled by the crowd. After Paul left Corinth and wrote his first letter back to them, his salutation read: "Paul, called to be an apostle of Jesus Christ through the will of God, and Sosthenes our brother, unto the church of God which is at Corinth." If this is the same Sosthenes who was beaten by the mob, he must have become converted through this experience and was now with Paul in Ephesus from where he wrote this letter. There is no doubt that this Sosthenes, now a fellow-worker with Paul, was from Corinth; otherwise there would have been no point in Paul mentioning his name. There is a slight possibility there were two men by this name, but this is very unlikely. It is apparently just another example of how one who has violently opposed the gospel can be converted by its power, even as Paul himself was. Paul continued to minister in Corinth for a good while after the episode before Gallio, and it was probably during this time that Sosthenes was converted. After his one and a half years in Corinth he set sail for Syria.

L. **Paul's Stop at Ephesus,** 18:18 b. - 21. Paul set sail from
Cenchrea, the eastern harbor of Corinth, about nine miles
from the city. There is nothing said about Paul's preaching
there, but he had apparently established a church there, for
we read in Rom. 16:1: "I commend unto you Phoebe our
sister, which is a servant of the church which is at Cenchrea."
But before he left Cenchrea he had his hair cut off because of
a vow he had taken. Paul's taking of a Jewish vow again shows
us the transitional character of the book of Acts. The laws
concerning vows are found in Lev. 7:16; 22:21,23; 27:2;
Num. 6:2,5,21; 15:3; 21:2; 30:2-13; Deut. 12:11; 23:18-22.
Vows were never considered a religious duty, that is, they
were never commanded, but when they were voluntarily
entered into they were considered most sacred and binding
and had to be carried out to the nth degree. Vows included
promises to do certain things or bring certain sacrifices to God
in return for certain benefits which were hoped for at His
hand, as in the case of Hannah (1 Sam. 1:11), or promises to
abstain from certain things. The Nazarite vow is described in
Num. 6. It involved four things: complete abstinence of wine
or of anything made from the grape, letting the hair of the
head and the beard grow, not touching a dead body of man or
animal, and prohibition of unclean food. Scripture says
nothing about the duration of the vow, but the Jewish
Mishnah prescribes a period of 30 days, or even twice or three
times that amount. At the termination of the vow the person
had to bring burnt, sin, and peace offerings with their
accompaniments. He then had to shave his head and burn the
hair in the fire under the peace offering. Thus the Nazarite
vow could only be concluded at the temple in Jerusalem.

Paul's vow and the shaving of his head at Cenchrea present
a problem as to what kind of vow he had placed himself
under. Some say it could not have been a Nazarite vow, while
others think there may have been some provision for those
traveling in foreign lands to wait until they could get back to
Jerusalem to make the offerings. This idea seems to be
reinforced by the fact that while Paul was here in Ephesus and
the people wanted him to stay longer with them, he said, "I
must by all means keep this feast that cometh in Jerusalem."
Paul left Priscilla and Aquila at Ephesus and continued on his
journey to Jerusalem.

M. **Paul's Fourth Visit to Jerusalem,** 18:22. Actually Luke does
not state that Paul went to Jerusalem. All he states is that Paul
landed at Caesarea and went up and greeted the church and
then went down to Antioch. It is clear, however, from his

stated intentions that he went up to Jerusalem and greeted the church there. For some reason Luke omits all reference to what took place on this visit, whether he got there in time for the feast or which of the feasts it was, and whether he completed the vow at the temple. Paul did take part in another vow in chapter 21.

IV. THE THIRD MISSIONARY JOURNEY, 18:23-20:38.

After spending some time in Antioch, Paul set out on his journey and traveled from place to place throughout Galatia and Phrygia, strengthening the believers. Again, Luke is very brief, giving us no details of anything that happened in this area. The main point to notice is that Paul felt the need to continually strengthen the believers. Getting people saved is one thing, but after that there is a need of continual ministry of the Word, so that the saved will continue to grow. There are comparatively few believers who can grow up in spiritual matters on their own and by themselves. Unless they are cultivated and fed by ministers of the Word they will regress and become unfruitful.

A. *Apollos at Ephesus,* 18:24-28. We are now introduced to a new character, Apollos, a Jew of Alexandria, Egypt. He was a man of excellent qualities and abilities. He was eloquent, mighty in the Scriptures, instructed in the way of the Lord, fervent in spirit, and taught diligently the things of the Lord. But strange to say, more than 20 years after the death of Christ, he knew only the baptism of John. He apparently knew nothing about what had happened at Pentecost, nor of the revelation given to Paul. However strange this may sound, there are some today after 1900 years who know very little more about the program of God, for they practically confine their reading and studying, if they do any, to the Gospel accounts.

There had been much progress in revelation since the days of John the Baptist, and thank God there was an enlightened couple at Ephesus who had the knowledge and the tact to deal with this man of God and to expound unto him the way of God more perfectly or accurately. And thank God, this man who was mighty in the Scriptures, was humble enough to receive instruction from a couple who were tent-makers. Apollos got up-to-date on his message. Instead of going back to John or to Pentecost, he went on with Paul. Apollos then decided to go over into Achaia, or Greece, so the Ephesian brethren wrote a letter to the disciples there to welcome him. Upon arriving he became a great help to those who through

God's grace had believed, for he powerfully refuted all of the Jewish arguments in public debate, showing by the Scriptures that Jesus is the Christ.

B. **Paul's Encounter with John's Disciples at Ephesus,** 19:1-7. Paul arrived at Ephesus soon after Apollos had left for Corinth. On Paul's first visit to Ephesus he stayed a very short time, since he was in a hurry to get to Jerusalem. He had reasoned with the Jews in the synagogue, but no church had been established during his brief stay. Now he has returned, as he promised (Acts 18:21), for an extended ministry. His first encounter was with a group of twelve Jews who were disciples of John the Baptist. In talking with them Paul apparently discovered that, while they were followers of Jesus, they were greatly lacking in their knowledge, even as Apollos had been before Priscilla and Aquila instructed him in the progressive revelation of God concerning the new dispensation.

We are confronted with three major questions in the exposition of this passage. First, did Paul ask these disciples if they had received the Holy Spirit subsequent to believing? Second, did the disciples answer that they were ignorant of the existence of the Holy Spirit? And third, did Paul rebaptize these disciples?

From the King James version the answer to the first question appears to be, "Yes." This rendering, "since ye believed," has given rise to the teaching that Holy Spirit baptism is a second work of grace. Thus, the sinner is saved when he believes, but after that he must grow and develop spiritually until he comes to full maturity, at which point he receives this miraculous baptism of the Spirit. But the King James is mistaken in its translation here and in a similar passage (Eph. 1:13). Practically all later versions of the Bible have corrected this error, rendering Paul's question: "Did you receive the Holy Spirit WHEN you believed?" The two verbs, "received," and "believed," are both in the same aorist tense and therefore denote instantaneous action.

The second question concerns the Holy Spirit Himself. Strangely enough, almost every modern version has retained the error of the King James by making these disciples say, "We have not so much as heard whether there be any Holy Spirit." This is an absurd statement, as it would have been impossible to know about John's baptism without knowing about the Holy Spirit. The main thrust of John's preaching was, "I indeed have baptized you with water: but he shall baptize you with the Holy Spirit" (Mk. 1:8). Besides, the Jewish Old Testament is full of the Holy Spirit from Gen. 1:2

to the end. Therefore they could not have been ignorant of the existence of the Holy Spirit. What they did not know was that the Holy Spirit had come or had been given, as He was given at Pentecost. They had been baptized only with water but had not been baptized with the Holy Spirit. John had promised that Christ would baptize with the Spirit, but they had not heard that this promise had been fulfilled. The emphasis here is not on the Person of the Spirit but upon the miraculous, empowering work of the Spirit. This is seen in the fact that both Paul and the disciples use the expression "pneuma hagion." As pointed out earlier when Holy Spirit is used without the definite article the emphasis is upon the gifts or empowerment of the Spirit. When the definite article is used "to pneuma to hagion," as it is in verse 6, the reference is to the Person of the Spirit. When Paul laid his hands on these disciples the Holy Spirit in Person came upon them and infused them with power so that they prophesied and spoke with tongues. It does not say that the Spirit entered into them, but came upon them, the same as He came upon the judges and prophets of old. It is important to see that this baptism with the Spirit was an outpouring upon a whole group all at once, even as it was at Pentecost. On the other hand, when the Spirit baptizes members into the Body of Christ it is an individual action: each is baptized at the moment he believes.

The third question asks whether Paul rebaptized these disciples. The King James seems to indicate that he did, and most commentators adopt this view. This passage has been used to support the claims of the Anabaptists who required the rebaptism of adults who had been baptized as infants. If Paul did rebaptize them it is the only recorded case of such action. None of the apostles who had received John's baptism were rebaptized at Pentecost. John's baptism is described by exactly the same words as the Apostles' baptism at Pentecost, "a baptism of repentance for the remission of sins." Those who believe Paul did not rebaptize these disciples base their argument upon grammatical construction. The participle for "hearing" is a first aorist, which refers to an indefinite past, and therefore could not refer to their hearing of Paul, which was present tense, but to their hearing of John. They combine verses 4 and 5, putting all of these words into Paul's statement. Paul thus said that when John baptized he told the people to believe on him which should come after him, that is, on Christ Jesus, and when they heard John say this they were baptized in the name of the Lord Jesus.

We do not know whether these twelve Jews were original

converts of John, or whether they were converts of Apollos
before he was enlightened by Priscilla and Aquila. What is
important to remember is that these were Jewish disciples of
John, that their number was the number of the Twelve Tribes
of Israel, that this took place during the Transition Period
when there was a different religious order for the Jews and the
Gentiles, and that the final and settled conditions which were
to become permanent in this present dispensation of the
Mystery had not yet been established.

C. ***Three Month Synagogue Ministry,*** 19:8-9 a. As Paul's
custom was during the book of Acts, he went first to the
Jewish synagogue, where for three months he spoke boldly,
trying to convince them about the Kingdom of God. But as
usual there were those who became obstinate and refused to
believe. They said evil things about the Way of the Lord
before the whole synagogue gathering, so Paul departed from
them, taking the disciples along with him.

D. ***Move to the School of Tyrannus,*** 19:9 b. - 22. We know
nothing about Tyrannus or what kind of school he had. We
don't know whether Paul rented the building or if Tyrannus
became a convert and opened his doors for a meeting place.
All we know is that Paul turned from the Jews to the Gentiles
and that this ministry at the Tyrannus school continued for
two years, and from that center the Word radiated out so that
all who lived in Asia, both Jews and Greeks, heard the gospel
message. We have remarked before that God gave to Paul the
signs of an apostle, and he wrought all of the miracles which
Peter had done.

There is a sense of irony, if not humor, in the story of the
seven sons of Sceva, the Jewish priest. These men were trying
to exorcise demons, and when they saw the great success of
Paul in casting out demons in the name of Jesus Christ, they
decided to horn in on the business, for it was a business with
them. And so they commanded the demon in a man to come
out in the name of Jesus whom Paul preached. The demon
cried out, "Jesus I know and Paul I know, but who are you?"
And with that the demon-possessed man with superhuman
strength attacked them and overpowered them and gave them
such a beating that they ran out of the house naked and
bleeding. All the Jews in Ephesus knew about this and great
fear fell on them all, and the name of Jesus was magnified.
James tells us that the demons believe there is a God and they
tremble at that Name. If Christ had died for the Devil and
demons, they would all be saved, for they believe. But He did

not die for these spirit beings. This is just one of the errors of Universal Reconciliationism.

As a further result many who believed came and openly confessed their evil deeds and those who had been practising sorcery brought their books containing magic incantations and made a great bonfire. When they calculated the value of the books it amounted to fifty-thousand drachmas, A drachma was about a day's wage. The reason many Christians never attain victory over sin in their lives is that they fail to do what these Ephesians did: they hang on to the old habits and friends and reading materials, which makes it very easy for them to slip back into their old ways.

After a three year period of ministry in Asia, a region he was once forbidden by the Spirit to enter, Paul purposed in the Spirit, after he had passed through Macedonia and Achaia, to go to Jerusalem, saying, "After I have been there, I must also see Rome." Having purposed this trip, he sent ahead of him Timothy and Erastus to make preparations, but he stayed on a little longer in Asia.

E. *The Riot at Ephesus,* 19:23-41. Ephesus was not only the chief city of Asia, it was also the center for the worship of the goddess Diana. The temple of Diana at Ephesus was classified as one of the seven wonders of the ancient world. The original temple was completed after one hundred years of construction in 480 B.C., at about the same time Ezra and Nehemiah were rebuilding the temple at Jerusalem. It was destroyed by fire the night Alexander the Great was born, and then restored with greater splendor than ever. And like the temple in Jerusalem, not one stone has been left standing of this beautiful marble structure which measured 160 feet wide and 340 feet long. In Paul's day the popularity of this temple and the worship of Diana was at its peak. The month of May was consecrated to the glory of this goddess and people from all over Asia came to Ephesus to join in the festivities. We learned from 1 Cor. 16:8 that Paul had decided to stay in Ephesus until Pentecost, which would coincide with these heathen celebrations.

This then is the scene: the city crowded with worshippers of Diana and the silversmiths eager to make a fortune by selling to this multitude silver images of Diana and the temple. Demetrius, who was president of the union of silversmiths took advantage of the situation to strike a death blow against Paul and his converts. He first of all inflamed the union members by telling them that this Paul was endangering their source of financial wealth by preaching that there are no gods made by human hands, and that not only their livelihood was in danger but the temple of the great goddess Diana and her magnificence would be despised and destroyed. The union members flooded the streets in rage, crying out: "Great is Diana of the Ephesians." The whole city was thrown into confusion. They apparently could not locate Paul, but they caught two of his companions, Gaius and Aristarcus, and rushed them into the great open-air theater which could seat 25,000. Paul wanted to enter the theater and speak to the crowd but the disciples held him back. Also certain of the Asiarchs (chief men of Asia) who had become Paul's friends, knowing the passions of the mob when excited at such a festival, sent an urgent message to prevent him from venturing into this scene of violence and disorder. As with most mobs of this nature there was great confusion, one shouting one thing, and others another. In fact, most of the mob didn't know why they were there. The Jews, apparently wanting to clear themselves of any complicity with the Christian group, pushed one of their number, Alexander, on the stage to speak, but when the crowd saw that he was a Jew they all with one voice began shouting, "Great is Diana of the Ephesians," and kept up the din for two hours.

After they had exhausted their energies, the town clerk was able to establish order. He allayed the fanatical passions of the people by this simple appeal: "Ye men of Ephesus, what man is there that knoweth now how that the city of the Ephesians is a worshipper of the great goddess Diana, and of the image which fell down from heaven." Then he reminded them that Paul and his companions had not been guilty of profaning the temple, or of blaspheming their goddess. Then he told Demetrius and his union members cases like this should be handled by the courts through the provisions of the law. And finally he warned them that Ephesus was in danger of being punished by the Romans for this unlawful uproar. Thus, in the providence of God, Paul was saved from suffering or death by the wise and prudent speech of the town clerk and by the intervention of certain of the Asiarchs.

There are several details we should notice in particular. The first concerns Diana. In the Greek the name is Artemis. Our translators have used the Roman name, Diana, but most modern versions read Artemis. In Roman mythology Diana was the daughter of Zeus or Jove, and the sister of Apollo. The Ephesian Artemis was more like the Lydian Cybele, the great mother of the gods. As with all of these heathen religions there were the temple prostitutes and the vilest debaucheries. Some think that the image of the goddess which fell from the sky was an aerolite or meteorite that was shaped to resemble a human body. The cult had its origins in ancient Asia and not in Greece.

Another point of interest is the use of the expressions translated "church" and "lawful assembly." The translators of the A.V. always translated the word "ekklesia" as church in the dozens of its occurrences, except in this passage where it is translated "the *assembly* was confused," "a lawful *assembly,"* and "he dismissed the *assembly."* Some theologians believe that the word church or ekklesia always means the same thing wherever it is found in the Bible. However, it is used to describe the children of Israel under Moses in the wilderness (Acts 7:38), and here it is used of an unruly mob that had assembled, and in Heb. 2:12 it is used of the future assembly of God's people in the millennial kingdom. The Church which is called the Body of Christ is an outcalling of saved people whose identity was never made known to men in past ages or generations. It is the subject of God's present activity and the truth concerning it was revealed to Paul and is to be found in his epistles. Strange to say, in the text we are considering, the translators have the town clerk to say that these men are not robbers of *churches,* when the word in the original is "temples." This is the only time the Greek word "temple" is translated "church."

One further point should be made, and that is that Paul wrote 1 Corinthians while he was at Ephesus, as noted earlier. In that letter Paul speaks of standing in jeopardy every hour, and of dying daily, and then he states: "If after the manner of men I have fought with beasts at Ephesus, what advantageth it me, if the dead rise not? Let us eat and drink, for tomorrow we die" (15:32). Then, when we read 2 Corinthians, which was written shortly afterwards, perhaps while Paul was in Philippi, we hear him say: "For we would not, brethren, have you ignorant of our trouble which came to us in Asia, that we were pressed out of measure, above strength, insomuch that we despaired even of life: but we had the sentence of death in ourselves, that we should not trust in ourselves, but in God which raiseth the dead: who delivered us from so great a death, and doth deliver: in whom we trust he will yet deliver us" (1:8-10). Evidently a great deal happened to Paul during his stay in Ephesus that Luke did not record. The same thing is true of Paul's experiences elsewhere. In 2 Cor. 11:22-33 Paul tells us he received thirty-nine stripes from the Jews on five occasions, that he was beaten with rods by the Romans three times, that he suffered shipwreck three times, and that he spent a night and a day adrift in the sea, but Luke is completely silent on all of these events, with the exception of a Roman beating at Philippi. Likewise he speaks of being in jail more often than the other apostles, but Luke mentions only the imprisonment at Philippi. The imprisonment at Caesarea and the shipwreck on the way to Rome happened after he had written 2 Corinthians.

We may speculate on reasons why Luke did not record these events, but we believe God has told us all He wanted us to know about these matters in His Word, and speculation, especially from silence, may land us on shaky ground. Some scholars of late have speculated that Paul was imprisoned while at Ephesus, although Luke gives no hint that he was, and that it was from this prison in Ephesus that he wrote his prison epistles. The almost universally accepted view which has been held until recently is that these epistles were written from the prison in Rome.[4]

Besides the objections noted by Guthrie to the Ephesus theory, our main objection is a dispensational one. The Ephesus theory would force us to end the transition in Acts before it actually ended. All during the latter half of Acts there was a difference of religious program for the Jews who believed and for the Gentiles who believed (Acts 21:25). The transition has ended when we come to the prison epistles, and the normal program for the Body of Christ has begun. The transitional practices of the Acts period have passed away (1 Cor. 13:8-13). Placing the prison epistles as early as Acts 19 violates the dispensational teachings of the book, but placing them in Acts 28 in Rome fits the dispensational facts perfectly.

It seems most unlikely that if Paul was in prison in Ephesus he would write an epistle to the church in the same city. The epistle makes it evident that the believers had access to Paul while he was in prison, so why should he write a letter? Not only so, but Paul specifically states in Ephesians 6:21,22 that he is sending Tychicus to deliver this letter to them, so that they might know his affairs. This fact surely suggests that Paul was not in Ephesus when he wrote Ephesians.

Paul had been in Corinth just before he came to Ephesus and he wrote a letter back to the Corinthians while he was in Ephesus. Paul was still practising water baptism while he was in Corinth (1 Cor. 1:14-16). There is no indication of any dispensational change taking place between the time he left Corinth and arrived in Ephesus. Yet in the Ephesian letter Paul states that there is now just one baptism, whereas just a few days earlier there had been at least two distinct baptisms. How could such a change be explained if Ephesians was written from Ephesus in Acts 19? If, however, Ephesians was written at the very end of Acts after Israel had been judicially set aside there is sufficient reason for the change. Water baptism, which had been very closely associated with Israel's religion for nineteen hundred years, passed away, along with everything Jewish, when Israel was set aside, leaving the one baptism, that of the Spirit, for the Body of Christ. This change could not have happened in Acts 19, as we see it.

F. *Paul Visits Macedonia and Greece,* 20:1-6. Luke tells us next to nothing of Paul's experiences for the next nine or ten months, from Pentecost of 57 A.D. to the days of unleavened bread of 58 A.D. All he states is: "He departed for to go into Macedonia. And when he had gone over those parts and had given them much exhortation, he came into Greece, and there abode three months." We learn a great deal of what happened during that time from 1 and 2 Corinthians, letters written at the time. We have already referred to 1 Cor. 16:5-8, where he tells the Corinthians he is going to stay at Ephesus until Pentecost and then travel through Macedonia and come into Greece where he would visit them and perhaps spend the winter with them. From 2 Cor. 2:12,13 we learn that Paul came from Ephesus to Troas, where he had a great opportunity to preach, but he was greatly troubled and had no rest in his spirit because he did not find Titus there. He had heard of all of the troubles in the Corinthian church through members of the family of Chloe who had come to Ephesus (1 Cor. 1:11). He had written a letter to the Corinthians to correct their immoral practices (1 Cor. 5:9,10). This first letter to them has not been preserved.

Now he writes another letter (1 Cor. 5:11), which we know as First Corinthians. He had dispatched Titus to Corinth, perhaps to carry this letter to them, and was eagerly awaiting the return of Titus with news of the reaction of the Corinthians to his exhortations and warnings. But as the days went by and no word concerning Titus came, Paul decided to go back to Macedonia, where, he says, "our flesh had no rest, but we were troubled on every side; without were fightings, within were fears. Nevertheless, God, that comforteth those that are cast down, conforted us by the coming of Titus (2 Cor. 7:5,6). Titus brought mainly good news from Corinth, that caused Paul to rejoice. First Corinthians was thus written shortly before Paul left Ephesus, and Second Corinthians was probably written from Philippi soon after Paul sailed from Troas to go into Macedonia. Paul doubtless visited all of the churches he had established in Macedonia, "giving them much exhortation," as Luke tells us. It is possible that at this time he also went into Illyricum (Rom. 15:19), which was a province on the Adriatic Sea west of Macedonia.

Luke then tells us that Paul went into Greece and abode there three months. Paul had at least three great burdens on his heart at this time. One was the immorality which was tolerated in the churches, especially in the one at Corinth. See 1 Cor. 5:1-13; 6:9-20; Gal. 5:19-21; Eph. 5:3-12; Col. 3:5-7; 1 Thes. 4:3-6. Another burden was that caused by the Judaizers who dogged his steps wherever he went. They caused divisions in the churches; they brought the believers into bondage, and they threatened the very existence of the Church by making it just another sect of the Jewish religion. They denied Paul's apostleship, they accused him of insincerity and dishonesty, and thus alienated his own converts. They denied the fact that a new dispensation of the grace of God had been committed to Paul by the risen Christ and insisted on a continuation of the dispensation of the Law. See how Paul defended his apostleship in such passages as 1 Cor. 9:1-27; 2 Cor. 10:1-11:33. The third burden on Paul's heart was the collection he was taking from the Gentile churches to help the poor saints at Jerusalem. We have already seen how Paul and Barnabas carried out such a mission near the beginning of his ministry in Acts 11:29,30. Also, at the Jerusalem Council in Acts 15 Paul had promised to remember the poor Jewish saints, a thing which he had made it his business to do (Gal. 2:10). Paul felt that if the Gentiles had become partakers of Israel's spiritual things it was their duty to make the Jewish believers partakers of their material blessings (Rom. 15:27).

We first read of Paul's purpose to go back to Jerusalem in Acts 19:21. While Paul was still at Ephesus he had given instruction both to the churches of Galatia as well as to the Corinthians on how the money should be collected and the appointment of an approved representative from each church to see that the money was delivered at Jerusalem. In 2 Corinthians 8 and 9 Paul further reminds the Corinthians of what is expected of them, that they have the money in hand before he arrives, so that he will not have to take a collection while he is there. He also highly commends the believers in Macedonia for their very liberal contribution. Then, when he arrived at Corinth and wrote his epistle to the Romans he told them of his plans to carry the gift which the believers in Macedonia and Achaia had made for the poor saints at Jerusalem. And he asks them to strive together with him in prayer that he might be delivered from the unbelieving Jews in Judea and that his service in Jerusalem might be accepted by the Jewish saints. Paul was apparently afraid that the Judaizing element in Jerusalem might so poison the minds of the saints that they would not receive him favorably. Paul no doubt had a two-fold motive in taking this gift for the poor saints in Jerusalem. It was first of all his nature to minister to the poor. He saw it as a duty. But also he was striving to heal the schism which the Judaizers had caused, and he hoped that this kindly gesture on the part of the Gentiles might be the means of cementing the Jewish and Gentile elements in the Church.

Getting back to the record of the Acts, Luke is silent on what happened during this third visit of Paul to Corinth. He tells us only that he stayed in Greece for three months and that when he was about to sail for Syria, the Jews laid wait for him in order to harm him. He therefore changed his plans and returned by land through Macedonia. On this trip Paul had six traveling companions: Sopater of Berea, Aristarcus and Secundus of Thessalonica, Gaius and Timothy of Derbe, and Tychicus and Trophimus of Asia. When they arrived at Philippi, his companions went on ahead to Troas. We learn that Luke rejoined Paul at Philippi, for he returns to the first person in the narrative: "And we sailed away from Philippi after the days of unleavened bread, and came unto them to Troas in five days; where we abode seven days." Luke had first joined Paul at Troas on Paul's first visit there and had gone with him to Philippi, where he apparently remained after Paul went on from Philippi to Thessalonica. That had been on Paul's Second Missionary journey, some five or six years earlier. Luke apparently made his home in Philippi. There is nothing in the record of Acts to indicate Luke had been with Paul during that interval. But now Luke is with Paul again, and as far as we know he was with him until his death in Rome, for Paul, writing from Rome in his final imprisonment and shortly before his execution, states: "Only Luke is with me" (2 Tim. 4:11). It is possible, of course, that Luke had seen Paul on occasions between his first and last visits to Philippi, but Luke never includes himself in the narrative during that time.

G. *Paul's Farewell at Troas,* 20:7-12. Paul and his fellow-workers stayed in Troas seven days. On the day before leaving the city, which was the first day of the week, Paul met with the church. The service was held in the evening. Paul preached to them and continued speaking until midnight. Luke tells us the meeting was held in a third story room, illuminated by many lamps. A young man, Eutychus by name was sitting in a window listening, and as Paul talked on and on he dozed off and slumped over and fell three stories to the ground. The people rushed down and picked up his dead body. But Paul went down and fell on him and embraced him, saying, "Don't trouble yourselves; his life is in him." There are a number of such incidents in the N.T. where it is difficult to know whether the person was actually dead before being restored to life, but in any event they all demonstrate miraculous power. (See Matt. 9:24; Acts 14:19.) After restoring the young man's life, Paul went back up stairs, where they broke bread (perhaps the observance of the Lord's Supper is intended), and had something to eat, and talked until the break of day. Perhaps he told them what he told the elders from Ephesus a few days later, that they would never see him again in the flesh, and this is the reason they sat up all night talking.

H. *Paul Meets With the Ephesian Elders,* 20:13-38. From Troas Paul's companions set sail for Palestine, but Paul walked the nineteen miles to Assos, where he joined his fellows in the ship. It may be that the emotional experience of saying goodbye to his converts for the last time was such that he wanted to be alone for a while. That night the boat arrived at Mitylene and the next day they arrived off Chios. The day after that they crossed over to Samos; then on the following day they came to Miletus. Apparently the ship was to be detained several days at Miletus, perhaps for taking on new cargo, so Paul sent word for the elders of the church at Ephesus to meet with him. He had not stopped off at Ephesus, since he was in a hurry to get to Jerusalem for the feast of Pentecost. He had left Philippi immediately after the days of unleavened bread, that is, seven days after Passover. Since Pentecost came fifty days after Passover, there remained only forty-three days to make the trip from Philippi. It took five days to get to Troas and approximately six days were spent in Troas, and six more days passed before sailing from Miletus. That left only twenty-six days to make it from Miletus to Jerusalem.

When the elders arrived from Ephesus, a distance of about thirty-five miles, they possibly met with Paul on the beach, where he delivered his farewell message to them. This is one of the most touching episodes in the recorded ministry of Paul. How difficult it must have been for Paul to conduct this service in the light of his knowledge of future events. These beloved converts for whom he had suffered so much and risked his life that they might be saved, he knew he would never see them again in this life. That in itself was a heartbreaking thought. But Paul knew too that after he departed, men whom he called savage wolves would come in the church and not spare the flock, and that even some of their own number would distort the truth and draw away disciples after themselves. That knowledge brought another heartbreak. And then Paul knew that he was headed for severe persecution and trouble in Jerusalem, for he said that in every city he had visited, the Holy Spirit, no doubt through prophetic utterances, testified that imprisonment and hardships awaited him. Paul really had much more concern for others than he did for himself, for he declared: "But none of these things move me, neither count I my life dear unto myself, so that I might finish my course with joy, and the ministry which I have received of the Lord Jesus, to testify the gospel of the grace of God." This is the only time this designation of the gospel is mentioned, but it is perhaps the most fitting title which could be given to the good news which was entrusted to Paul.

Every believer's life should be an example worthy of following. Paul said, "Follow me, even as I follow Christ." And here he reminds these elders of how he behaved himself among them. He could say that he was innocent of the blood of every man, for he had not shunned to declare unto them the whole council of God. Even though God had ordained that those who preach the gospel should live of the gospel (1 Cor. 9:14), Paul had worked with his own hands to support himself so that no one could charge him of being a huckster, in business simply for the money. He was an example of the grace of giving and reminded them of the words of the Lord Jesus, how He said, "It is more blessed to give than to receive." (This, by the way, is the one of only two times where Paul directly quotes something Jesus said during His earthly ministry. The other occasion is in connection with the Lord's Supper in 1 Cor. 11:24-26.)

After thus pouring out his heart to these Ephesian elders, Paul kneeled with them on the beach and prayed with them. They were all in tears as they embraced him and kissed him, sorrowing most that they would never see his face again in this life. Since Luke says they sorrowed most of all, there is the inference that they also sorrowed because of the predictions Paul made concerning the coming in of false teachers who would disrupt the church. They accompanied him to the ship, and no doubt stood on shore waving goodbye until the ship was well out to sea.

V. THE TRIP TO JERUSALEM, 21:1-17.

A. *Voyage from Miletus to Tyre,* 21:1-6. By consulting a map of
the eastern Mediterranean we can trace Paul's voyage. The
first day they sailed south to the island of Coos or Cos, and
the following day arrived at the island of Rhodes, an
important place in ancient history. Here had stood the
Colossus a figure over a hundred feet high, but in Paul's day it
lay prostrate on the ground as a result of an earthquake in 224
B.C. From Rhodes the ship docked at Patara on the mainland
of Asia Minor. There Paul found another ship which was
sailing for Phoenicia. Sailing in a south-easterly direction they
passed south of the island of Cyprus and landed at Tyre,
where the ship docked for a week to unload its cargo. Tyre
had been an important commercial center as early as the days
of Joshua (cf. Josh. 19:29, where it is called "the strong
city"). In the time of David and Solomon, Hiram, king of
Tyre, had been very friendly with Israel, supplying workmen
and materials for the temple (1 Kgs. 5:1; 9:11,12). But
because of the wickedness of the city, God had
Nebuchadnezzar besiege the city for thirteen years and then
had Alexander the Great destroy it. It was rebuilt by the
Seleucidae and was still a large city in Paul's day. See Ezek. 26
for the judgment pronounced upon Tyre. Paul found some
disciples there who said through the Spirit that he should not
go up to Jerusalem. We will comment on this statement later.
Paul was not deterred by their words, but boarded the ship
after taking leave of them.

B. *From Tyre to Caesarea,* 21:7-14. The ship stopped for a day
at Ptolemais giving Paul time to greet the believers in that city.
This town was known as Accho when Israel entered the land
under Joshua. It was given to the tribe of Asher, but they
never possessed it (Judg. 1:31). At the time of the Crusades it
was known as St. Jean d'Acre. The modern name is Akko. It is
not clear whether Paul and his party went on to Caesarea by
boat, or whether they took the land route over the plain of
Esdraelon and Mt. Carmel. In Caesarea they stayed at the
home of Philip the evangelist, who had four daughters who
prophesied, but we are not told whether they prophesied
anything about Paul. We are told that after several days the
prophet Agabus came from Judea and acted out his prophecy
by binding his hands and feet with Paul's belt, saying, "Thus
says the Holy Spirit, So shall the Jews at Jerusalem bind the
man that owns this belt, and shall deliver him into the hands
of the Gentiles."

Upon hearing this prophecy every one tried to persuade Paul to turn back and not venture into Jerusalem. But Paul told them all that their pleadings were breaking his heart, for he was ready not to be bound only, but also to die at Jerusalem for the name of the Lord Jesus. So they ceased pleading and said, "The will of the Lord be done." It should be noted that Agabus did not say, "If the man who owns this belt goes up to Jerusalem such and such will happen to him." If his prophecy was true and was inspired by the Holy Spirit, Paul would go to Jerusalem; he would be arrested, and he would be turned over to the Gentiles. The prophecy makes it a foregone conclusion that he would go. One writer who thinks Paul should have turned back adds to the Word of God by saying what Paul's friends meant was, "The permissive will of the Lord be done." But every sin that has ever been committed has been done by the permissive will of God. We are quite certain that Paul's friends were not saying, "We know Paul is disobeying God, but we pray that God may permit him to go against God's directive will."

C. *From Caesarea to Jerusalem,* 21:15-17. After several days Paul and his group packed up their baggage and went up to Jerusalem, along with other disciples and a man by the name of Mnason, an early disciple, with whom Paul was to stay in Jerusalem. Upon arriving, the brethren received Paul and his fellows very warmly. We are not told how many or just who the brethren were, but they must have been members of the Jerusalem church. It is altogether possible and probable that James, the leader of the church, along with the elders of the church were on hand to welcome him.

VI. PAUL'S EXPERIENCES AT JERUSALEM, 21:18-23:22.

A. *His Meeting with James and the Elders,* 21:18-25. The very next day after Paul's arrival James and the elders had a meeting with Paul to hear Paul's report and to discuss some of the problems which would arise as a result of Paul's visit to Jerusalem. It had been almost ten years since Paul had met with these church leaders, as recorded in Acts 15. After exchanging greetings, Paul gave a full report of what things God had accomplished through his ministry among the Gentiles during those years. Paul's good report must have included mention of the offering which the Gentile churches had taken to assist the poor saints at Jerusalem. It is possible that some of Paul's companions who carried this offering were also given opportunity to speak. When Paul's report was ended, we read, "They glorified the Lord." This statement surely indicates that they accepted Paul's report as being from the Lord. Paul, in writing to the Roman church a few months before this, had asked them to pray that his service for Jerusalem might be accepted of the saints (Rom. 15:31), and their prayers had been answered.

Then the church leaders brought up the problems which Paul would confront. There were two groups of Jews who would confront Paul, the unbelieving, the Christ-rejecting leaders of the nation, and the believing, or Christian Jews. They were primarily concerned with the Christian Jews. Even when Paul had met with the church in Acts 15 there were some who contended that Gentiles could not be saved apart from circumcision and observance of the rituals of the Mosaic law. However, James and the other leaders of the church agreed unanimously that Gentile converts were under no obligation to be circumcised and to keep the law. And James, on this present occasion, refers to that decision (Acts 21:25), as still being the stand of the Jerusalem church. But at that Acts 15 Council there was nothing said about releasing Jewish believers from circumcision and the Jewish customs. There was the plain inference that they were to continue in these practises. And so for the past nine or ten years they had continued, and now there were thousands of Jewish believers in Jerusalem. And no doubt the Pharisaic party of believers who favored Gentile circumcision had grown. During the years many false reports about Paul had filtered into Jerusalem. The thing that disturbed James and the elders was that so many of the Jewish saints believed these false reports and accused Paul of apostatizing from Moses and therefore forbidding Jewish parents to circumcise their children. It is apparent that these charges were false, for Paul himself had circumcised Timothy, one of his most trusted co-workers, and he had written to the Jewish believers at Corinth that it was not necessary for them to become uncircumcised now that they were Christians (1 Cor. 7:18). It is true that Paul preached against circumcision as a saving ordinance, and he did this by showing that Abraham was saved by faith alone a number of years before circumcision was instituted (Rom. 4:9-11). Paul's teaching about the law were grossly misunderstood and misrepresented. He speaks of being "slanderously reported," as teaching, "Let us do evil, that good may come" (Rom. 3:8). He must have been accused of making void the Law of God, for he asks: "Do we make void the Law through faith? God forbid: yea, we establish the Law" (Rom. 3:31).

How would these thousands of Jewish believers in Jerusalem who believed these false reports about Paul react to his presence in Jerusalem? What could be done to persuade them that Paul was not an apostate? There were four of their number who had taken the Nazarite vows and were in the temple ready to be purified. They suggested that if Paul would join them, go through the purification ceremonies, and pay their expenses, this would be proof which should convince everyone that the charges against Paul were false and that he himself was walking orderly according to the law. Paul agreed to follow their advice.

B. *An Excursus on Paul, James and Circumcision.*

1. *Paul:* We must pause at this point to consider the views of some Christian writers, and even some Pauline dispensationalists,[5] who take the view that Paul was out of the will of God in going to Jerusalem and in everything he did there, and that James and the Jerusalem elders were a bunch of conniving compromisers who were really enemies of the grace of God. Although we might quote from various writers, we will limit our quotations to one in order to conserve space. It should be said that there are some commentators who take the position that Paul was in the will of God in going to Jerusalem but out of God's will in what he did there.

   a. *The View That Paul Was Out of the Will of God:* The book we have chosen from which to quote is *ACTS, an Expositional Commentary,* by Donald Grey Barnhouse with Herbert Henry Ehrenstein, published by Zondervan Publishing House, Grand Rapids, Michigan, 1979. The preface states that the editor, Mr. Ehrenstein, transcribed the materials from tape recordings made by the late Dr. Barnhouse, and that where tapes were missing the editor had to write these sections in Dr. Barnhouse's style. Therefore we cannot be sure that the quotations are actually those of Dr. Barnhouse or of his editor.

   Regarding the vow which Paul made in Acts 18:18 we read: "Here, Paul was definitely out of the will of the Lord. He had no right to take this vow, or to have his head shaved as a symbol of it. This was deliberate sin on his part."[6] Commenting further on this event, we read: "I think we have the secret of Paul's ultimate failure in the vow he took because he would ultimately get caught in Jerusalem in a place he never should have been. He would be arrested and would never be a free man again as long as he lived. I believe firmly that the taking of this vow was really the beginning of the end for Paul. I think we can discern, if we look closely at the Bible, that Paul, who was an extremely well-educated man, wanted to work with the Jews. After all, the Jews were people who knew how to reason down to fine points of theology. Paul liked that, and for him to talk with Jews about the Old Testament gave him great pleasure. Yet, God had told him to go to the Gentiles."[7] In reply to these statements we would ask just one question: Did God commission Paul to go only to the Gentiles? If He did then Paul was continually out of the will of God on all of his missionary journeys, for we read in Acts 17:1,2 that Paul's custom was always to go first of all to the Jewish synagogue in his travels. In fact, he stated it "was necessary that the Word of God should first have been spoken to you (Jews)" (Acts 13:46). God plainly declared at the time of his conversion: "He is a chosen vessel unto me, to bear my name before the Gentiles, and kings, and the children of Israel" (Acts 9:15). The question then is, Was Paul out of the will of God for preaching to the children of Israel? There is one other minor question we should ask about the statement: "He would be arrested and would never be a free man again as long as he lived." How could this be true in the light of his statement eleven pages later that Paul was released from his Roman prison after two years and continued his missionary travels, going as far as Spain?

We find these remarks on Acts 20:22: "Notice the statement (v. 22) that he was going to Jerusalem 'bound in the spirit', [small 's' by the way]. This was not a Holy Spirit compulsion but, I believe, a self-will moving of Paul's own spirit. I think here is one indication that shows that Paul was willfully going to Jerusalem."[8] "Paul was making up his own mind to go to Jerusalem when, I firmly believe, God wanted him to move on to Rome and perhaps to Spain—Gentile territories, since he was the apostle to the Gentiles."[9] We would remind our readers that there are no capital letters in the Greek language, and further, all ten of the newer English versions consulted translate this word as "the Holy Spirit." Even if Paul "purposed in his own spirit" to go to Jerusalem, this in itself, is no proof that he was defying the will of God. When Paul was pressed in the spirit (Acts 18:5), or when Apollos was fervent in the spirit (Acts 18:25), did that mean that they were acting willfully against the will of God?

The view under consideration presents this estimate of Paul's character: "The Psalmist describes such a condition in Psalm 106:15, 'He gave them their request but sent leanness to their soul.' How many of the Lord's people have lean souls! Paul was one of these at this point in his life. It's sad that he could be such an ardent, devoted follower of the Lord Jesus Christ, but then would go off on a tangent of his own stubbornness."[10]

"Here in Acts 21, we find the Holy Spirit twice issuing a distinct warning to Paul about going to Jerusalem (verses 4 and 11). He could have had God's 'first-best' if he had listened to these warnings. But, as it was, he wilfully settled for God's 'second-best.' "[11]

"By this time Paul was an opinionated, stubborn man and was determined to have his own way."[12]

Asking whether Paul's statement that he was ready not only to be bound, but also to die at Jerusalem for the name of the Lord Jesus proves that he was anxious for the will of the Lord to be done in his life, the answer is given: "Dying is easy. One sharp moment and that's the end of it. To stand up in front of a firing squad and let the enemies of the cross of Christ shoot you is easy."[13] The inference is that Paul was actually showing very little devotion to Christ in being willing to die for Him, which was easy: he rebelled against living for Christ, which was hard.

"Under ordinary circumstances, Paul would have bluntly lashed out against such false teaching (that of James and the Jerusalem church). But Paul was out of the will of the Lord. He seems to have lost his spiritual discernment, for, not only does he not castigate James and these law-keeping Christians, he joins them in their heresy. This is one of the saddest sections in the Bible."[14]

"They (James and the Jerusalem church) wanted all Gentiles to be circumcised."[15] Read Acts 21:25 to see if this is a truthful statement.

The Asian Jews who started the riot which resulted in Paul's arrest are depicted as being right and more honorable than Paul. "But these Asian Jews were right . . . They knew that Paul, in spite of all his vows and shaved head and association with legalistic church members, was a strong opponent of Judaism and the temple, and the priesthood and the law. They had heard him preach. And they were shocked to see him now going through the legalistic practices of Judaism once again. They rightly assumed he was a phoney. A turncoat."[16]

Paul is depicted as being a very egotistical person: "Incidentally, it is significant that the first word of Paul's defense in verse 3, is 'I' because you are going to see this entire chapter filled with I and Me! ... Paul not only had 'eye' trouble; he also had 'I' trouble."[17] "Count the number of times the personal pronoun 'I' appears: 'I did this: I did that; I ... I ... I ... I ... I.' This is the way people talk when they are out of the will of God. Their activities center about themselves instead of upon what God did, what God said, and what God wants."[18]

We have given these extended quotations so that our readers might understand the thinking and the reasoning of those who teach that Paul was out of the will of God in this whole episode of Acts 21. However, in all fairness, it should be said that not all who hold this view are as brutal with Paul as is Dr. Barnhouse. Dr. Barnhouse seems to believe that Paul's motive for going to Jerusalem was the pleasure he derived from reasoning with the intellectual Jews about Old Testament theology. Others impute a much higher motive to Paul. They believe that his great love for his own countrymen and the burning desire to save them was the thing that blinded him to the will of God. Thus, while they believe Paul was out of the will of God his guilt was greatly mitigated by the worthiness of his motive.

b. *The View That Paul Was in the Will of God:* We have seen that the most obvious reason for believing Paul was out of the will of God is based upon the fact that the Holy Spirit warned Paul against going to Jerusalem. We first read of Paul's purpose to go to Jerusalem in Acts 19:21. He also mentions it in Rom. 15:25-31 and in 1 Cor. 16:3. It would appear that one of the main projects on Paul's whole third missionary journey was to raise money from the Gentile churches which he purposed to carry to Jerusalem to assist the poor saints there who were in great straits. His decision to go to Jerusalem was not made on the spur of the moment. It was a long, well-thought-out plan which covered several years of work. Those who place Paul out of the will of God in going should consider carefully if they are willing to label this whole enterprise as a work of the flesh.

The next reference is where he was hastening, if possible, to get to Jerusalem for the day of Pentecost (Acts 20:16). Then in chapter 20:22,23 he informs us that the Holy Spirit had been witnessing in every city he had visited that bonds and afflictions were awaiting him in Jerusalem. Then when he arrived at Tyre the disciples said to Paul through the Spirit, that he should not go up to Jerusalem (Acts 21:4). Of all the warnings given, this is the only one which specifically states that Paul should not go to Jerusalem. How then, can we believe Paul was in the will of God in going when it was said through the Spirit that he should not go?

F. F. Bruce gives this answer: "Their inspired vision foresaw the difficulties and dangers that lay ahead of Paul (cf. v. 11); they drew the conclusion that he should not go up to Jerusalem (cf. v. 12). We must not infer that his continuing the journey was contrary to God's will; it was 'under the constraint of the Spirit' (20:22) that he was going to Jerusalem."[19]

Homer A. Kent, Jr. gives this answer: "Did Paul disobey the Holy Spirit by going to Jerusalem? It must be remembered that Paul's ministry was characterized by a sensitivity to the Spirit's leading (16:6-10), which increases the probability for right action here also. His reasons for going to Jerusalem were proper (20:16,24; 24:11,17). Furthermore, he was making this trip by the Spirit's constraint (19:21; 20:22). The Spirit had been revealing the dangers which awaited (20:23), but these were part of Paul's commission (9:16). Paul never gave any indication that he felt it was a mistake (23:1; 24:16). What happened in 21:4 was probably similar to the later instance in Caesarea with Agabus, where the information revealed by the Holy Spirit through the prophet was utilized by the people to urge Paul not to endanger himself (21:10-12). Paul, however, regarded it not as a prohibition but a divine forewarning so that he would be spiritually prepared for what would happen."[20]

George Williams states that this and the other warnings were tests of Paul's resolution to obey the inward voice which bound him to go. He cites a similar

case concerning Elisha in 2 Kgs. 2:1-13. On three
occasions Elijah commanded Elisha to remain behind at
a certain place in order to test him. But Elisha refused
to obey because he knew he would miss the blessing if
he was not with Elijah when he was taken up into
heaven in the chariot of fire. If he had obeyed the
prophet's command, he would have missed the blessing.[21]

Henry Alford comments on Acts 21:4: "The notice
here is very important that these Tyrian disciples said
to Paul *by the Spirit,* that he should not go to
Jerusalem—and *yet he went thither,* and as he himself
declares, *bound in the spirit by the leading of God.* We
thus have an instance of that which Paul asserts in 1
Cor. 14:32, that the spirits of the prophets are *subject
to the prophets,* i.e., that the revelation made by the
Holy Spirit to each man's spirit was under the influence
of that man's will and temperament, moulded by and
taking the form of his own capacities and resolves. So
here: These Tyrian *prophets* knew by the Spirit, which
testified in every city (chapter 20:23) that bonds and
imprisonment awaited Paul. This appears to have been
announced by them, shaped and intensified by their
own intense love and anxiety for him who was
probably their father in the faith. But he paid no regard
to the prohibition, being himself under a leading of the
same Spirit too plain for him to mistake it."[22]

It is significant that all of the other English versions
consulted make the statement, "I go bound in the
Spirit," (Acts 20:22), refer to the Holy Spirit, which
include *The New English Bible, The Revised Standard
Version, The New International Version, Today's
English Version, The Living Bible, Phillips' Modern
English, The Confraternity Version, Young's Literal
Translation, The Berkley Version,* and *The Amplified
Version.* The unanimous conclusion of the host of
Greek scholars involved in these many translations gives
weighty evidence that it was the Holy Spirit who
constrained Paul to go to Jerusalem. We believe that all
that has been said above gives a sufficient answer to the
question raised by Acts 21:4.

One of the writers quoted pointed out the fact that
no statement can be found in Scripture indicating that
Paul erred in going to Jerusalem or in what he did
there. Not only is this so, but we do have a very
significant statement by the Lord Himself in Acts

23:11 commending Paul for his witness for the Lord in Jerusalem. We will deal further with the passage when we come to it in our study.

Another argument used to try to prove Paul erred in going to Jerusalem is based on Acts 22:18,21. Paul there tells what happened to him when he first visited Jerusalem after his conversion. The Jews sought to kill him, and while he was in the temple praying the Lord appeared to him in a trance telling him to get out of Jerusalem, for the Jews would not receive his testimony and God would send him far hence to the Gentiles. This is interpreted as a permanent injunction that Paul was commanded never again to set foot in Jerusalem. If this be true then doubtless Paul was disobedient on all four of the subsequent visits to the city recorded in Acts. If Paul had so understood this instruction, when he was commissioned by the church at Antioch to carry relief supplies for the famine-stricken saints in Jerusalem, he should have refused to go. And when he went to Jerusalem in Acts 15 we are told he went up "by revelation," which is evidence that God had not permanently banned him from Jerusalem. The basis for the argument seems to be that since Paul was appointed as the apostle of the Gentiles he had no business going to the Jews. Advocates of this view seem to forget that Paul was commissioned by the Lord to go to the Jews as well as the Gentiles (Acts 9:15), that Paul declared it was necessary for him to go to the Jews first (Acts 13:46), and that he always went first to the Jewish synagogue in every city he visited. We could give some credence to this argument if Paul had bought a house in Jerusalem and had taken up permanent residence there. But the fact is that over a period of some twenty years or more he made only five brief visits, none of which lasted over two weeks. The remainder of those years was spent out in the Gentile world.

Not only do we believe that Paul did not err in going to Jerusalem in Acts 21; we believe it was necessary for him to go in order for him to fulfill his ministry. Paul himself expressed this fact in Acts 20:24 when he spoke of his going to Jerusalem in order to finish the race and complete the task the Lord Jesus had given him. On previous visits to Jerusalem he had gone to minister to the material needs of the saints, as indeed he was doing on this occasion, and to settle certain doctrinal matters with the church there. But he had never testified to the rulers of Israel. We believe it was necessary for Paul to do this to fulfill his commission before the final doom was pronounced upon the city. Paul's commission called for him to witness before kings and rulers. How could he ever set up a meeting with the high-priest and the sanhedrin to testify the gospel to them? Such a thing was humanly impossible, but God had a way of doing it. He had the rulers set up the meeting by having Paul arrested. And not only through his arrest did he have opportunity to witness to the rulers of Israel, he also was enabled to testify before other rulers and kings, such as Felix and Festus and King Agrippa, and finally before Caesar himself. Paul was commissioned to testify before kings, but it would seem humanly impossible for this little Jew to gain audiences with kings. God's way of doing it was apparently through his arrest, and the remaining chapters of Acts tell how it came about. There can be no doubt that God used Paul's final visit to Jerusalem as the means of completing His commission to Paul. If Paul had heeded the pleadings of his friends and had turned back from going to Jerusalem to avoid arrest and imprisonment which he knew would happen, it is difficult to see how he could ever have completed his mission.

Paul stated very clearly his reasons for going to Jerusalem this final time: to fulfill his commission from the Lord (Acts 20:24), to bring alms and offerings to his nation (Acts 24:17), and to worship (Acts 24:11). In spite of his intense love for his own people of Israel, there is no hint that he was motivated by the hope of converting Israel's leaders. How could he have had such a hope when the Holy Spirit testified in every city he passed through that bonds and afflictions were awaiting him in Jerusalem?

With the knowledge that he would be imprisoned in Jerusalem Paul wrote to the Roman believers to pray for him (Rom. 15:30-32). He made three requests: that he might be delivered from the unbelieving Jews, that the offering he was carrying might be accepted by the believing Jews, and that he might come to Rome by the WILL OF GOD. We believe that all three of the requests were granted.

Had the prayer not been answered Paul would have been killed and our Bibles would be lacking: Ephesians,

Philippians, Colossians, Philemon, and the letters to Timothy and Titus. Since the saints "received him gladly" and "glorified the Lord" on his behalf, it is apparent that the offering was accepted. And we know that he got to Rome by the will of God. And he came with joy, for the Roman saints came down as far as Appii Forum and the Three Taverns to meet him. And we read, "Whom when Paul saw, he thanked God and took courage." What a joyous occasion that must have been for Paul, in spite of his chains. Thus we believe that all that happened to Paul was according to the will of God. There is nothing in the context to hint at the contrary.

2. *James:* Those who condemn Paul for his actions at Jerusalem must of necessity also condemn James. One writer seeks to do this by first of all pointing out the fact that this man who was the physical brother of Jesus was an unbeliever while Jesus was on earth (John 7:5). But what is not pointed out is that Jesus, after His resurrection, made a special revelation of Himself to James (1 Cor. 15:7), which resulted in his conversion, so that we find him among the disciples in Acts 1:14. And this special revelation of Jesus to James alone no doubt resulted in a special commission for him, which we believe was to head up the Jerusalem church.

Next, in order to cast suspicion on the character of James it is pointed out that the name James is Jacob in Hebrew, and Jacob means "supplanter." Therefore James is a supplanter! Does this mean that James the brother of John who was killed by Herod was also a supplanter? And what about the other Apostle James? It is argued that Peter was appointed by God to be the head of the Jerusalem church, but that James used his prestige as the earthly brother of Jesus to push Peter aside and take over as dictator of the church. It is true that Peter was the main spokesman for the Twelve Apostles in the early Acts when the Kingdom hope was burning brightly. But nowhere is it stated that Peter was appointed head of the Jerusalem church. After Paul's ministry began it became evident that the kingdom hope had been postponed and so we find Peter going out on preaching missions around the land, and it seems that by Acts 21 there were none of the Apostles left in Jerusalem: at least, none are mentioned. It was necessary to have a resident pastor for the church in Jerusalem, and that is what James became.

It is alleged that James was a Judaizer who led the Jerusalem church away from the grace of God and put it under the law. The fact is that from the very first, while Peter was apparently in charge, the Apostles were to be found daily in the temple, fulfilling the command Jesus gave them just before His death, to obey those who sat in Moses' seat (Matt. 23:1-3). When the Council in Acts 15, under the direction of the Holy Spirit, freed the Gentiles from Mosaic observances, there was no such action taken regarding the believing Jews. Instead, there is the clear inference that they were to continue just as they had from the beginning. The Holy Spirit definitely set up a two-fold religious order, one for the Jews who believed and another for the Gentiles who believed. James recognized that this two-fold order was still in effect in Acts 21:25: The Gentiles were to observe no such things as did the Jews. This is one of the factors which characterized the latter half of Acts as a transition period. It is evident that this two-fold order is not in effect today. Where did it cease and where do we find the first command for the Jewish believers to forsake the temple and its worship?

We believe we find the first instruction for the Jews to break away from the Mosaic system in the book of Hebrews. This book gives special instruction to Jewish believers in light of the approaching destruction of Jerusalem and its temple. The temple was still standing when this book was written, and the writer in conclusion states: "For the body of those beasts, whose blood is brought into the sanctuary by the high priest for sin, are burned outside the camp. Wherefore Jesus also, that He might sanctify the people with His own blood, suffered outside the city gate. Let us (believing Jews) go forth therefore unto Him outside the camp, bearing His reproach" (Heb. 13:11-13). This seems to us to be a definite command for believing Jews to now forsake Jerusalem and its temple worship and identify with Jesus outside the camp of Judaism.

It is very significant that the expression "without the camp," or "outside the camp" appears sixteen times in Exodus through Deuteronomy. One event is especially significant which illustrates the text in Hebrews. In Exodus 33, right after Israel had rejected Jehovah and had made a golden calf to worship, we are told in verse 7: "And Moses took the tabernacle, and pitched it without the camp, and called it the tabernacle of the congregation. And it came to pass, that every one which sought the Lord went out unto the tabernacle of the congregation which was without the camp." At the end of Acts, Israel had again rejected Jehovah Jesus, the true Tabernacle, and the Tabernacle was pitched outside the camp, and those who sought the Lord had to go outside the camp of Judaism and bear His reproach. Therefore, we believe that during the book of Acts it was God's will for the Jerusalem saints to maintain the Mosaic order. But lest this statement be misunderstood, we shall have more to say later about the Law and Circumcision in this excursus.

The character of James and the elders is further disparaged by the fact that Luke makes no mention of them accepting the gift from the Gentile churches, nor is anything said about them trying to help Paul after his arrest. It is argued from the silence on these points that they either didn't accept the gift or that they took it without even thanking Paul and his companions who had brought it, and that they deserted Paul to the mob after he was arrested. This type of argument can be very misleading. We are not to suppose that Luke recorded every word spoken by Paul and the others, as would a court reporter, just as the Gospel writers did not record everything that Jesus said and did. John tells us that the world would not be able to contain all the books which would be written in such a case (John 21:25). Had Luke recorded everything that was said at that conference it would have been a book by itself. Besides, it is very doubtful that Paul would have cooperated and followed their suggestion if James and the elders had manifested such a spirit. It may strike us as strange that Luke does not mention the gift, but it seems that the most important and pressing matter was how the many misinformed Jewish believers would treat Paul. Then as to the matter of not coming to Paul's help when the mob seized him and the Romans took him into custody: what could they have done? Luke and Paul's companions were also present and nothing is said about them doing anything to help. Does that mean that they also deserted Paul? We leave it to our readers to judge.

One other thing should be said about James. He was the writer of one of the inspired books of the New Testament. We know that all of the writers of Scripture were · fallible men, capable of making mistakes and sinning. Paul was no exception and neither was James. David committed a terrible sin when sexual lust blinded his eyes. But David confessed his sin and God exposed and judged it. If Paul committed such a terrible sin at Jerusalem, he never confessed it, and God never exposed it or judged it. And if James was the conniving, usurping, deceptive autocrat that some make him out to be, it is difficult for us to put him in the category of holy men through whom God gave the Scripture. And when we read his epistle all of these allegations dissolve into thin air. One allegation has been that James used his fleshly relation to Jesus for his own personal gain. He could have opened his epistle with the words: "James, a son of Mary and brother of Jesus Christ." But how does he begin? "James, a bond-slave of God and of Jesus Christ." Instead of being a brother he sees himself as a slave of Jesus Christ.

How does James define religion in James 1:27? Is it observation of circumcision and ritual? The fact is he doesn't even mention any kind of legalistic practises. Instead, true religion is visiting orphans and widows and living clean lives. He does mention the law several times, but notice the difference between his words and those of Peter who spoke of the law as being a yoke of bondage (Acts 15:10). James speaks of "the perfect law of liberty" and "the royal law" (James 1:25; 2:8,12). There is a vast difference between a yoke of bondage and perfect liberty. Peter referred to the law under the Old Covenant, which was external, written on tables of stone. But it must be remembered that James and the other Jewish believers were now under the New Covenant, and in that covenant the law is internal, written upon the tablets of the heart, so that the believer has perfect liberty in obeying God (Heb. 8:10 cf. Jer. 31:33). Paul speaks of the New Covenant in the same way in 2 Cor. 3:5-18. The Spirit of the Lord indwells the believer under the New Covenant, and Paul says, "where the Spirit of the Lord is, there is liberty." When James speaks about salvation he makes no reference to circumcision or baptism. He simply says, "Of His own will begat He us with the word of truth" (Jas. 1:18).

But doesn't James contradict Paul's teachings of justification by faith when he states: "Was not our father Abraham justified by works, when he had offered Isaac his son on the altar?" (Jas. 2:21). Martin Luther seemed to think so. But what Luther apparently failed to see is that the Bible speaks of two kinds of works. There are "works of the flesh," which originate from the unregenerate human nature, and there are "works of faith" which spring from the renewed nature. It should be evident that no one can be saved by the works of the flesh, and it is just as evident that no one can produce works of faith until he is first saved. What kind of works was James imputing to Abraham?

Abraham was justified by faith in Gen. 15:6 when he was 85 years old, 15 years before Isaac was born. James says that Abraham was justified by works when he offered up Isaac in Gen. 22, which was 45 years after he had been justified by faith. Therefore it was the faith Abraham had possessed for 45 years that came to fruition in his most outstanding act of faith in offering up his only son in whom all of God's promises to him resided, "accounting that God was able to raise him up, even from the dead; from whence also he received him in a figure" (Heb. 11:19). James puts these two justifications together in these words, "You see that his faith and his actions were working together, and his faith was made complete by what he did. And the scripture was fulfilled that says, Abraham believed God and it was credited to him as righteousness" (Jas. 2:22,23, N.I.V.).

Not only does James speak about two kinds of works; he speaks also of two kinds of faith: dead faith and living faith. He uses the human body as an illustration. "For as the body without the spirit is dead, so faith without works is dead" (Jas. 2:26). Faith is invisible. It is something like electricity. The only way we can tell whether the power line is dead or alive is to connect something to it and see if it produces any action or work. The only way we can tell that a person has a living, vital faith in Jesus Christ as Savior is by the kind of life he manifests. James speaks of showing his faith by his works.

Paul has much more to say about good works than does James. See Eph. 2:10; 1 Tim. 2:10; 5:10; 5:25; 6:18; 2 Tim. 3:17; Tit. 2:7,14; 3:8,14. Paul's good works are works of faith engendered by the Holy Spirit.

Therefore we conclude that charges against James that he was a Judaizer, teaching salvation by works, law-keeping and circumcision are false. Charges that he was a usurper, that he used his fleshly relation to Jesus for gain, and all other such allegations are also proved false from an examination of his divinely inspired epistle. Is it not strange that sincere students of the Scripture can come to such diverse opinions. Whereas some have such bad things to say about James, the Lord's brother, compare this with what Conybeare and Howson say about him:

"He was, indeed, divinely ordained to be the apostle of this *transition-church.* Had its councils been less wisely guided, had the gospel of St. Paul been really repudiated by the church at Jerusalem, it is difficult to estimate the evil which might have resulted."[23]

3. *Circumcision:* Before returning to the narrative of Acts 21, we must further digress to speak in particular about the subject of Circumcision, since that is one of the key factors in the text before us. The question is, Was Paul telling the truth when he agreed to the statement that he had not taught the Jews among the Gentiles to forsake Moses, saying that they ought not to circumcise their children, neither to walk after the customs? What was Paul's attitude toward circumcision as revealed in his epistles? This word does not always have the same connotation and it is therefore very important to sense the meaning in the context where it is found.

The primary meaning of circumcision is the religious rite of cutting off of the foreskin (Gen. 17:11). Because the practise of circumcision set the nation of Israel apart from all of the other nations, the word is often used as a synonym for Israel, and the word "uncircumcision" is used as a synonym for the Gentiles (Gal. 2:7-9; Eph. 2:11). In a few places circumcision is used figuratively for a spiritual condition of the heart (Rom. 2:29; Phil. 3:3; cf. Jer. 9:26; Acts 7:51). Whereas Paul vigorously opposed circumcision for Gentile believers, he states: "We are the circumcision, which worship God in the Spirit, and rejoice in Christ Jesus, and have no confidence in the flesh" (Phil. 3:3). He shows how we have become the circumcision: "circumcised with the circumcision made without hands, in putting off the body of the sins of the flesh by the circumcision of Christ" (Col. 2:11). In some places circumcision refers to Christ-rejecting, unsaved Jews (Tit. 1:10), whereas in other places it refers to those Jews who have believed on the Lord Jesus Christ, (Acts 10:45). In yet other places it refers to Jews who are said to have believed, but who insisted that Gentiles must be circumcised in order to be saved (Acts 15:1,5). Failure to recognize these distinctions by making the word mean the same thing in every occurrence will result in great confusion. For example, Paul states in one place, "For there are many unruly and vain talkers and deceivers, especially they of the circumcision, whose mouths must be stopped, who subvert whole houses, teaching things they ought not for filthy lucre's sake" (Tit. 1:10,11); and yet he says that certain ones "who are of the circumcision: these only are my fellow-workers unto the kingdom of

God, which have been a comfort unto me" (Col. 4:11). There must have been a vast difference between those fellow-workers of Paul who were of the circumcision, and those others of the circumcision who were unbelievers, subverters, vain talkers, and deceivers. To make legalizers and Judaizers out of all who are said to be of the circumcision, as some commentators seem to do, is a tragic mistake. It should also be remembered that circumcision did not originate with Moses and the Law. It was given to Abraham over four hundred years before the Law was given, and it was continued under the Mosaic Covenant (Acts 7:8; John 7:22). Rom. 4:9-12 is an important Scripture on this point.

Paul stated, "If ye be circumcised, Christ shall profit you nothing" (Gal. 5:2). And yet he circumcised Timothy (Acts 16:3). Did Christ become of no profit to Timothy? Every Jew that Paul preached to was already circumcised, for he could not have been a Jew without circumcision. Paul himself was circumcised. How could any of these Jews who were all circumcised benefit from Christ if Christ was of no profit to those who were circumcised? It should be evident from the context of Gal. 5:2 that Paul means, "If you as a Gentile become circumcised or if you as a Jew trust in circumcision as a means of justification, Christ will profit you nothing." Otherwise, no Jew could ever have been saved. At the Council in Acts 15 Peter makes it clear that as believing Jews who were still practising circumcision, they were not trusting in circumcision for salvation, for he said: "We believe that through the grace of the Lord Jesus Christ we (Jews) shall be saved, even as they (the Gentiles)." And James makes it clear that neither he nor any of the leaders of the church at Jerusalem had sent out men to preach that the Gentiles must be circumcised and keep the law. In fact, he calls such men trouble-makers who were subverting the souls of the Gentiles. And Paul plainly states that God shall justify the circumcision by faith (Rom. 3:30).

It cannot be denied that there were Jews in Jerusalem who professed to believe in Jesus but also believed it was impossible to be saved apart from circumcision. Perhaps there had come to be many such professing believers by the end of the book of Acts, and they naturally would be opposed to Paul. But it should be plain from Acts 15 that neither Peter, nor James, nor the elders of the church believed this. The problem about circumcision during that time was akin to the problem about baptism today. There are millions of professing Christians today who believe it is impossible to be saved apart from water baptism, just as there were Jews who believed the same thing about circumcision. There are others who say that water baptism has nothing to do with salvation, but that after one is saved he must be baptized. Some Jews said the same about circumcision for Gentiles. Others, like Paul, who said "circumcision is nothing and uncircumcision is nothing" (1 Cor. 7:19), say, "Baptism is nothing and non-baptism is nothing, but faith which works by love."

We can sympathize with the Jews at the time of the change of dispensation under Paul. For 1900 years God's Word had plainly taught that no uncircumcised person had any relationship to the congregation of Israel. If they were not circumcised they were to be cut off from God's people (Gen. 17:10-14). The mistake the Jews made was to suppose that circumcision was a saving ordinance. If they had understood their own Scriptures, as Paul did, they would have seen, as Paul demonstrates in Rom. 4:9-12 that Abraham was justified by faith while he was still in uncircumcision, and that he later received circumcision, which was a seal of the righteousness of the faith he had while he was yet uncircumcised. Circumcision was a covenant into which God entered with the nation of Israel. In the new dispensation under Paul God has suspended Israel's covenants; therefore circumcision has been suspended along with the covenant. God is dealing today in pure grace, apart from covenants and special privileges.[24] But the Abrahamic Covenant is an everlasting covenant, and when Christ returns to establish His kingdom and covenants with Israel, circumcision will no doubt be reestablished with Israel (Gen. 17:13). Likewise, the Sabbath will be restored, for "It is a sign between me and the children of Israel for ever" (Ex. 31:17). Jerusalem and the Temple will be restored, along with priests and sacrifices (Zech. 14:16; Ezek. 40-48). Now if circumcision, sabbath keeping, and temple worship in Jerusalem are to be restored in the coming Kingdom, and if God was still dealing with the nation of Israel in regard to their kingdom promises in the Acts period, does it seem strange that God would continue these practices during that time? It would have been much simpler and easier for us to understand, had God destroyed the temple and Jerusalem and had cut the Jews off completely the moment He began the new dispensation under Paul. But God didn't do it that way. God is long-suffering, as Peter points out (2 Pet.

3:9,15,16), and he gave the individual Jews a period of years to repent after He had started the new dispensation, before He pronounced His final judgment upon the nation at the end of Acts, and even then He extended His grace a few more years before He actually destroyed the city and the temple and drove those who were left from the slaughter as exiles among the nations.

We have tried to show the various ways the term circumcision is used in order that we might better understand Paul's declaration that he had not taught the Jews they must cease the practice of circumcision. Some of these usages seem to be contradictory. For example, he told the Romans, "What profit is there in circumcision? Much in every way" (Rom. 3:1,2); and yet he told the Corinthians: "Circumcision is nothing, and uncircumcision is nothing" (1 Cor. 7:19); and to the Galatians he wrote: "For in Christ Jesus neither circumcision availeth anything, nor uncircumcision" (Gal. 6:15). In one place it avails much and in another it avails nothing. But he also wrote to the Galatians, "If ye be circumcised, Christ shall profit you nothing" (Gal. 5:2). Is this not a command for Jews to give up circumcision?

Let us imagine a situation in which Paul was preaching to a mixed group of Jews and Gentiles. He tells them their good works cannot save them; their keeping of religious ceremonies cannot save them; their baptisms cannot save them; their circumcision cannot save them; in fact, if they are circumcised Christ will profit them nothing. Then all of the Jews raise their hands and say, "But Paul, we are all circumcised already. Do we have to get uncircumcised to get saved?" We believe Paul would answer, as he did answer the Corinthians: "Is any man called being circumcised? Let him not become uncircumcised. Is any man called in uncircumcision? Let him not be circumcised. Circumcision has nothing to do with salvation; neither does uncircumcision. Let every man remain in the situation he was in when God called him" (1 Cor. 7:18-20). Paul makes no command for the believing Jew to give up circumcision, except in the sense of it having any merit whatsoever as far as salvation is concerned. We can imagine that Paul might have addressed the Jewish fathers in his audience: "You fathers who have little infant boys whom you circumcise, be sure that you make it plain to them as they grow older, that, while circumcision was a sign between God and the nation of Israel, God has now broken down all distinctions between Jews and Gentiles, and therefore circumcision gives you no special privilege, nor does it avail in any way for your salvation." Thus God has taken the Jew who was circumcised and the Gentile who was uncircumcised, and has placed them both in Christ where all such differences have been dissolved, so that Paul can say, "There is neither Greek nor Jew, circumcision nor uncircumcision, Barbarian, Scythian, bond, nor free: but Christ is all, and in all" (Col. 3:11).

It is thus my personal belief, in spite of what good men have written, that Paul did not make a mistake; did not compromise the truth; did not falsify his ministry; did not use duplicity; did not use expediency; did not step out of the will of God in what he did at Jerusalem. These convictions are based upon Scriptural facts, not speculations. Had Paul come to Jerusalem unprepared, with no knowledge of the problems which would confront him, so that he would have to make decisions on the spot without time for reflection, we can imagine he might have done things for which he would have been sorry afterwards. But he didn't go to Jerusalem unprepared. Even before he left Ephesus in Acts 20:23 he knew that he would meet with great trouble in Jerusalem, and he received warnings all along the way. He had months in which to reflect upon possible actions he might take were he confronted with this or that problem or temptation to compromise the truth. In the light of these facts, and in the knowledge of Paul's sensitive conscience, his uncompromising stand for the truth, and his placing of the will of God above everything else, we find it personally impossible to believe that Paul could have fallen prey to such a mistake. Apart from a proper dispensational understanding of the character of the Book of Acts, we can see the problem which faces those who begin the new dispensation and the Body of Christ on the day of Pentecost, who see no difference between revelation given to Paul and that given to the Twelve, who suppose that from Acts 1 the preaching included everything contained in Paul's epistles. Surely under a situation like that those early Christians had no business going to the Jewish temple, or of continuing with circumcision and the other Jewish customs. It is easy to see why they should think the Twelve Apostles were bigoted Jews who hated the Gentiles and refused to preach to them, so that God had to replace Matthias, who took the place of Judas, with Paul, in order to get the message to the Gentile world. But all of these problems disappear when we accept the literal facts presented in the Book, that Pentecost was not the birthday of the new, unprophesied Body of Christ, but was rather the offer of the Kingdom to the nation of Israel, and that the new dispensation began with the raising up of a new apostle, separate from the Twelve.

C. *The Uproar and Arrest,* 21:18-36. We return now to the narrative with Paul and the four Jews in the temple who had taken a vow. Paul himself did not take the Nazarite vow, but as often was the practise, he went into the temple and went through the rite of purification and stood the expense for the offerings which had to be made for these four men who had taken the Nazarite vow (Num. 6:13-21). The purification ceremonies lasted for seven days, and when the time was nearly ended, certain Jews from Asia who had come for the Feast of Pentecost caught sight of Paul in the temple. These were not Jews who had believed on Jesus through Paul's preaching, but the unbelieving Jews who had caused him so much persecution. Back in Asia they had to restrain themselves in their persecutions because of the Roman governors, but now they found him where they felt free to do their very worst. What hatred they had for this man who dared put Gentiles on a level with the Jews, God's chosen people, and claim that they could be saved apart from the Jews' religion. They began shouting, crying out for every one to help get rid of this one whom they accused of teaching all men everywhere against the people of Israel, and the law, and the temple. They even accused Paul of bringing a Gentile, Trophimus of Ephesus, into the temple, thus polluting the holy place.

What a contrast between the first Pentecost of Acts and the last. Then the Holy Spirit was poured out and there were about three thousand saved, but now they were blaspheming the Holy Spirit and trying to murder God's messenger of grace. Then the whole city was stirred and amazed by the miraculous manifestations of the Spirit; now the whole city had become a howling, blood-thirsty mob. They laid hold of Paul and dragged him out of the temple and immediately the Levites closed the temple doors, lest blood would be shed in that holy place.

At the northwestern corner of the temple area was located the fortress of Antonia, built by Herod the Great and named in honor or Mark Antony. There a garrison of Roman soldiers was stationed, especially at Jewish festivals, to maintain order. The sentries in the tower could observe everything that happened in the temple area, and when they saw the uproar below they flashed word to the chief captain, Claudius Lysias (ch. 23:26), who immediately ran down with a cohort of armed soldiers, and when the Jews saw the Romans they stopped beating Paul. The captain apprehended Paul, had him bound with two chains and demanded to know who he was and what he had done. The Jews were hurling out so many charges that the captain couldn't know for sure what the charges were, so he ordered him to be carried into the fortress. The soldiers had to literally carry him up the steps to protect him from the violence of the mob, as they cried, "Away with him."

D. *Paul's Defense Before the People,* 21:37-22:21. As Paul was about to be taken inside the fortress he spoke to the captain, who was surprised to hear him speaking in Greek, for he had mistaken him for an Egyptian bandit who previously had raised an insurrection and had led a band of four thousand murderers into the wilderness of Judea. But Paul answered that he was a Jew, born in Tarsus, an important city in Cilicia, and he besought him that he might speak to the people. Paul's calm and collected demeanor apparently impressed Lysias, for he granted him permission to speak. Standing at the top of the stairs, Paul beckoned with his hands and the mob suddenly became silent and Paul spoke to them in Hebrew, which caused them to remain the more silent.

He told them he was a Jew of Tarsus, yet reared in Jerusalem under the tutelage of no less an important teacher than Gamaliel (cf. ch. 5:34), and was taught according to the perfect manner of the law. He then identified himself with them, for he had had zeal for God, just as they were manifesting, and had persecuted followers of this Way unto death. He had done to Stephen and others exactly what the mob was trying to do to him. Then he related how, when on one of his missions with orders from the chief priest to arrest any followers of Jesus in Damascus he was blinded by a bright light from heaven, and falling to the ground he heard the voice of Jesus speaking from heaven. All of those in his party saw the searing flash of light and were afraid, but Paul says they did not hear the voice. (This may sound like a contradiction of chapter 9:7: "The men which journeyed with him stood speechless, hearing a voice, but seeing no man." There is no contradiction. The men heard the sound of a voice, but they did not hear or understand what it said. The same word is translated "understand" in 1 Cor. 14:2.) Paul then rehearsed the details of his conversion, some of which are not given in the earlier record. Chapter 9:18 tells us the fact that he was baptized, but chapter 22:16 tells us the purpose of his baptism: "be baptized, and wash away thy sins, calling on the name of the Lord." This is evidence that water baptism was never understood as a burial or watery grave, as many interpret it today, but as a washing or cleansing ceremony. We know that physical water cannot actually wash away the guilt and defilement of sin, any more than the blood of animal sacrifices: nevertheless, under the particular economy of God in effect, these ceremonies were required as an expression of faith. Another detail not mentioned earlier is that when he was in the temple in Jerusalem after his conversion, he was in a trance and saw Jesus speaking to him and telling him to hurry and get out of Jerusalem, because they would not receive his testimony concerning Jesus. Paul apparently felt that since he was so well known as a leader against the followers of Jesus, now that he had been converted to Jesus, the leaders of the nation would listen to him. But the Lord said: "Depart; for I will send thee far hence to the Gentiles."

The mention of Gentiles ended Paul's discourse. When they heard that hated word they began shouting, "Away with such a fellow from the earth; he is not fit to live." We do not believe that this mob was composed of members of the Jerusalem church, as some seem to think. The riot was started by Asian unbelieving Jews. We cannot imagine James, the Lord's brother, the writer of inspired Scripture, to have been one of the rabble, clamoring for Paul's blood. If Paul had been in a compromising mood, as some seem to think he was, he could have avoided this further uproar and perhaps imprisonment by simply omitting any reference to the Gentiles. He must have known that the mention of that word would be like a spark in dry tinder. He wisely put off its mention until he had given a clear testimony concerning Jesus Christ as the Just One, Israel's Messiah, raised from the dead. But the fact that he had the courage to pronounce that word, which spoke so fluently of God's matchless grace, shows that he was uncompromising. He had witnessed the Gospel of the Grace of God to these Jews at Jerusalem, by stating that God had sent him to the alien Gentiles with the message of salvation. What better definition of free grace could a Jew have than salvation of the hated, despised, unclean Gentile dogs?

Captain Lysias didn't understand Hebrew, so he didn't have the slightest idea of what had triggered this explosion of the Jewish mob, so he ordered that Paul be brought into the fortress and be examined by scourging to learn the facts. As the centurion was binding Paul, Paul asked if it was lawful to bind a Roman citizen before being tried and condemned.

When the centurion discovered Paul was a Roman citizen he hurried off to Captain Lysias and warned him to be careful what he did to Paul, because he was a Roman. When the chief captain heard that, he was afraid and dismissed those who were going to torture Paul, after confirming from Paul that he was indeed a Roman citizen. The captain told Paul that he had obtained Roman citizenship. But Paul said, "I was born a citizen." Is it not remarkable how this little, despised Jew was able to make Roman centurions and chief captains, and even kings shake in their boots? Think of the jailer at Philippi, and this chief captain, and later of King Agrippa. This proud chief captain could boast of his citizenship which he had purchased, but not before Paul. Paul was born free.

E. *Paul Brought Before the Jewish Sanhedrin,* 22:30-23:11. The next day in order to find out just what it was the Jews had against Paul, Lysias ordered the Jewish priests and council to gather and stood Paul in their midst. Paul, looking straight into the eyes of his accusers began by addressing them as brothers, a conciliatory remark, and by stating that he had a clear conscience about his life before God to that very day. At that, the high priest ordered those standing next to him to strike him on the mouth. But Paul in righteous indignation replied, "God will strike you, you whitewashed wall. You sit there to judge me according to the law, yet you yourself break the law by commanding that I be struck." The expression, "whitewashed wall," is an interesting one. When a dead body was found in the field it was buried on the spot where it was found. When pilgrims traveled to the feasts in Jerusalem they would often come into contact with such a grave, which would make them ceremonially unclean. To avoid this it was ordered that all such graves should be whitewashed a month before the feasts, so that pilgrims might avoid coming in contact with them. Jesus used this word when he spoke of the scribes and Pharisees being like whitewashed sepulchres (Matt. 23:27). To call one a whitewashed wall was not exactly an expression of respect. Whereupon those who struck Paul said, "Do you mean to insult God's high priest?" Paul did not realize that it was the high priest who had given the order, and he apologized by showing his respect for the law, from which he quoted: "Thou shalt not speak evil of the ruler of thy people." Paul here not only confessed that he had done wrong in speaking disrespectfully of the high priest, but he acknowledged the fact that Israel still stood as a nation and that the high priest was still the God-appointed leader, even though he was a Christ-rejecter. But it would not be long before God would finally smash that whole order of things in His judgment upon Israel.

Paul knew that the membership of the Sanhedrin was divided between Pharisees and Sadducees, and knowing their dislike for one another because of differences in belief, he decided to turn the tables on them and cause them to vent their hatred on each other instead of upon himself. So he cried out: "I am a Pharisee and the son of a Pharisee. I am on trial because of my hope in the resurrection of the dead." Immediately a hot dispute began between the Sadducees, who were materialists, denying both the resurrection and the existence of spirit and angels, and the Pharisees who confessed all three. The Pharisees even went so far as to take sides, in a sense, with Paul, for they said, "We find no fault with the man: perhaps a spirit or angel did speak to him." The session turned into such a brawl that the chief captain was afraid Paul would be torn to pieces, so he ordered the troops in to rescue Paul and bring him back into the fortress.

This section marks the official rejection of Paul and his gospel by the Jewish Sanhedrin. Paul has finished his testimony to Jerusalem. That night the Lord appeared to Paul and said, "Be of good cheer, Paul: for as thou hast testified of me in Jerusalem, so thou must bear witness also at Rome." This commendation of Paul by the Lord creates a real problem for those who have expressed condemnation for Paul's activities at Jerusalem. They have to go to great lengths to try to explain that the Lord was not commending Paul for his testimony in Jerusalem, but rather was rebuking him. They say that the Lord knew how dejected he was for the terrible mess he had made of things in Jerusalem, but because he had been motivated by love for his people Israel, God appeared to him to let him know that He had not forsaken him because of his failure and that He would be with him. It seems that anyone who reads the Lord's words to Paul with an unprejudiced mind could come to no other conclusion than that the Lord was placing His approval upon Paul's actions and because of this the Lord encouraged him. It is not very frequent in Scripture that the Lord grants cheer to those who are out of His will. Besides, there is a comparative statement here. "As thou hast testified of me in Jerusalem, so thou must bear witness of me also at Rome." This must mean, if Paul had given a poor witness in Jerusalem he must also give a poor witness in Rome. We do not believe it means this. Notice also the imperative: "thou must bear witness of me also at Rome." The plain inference is that there was a "must" for his witness in Jerusalem. When this statement is compared with the statement of Paul's purpose in Acts 19:21, it becomes unmistakably clear that this whole trip to Jerusalem and to Rome was God's must for Paul.

F. *The Plot to Kill Paul,* 23:12-22. The Jews were so enraged by the action of the Roman captain in snatching Paul away from them before they could kill him that over forty of them bound themselves under a curse that they would not eat until they had slain Paul. They presented their plot to the Sanhedrin that they should ask the chief captain to bring Paul down for another conference with him, while they laid in wait to slay Paul. But isn't God's providence wonderful? We were completely unaware that Paul had a sister, or that she had a young son. It would almost seem that by chance this young man overheard the plotters' scheme and he came to the fortress to warn Paul. Paul had him sent by one of the centurions to Lysias to deliver a message. The chief captain must have sensed there was something secret about this, for he took the youth aside where no one could overhear them and asked what it was he had to tell him. When he had exposed the plot, Lysias charged him to tell no one what he had done. A band of forty murderous Jews, nor a band of any number, could thwart God's purpose to bring Paul to Rome. He had to get there in spite of plots and storms and shipwrecks and snake bites. Another outstanding example of God's providence is in a book which doesn't mention God's name once, but He is there just the same. Read how the whole Jewish nation was saved from destruction just because King Ahasuerus had insomnia (Esther 6:1-7:10).

VII. PAUL'S TWO-YEAR IMPRISONMENT AT CAESAREA, 23:23-26:32.

A. *Paul Whisked Off to Caesarea by Night,* 23:23-35. The chief captain lost no time after he had learned of the murderous plot against Paul. He made ready two hundred soldiers and seventy horsemen, and two hundred spearmen to leave for Caesarea at nine P.M. He provided a horse for Paul to ride and they were ordered to deliver Paul safely to Felix, the governor of the province. We learn the name of the chief captain from the letter he addressed to Felix. He explained how the Jews had seized Paul and would have killed him had he not rescued him when he learned he was a Roman. Finding nothing worthy of death or imprisonment in the charges made by the Jews, he sent him to the governor and commanded his accusers to come to Caesarea to lodge their charges before him. The soldiers covered about 40 miles that night and arrived at Antipatris. From there the cavalry went on to Caesarea with Paul and the soldiers returned to Jerusalem. When Felix had read the letter from Claudius Lysias he asked Paul from what province he was and said he would hear his case as soon as his accusers arrived. He ordered Paul to be kept in Herod's palace.

B. *Paul's Defense Before Felix,* 24:1-27. Five days later Ananias the high priest and the elders of Israel came down to Caesarea and brought with them a lawyer named Tertullus, who argued the case for the Jews against Paul. The Jews hated the Romans, but Tertullus feigned great appreciation on the part of all Jews for the beneficence enjoyed under the reign of Felix, thinking to gain favor with the governor. Then he began to accuse Paul of being a trouble-maker, stirring up riots among the Jews all over the world. He called him a ringleader of the sect of the Nazarenes and accused him of desecrating their temple. Some Greek texts omit the statements about the violent actions of Lysias from the second half of verse 6 to the last half of verse 8. It is unlikely that Tertullus would have criticized the actions of the Roman chief captain before the Roman governor. However, what he is reputed to have said is true; in fact, it is the only true thing in the lawyer's speech.

After Tertullus had lodged his charges and all of the Jews agreed they were true, Felix motioned to Paul to speak. Paul addressed Felix in a courteous manner but used none of the flattery of Tertullus. To paraphrase Paul's defense, he said, "You can easily verify the fact that it was not more than twelve days ago I came to Jerusalem to worship. But my accusers did not find me in the temple arguing with anyone, or stirring up a crowd in the synagogue, or doing so anywhere else. They cannot prove any of the charges they have made; however, I do admit that I worship the God of our fathers by following the Way which they call heresy, believing all that is written in the Law and in the prophets, having hope towards God that there shall be a resurrection of the just and of the unjust, which they also believe. And in all of these things I do my best to maintain a good conscience toward God and man. Now after several years I came to bring financial help to my countrymen and offerings. While I was engaged in this service, certain Jews from Asia saw me purified in the temple, but there was no mob or disturbance. These Jews ought to be here to accuse me, but since they are not, let those who are here say if they found any evil-doing in me when I stood before the

Sanhedrin, except it might be they would object to my shouting, 'Touching the resurrection of the dead I am called in question by you this day!' ''

Then Felix, who was better acquainted with the Way than most people, adjourned the trial and said he would pronounce judgment after Lysias had come down to Caesarea. He turned Paul over to a centurion with orders that he be given reasonable liberty and that his friends be allowed to minister to his needs. It might appear from his knowledge of the Way and of his kindness to Paul that Felix was a generous and good Roman governor. However, such is not the case. We see from the context that Felix had an ulterior motive in his treatment of Paul. He sent for Paul on numerous occasions to talk with him, not because he wanted to know more about the Lord Jesus Christ, but because he hoped Paul would pay him a bribe to release him. Modern politics hasn't changed much. Both Tacitus and Josephus testify to his cruelty and rapacity which knew no bounds. It is said that he did not hesitate to employ the *sicarii* for his own ends.[25] The sicarii were a band of assassins which sprang up in Jerusalem who carried daggers under their garments and slew men during the day, especially at festival times, when the streets were crowded. Their name comes from the Latin for dagger. Lysias at first mistook Paul for "the Egyptian who . . . led out into the wilderness the 4,000 men of the sicarii," (Acts 21:38). During the reign of Felix revolts by the Jews became increasingly common and it is thought that these revolts marked a distinct stage in that movement which precipitated the outbreak of 70 A.D. Felix was guilty of the murder of Jonathan, the Jewish High-priest. He hired assassins who killed him in the sanctuary of the temple. Tacitus wrote of Felix, "in the practice of all kinds of lust and cruelty he exercised the power of a king with the temper of a slave."[26]

Some days after the hearing in which Paul defended himself against the charges made by Tertullus, Felix came to Caesarea with his wife Drusilla, a Jewess. Drusilla was one of the three daughters of Herod Agrippa I, who had had the Apostle James beheaded and who was smitten by God for accepting the worship of the people. We will meet her sister, Bernice, in chapter 25. According to Josephus, Drusilla was married to King Azizus of Emeza at the age of 14. Shortly after this Felix induced her through a Cyprian magician whom he hired, to desert her husband and marry him. Although she is called a Jewess, the Herods were actually Idumaeans or Edomites. In 126 B.D., Idumaea was subdued by John Hyrcanus, who compelled the people to become Jews and submit to circumcision. Hence, Drusilla could be called a Jewess. When Felix told her about this Jew, Paul, she was apparently curious to hear more about him and what he was preaching. Therefore Felix sent for Paul to hear him privately.

Paul was no doubt well acquainted with the character of both Felix and Drusilla, so he took advantage of the opportunity by preaching to them concerning righteousness, and self-restraint and final judgment. His preaching caused Felix to tremble, but instead of repenting, he dismissed Paul and told him he would call for him again at a convenient time. Drusilla was no doubt enraged by Paul's preaching, just as Herodias was over the preaching of John the Baptist (Matt. 14:1-12). John was beheaded, but Paul was left in prison for two years. The Bezan text says that Felix left Paul bound to please Drusilla, which is probably true.[27] He did it also to please the Jews. The Jews were bringing so many charges against him for his long record of bad government that he did everything possible to curry their favor.

C. ***Paul Appeals to Caesar,*** 25:1-12. After Paul had been in prison for two years at Caesarea, Porcius Festus took the place of Felix as governor. Three days after his arrival in Caesarea he went up to Jerusalem. There the Jewish leaders brought their charges against Paul and requested Festus to have him brought to Jerusalem, hoping to murder him on the way. But Festus replied that Paul would be kept at Caesarea and that those who wanted to accuse him could return with him and have their day in court. Then ten days later Festus returned to Caesarea accompanied by the Jewish leaders. The next day Paul was brought before the judgment seat and the Jews repeated all of the charges they had brought before Felix, but they could prove none of them. Paul denied he had done any wrong against the law of the Jews, or the temple, or against Caesar. Then Festus, desiring to please the Jews, asked Paul if he was willing to go to Jerusalem to be judged before him there. Paul, knowing the murderous intention of his accusers, replied: "I am standing before Caesar's tribunal, where I ought to be tried. To the Jews I have done no wrong, as you very well know. But if I have committed anything worthy of death I do not refuse to die. But if the charges brought against me by these Jews are not true, no one has the right to turn me over to them. I appeal to Caesar!" Festus was no doubt surprised by this turn of events and he may have been piqued by Paul's action which indicated a lack of confidence that he would get a fair trial before him in Jerusalem. But Festus did not know the real motivation of the Jews. According to Roman law, if the appeal to Caesar was admissable, it at once suspended all further proceedings by Festus. Hence we read that Festus conferred with his council concerning the admissability of Paul's appeal, and finding no objections to the appeal, Festus replied to Paul, "You have appealed to Caesar. To Caesar you will go!"

Festus was duty bound to keep his prisoner safe and to deliver him to Rome without delay and to forward all documents bearing on the case, along with his own judgment in the matter. But the information he had received from the trial was so vague and confusing, he hardly knew what to write to the Emperor. A visit by King Agrippa, we shall see, provided him with the needed information.

It is significant that God chose a man to be the Apostle to the Gentiles who could say, "I am a Jew" (Acts 21:39), and at the same time say, "I am a Roman" (Acts 22:27). He was a Jew of the dispersion and a Roman citizen and was thus ideally suited to be the Apostle of the Gentiles. Not only so, but humanly speaking, apart from his Roman citizenship, Paul could not have been saved from severe punishment or death at Jerusalem, nor could he have had the opportunity to witness before the Roman rulers. Immediately we will see he is given another opportunity to witness before a king, and finally, we know, before Caesar himself.

D. *Paul Testifies Before King Agrippa and Bernice,* 25:13-26:32.
King Agrippa and his sister Bernice came to Caesarea to pay a visit to the new governor, Festus. We have already remarked that Bernice was a sister of Drusilla and a daughter of Herod Agrippa I. If anything, she was more immoral than her sister. She was an incestuous person. She first married her uncle, Herod, king of Calchis. After his death she consorted with her own brother, the Agrippa of our present story. She had an affair with King Polemo of Sicily, who for her sake was circumcised and embraced Judaism. She then deserted him and went back to live with her brother. Later on she had a shameful relationship with Vespasian and Titus, father and son. She is not only an example of the ungodly character of the whole Herod clan, but also of how one can be devoutly religious and at the same time devoutly immoral.

After Agrippa had visited for several days, Festus mentioned his problem with his prisoner Paul. He explained all that had happened during the past two years and how Paul had testified before him. He could not see that Paul had done anything deserving of death, but Paul had refused to go to Jerusalem to be tried by the Jews and instead had appealed to

Caesar. Since he had no definite charges to present to the Emperor, he thought Agrippa might be able to help with the letter after he had heard him.

Agrippa agreed and the next day, with great pomp and ceremony, Agrippa and Bernice entered the hall which was filled with all of the high ranking officers and the leading citizens of Caesarea. What an opportunity for Paul! How could he ever have arranged for such an audience as this by himself? He didn't have to rent a hall, or advertise the meeting. And even if he had done so, none of these important persons would have attended. While all of this happened in the providence of God, yet it was the Roman government that had made all of the arrangements for this unusual meeting. His audience was not the riff-raff of the streets but the cream of society. It would be interesting to know if any in that audience were not only almost persuaded, but fully persuaded to become a Christian. We have to remember that the gospel is a two-edged sword: It is a savor of life unto life to those who believe, and a savor of death unto death to those who do not believe (2 Cor. 2:16). It is not in vain when no one is saved when the gospel is preached.

Festus opened the hearing by explaining what he knew of Paul's case and how the Jews had said he ought not be permitted to live any longer, but that he himself had found nothing worthy of death in him. And since Paul had appealed to Caesar he had determined to send him, but having no specific accusations to present to Caesar, he had brought Paul before them all, and especially before King Agrippa, that through this investigation he might have something to write, for it seemed unreasonable to him to send a prisoner to the Emperor without specifying the charges against him.

Agrippa then signaled to Paul that he was permitted to speak for himself. Paul addressed King Agrippa with all due respect without the use of flattery. He felt himself fortunate to testify before the king because he knew the king was well acquainted with all the Jewish customs and controversies. Therefore he begged the king to listen to him patiently.

Paul first spoke of the manner of his life from his youth, which at the first was among his own nation at Jerusalem. All of the Jews could testify, if only they would, that he had lived after the manner of the strictest sect of the Jews' religion as a Pharisee. But now, Paul says, "I am being judged by the Jews for the very hope of the promise God had made to our fathers, unto which promise our twelve tribes, instantly serving God day and night, hope to come." It is for the sake of this hope that the Jews are now accusing him. Then he directs a personal question to the king, "Why should it be thought a thing incredible with you, that God should raise the dead?" Paul does not yet mention the thing that antagonized the Jews the most, namely, his placing the Gentiles on a par with the Jews. Actually, the subject of resurrection was the basic reason for opposition. If Christ had not been raised He could not have appeared to Paul and have commissioned him to be His apostle to the Gentiles. And while the Jewish Pharisees professed to believe in both spirit and resurrection, they denied the resurrection of Jesus, in spite of the many infallible proofs. They had to either accept the fact of His resurrection and thus admit their guilt of murdering their Messiah, or reject His resurrection and justify their act of putting to death a blasphemer. Paul laid great emphasis upon the resurrection of Christ (cf. Acts 13:23,30,33,34,37; 17:3,18,31,32; 23:6; 24:15-21; 26:8,23; 28:20).

Paul's statement about the twelve tribes of Israel instantly serving God day and night is difficult to understand in light of the nation's rejection of Christ. Paul's apostate Jewish accusers were surely not serving God day and night or at any other time. It has been suggested that Paul must be speaking in view of that believing remnant of Rom. 11:5. It is doubtless in this sense that James wrote to the twelve tribes scattered abroad (Jas. 1:1). Compare also the 144,000 remnant of the twelve tribes of Israel (Rev. 7:5-9).

In a sense Paul could sympathize with his accusers, for he was once the ringleader of the group that persecuted and put to death the believers in Jesus. Notice his statement, "I verily thought with myself, that I ought to do many things contrary to the name of Jesus of Nazareth." The position of the "I" in the Greek makes it emphatic. Paul's judgment as the persecutor was based totally upon what he thought with himself. Paul had a good conscience even while putting the disciples to death (cf. Acts 23:1), for he thought he was serving God. There are many people today who may think they are serving God and therefore have a good conscience, who in fact are working against God's will. There are sincere believers who have persuaded themselves they are serving God by fighting against other believers with whom they do not see eye to eye. It behooves every believer to make sure he is not simply "thinking with himself," for he may be as wrong as was Paul. Paul's confession of his acts of persecution against those who followed the Way served to show his honesty and sincerity. It also demonstrated the miracle of his conversion, which turned him around 180 degrees. It is interesting to note that the Greek word for persecute means "to pursue." and that after Paul's conversion he used that same word to describe his activity. Where he once pursued Christians to put them to death, he now pursued the things that make for peace (Rom. 14:19), love (1 Cor. 14:1), righteousness, godliness, faith, love, patience, meekness (1 Tim. 6:11). Believers should be just as energetic in pursuing God's will as they were in pursuing pleasures and self-gratification before they were converted.

Next Paul tells about his conversion (verses 12-18). This is the third record of this event. The first four verses are almost identical with the account in chapter 22, but the three remaining verses give us new information. Paul tells us the glorified Christ told him, "I have appeared unto thee for this purpose, to make thee a minister and a witness both of these things which thou hast seen, and of those things in the which I will appear unto thee." Apart from this statement we might suppose that Paul got his complete revelation at the time of his conversion. But this verse tells us that there was progressive revelation given to Paul. Paul was ministering during a period of transition. New truth was revealed when the time for it was ripe. The former dispensation was passing away and the new one was coming into prominence. There were numerous practises which were common to Paul and the Twelve during the latter half of the Acts period which passed away after that period. We are plainly told of certain things which would pass away or cease in 1 Cor. 13:8. The later epistles of Paul give us a more detailed revelation about the dispensation of the mystery and the fact that there is only one baptism for the Body of Christ, whereas during the Acts period there were three baptisms: that of water, that of Christ baptizing with the Holy Spirit, which was an enduement of power to perform miraculous works, and that of the Holy Spirit baptizing believers into the Body of Christ.

Continuing with Christ's words to Paul, we read, "Delivering you from the people (of Israel), and from the Gentiles, unto whom I now send you, to open their eyes, and turn them from darkness to light, and from the power of Satan unto God, that they may receive forgiveness of sins, and inheritance among them which are sanctified by faith that is in me."

Here we have a series of things which were to be accomplished through Paul's ministry. He was first of all to open the eyes of the Gentiles who had been blinded by Satan (2 Cor. 4:4). God is speaking here of the eyes of the understanding (Eph. 1:18), not the physical eyes. He was to turn them from darkness to light (Eph. 5:8). He was to deliver them from the power of Satan to the power of God (Col.

1:13). And all of this was to the end that they might receive forgiveness of sins and inheritance among those who have been set apart by faith that is in Christ Jesus. No man could accomplish this work by his own effort or ability, and yet it was Paul's responsibility. It must always be remembered that the believer is a "fellow-worker with God" (1 Cor. 3:9), and that it is God who works in and through the believer both to will and to do what is pleasing to Him (Phil. 2:13). And so Paul says in verse 22: "Having therefore obtained help of God, I continue unto this day, witnessing to both small and great."

Although verse 17 sounds like Christ sent Paul immediately to the Gentiles after his conversion, Paul makes it plain in verse 20 that he went first to the Jews in Damascus, then to those in Jerusalem and then to the Jews throughout all the coasts of Judea, and then to the Gentiles. Acts does not record Paul's Judean ministry and Paul makes it clear in Gal. 1:22 that he was unknown by face to the churches of Judea, which fact seems to contradict a Judean ministry. However, the Galatian passage apparently means that he had had no Judean ministry until after he left Cilicia and came to minister at Antioch.

In verse 20 Paul states a three-fold objective of his ministry to the Gentiles: to cause them to repent, to turn them to God, and then to have them do works which would prove the genuineness of their repentance. There is a great deal of misunderstanding about repentance which often confuses the unsaved concerning the terms of salvation. Repentance is made to be a separate and distinct work which the sinner must do before he is qualified to become a Christian. Repentance is represented as an emotional response the sinner must make to show that he is sufficiently sorry for all of the sins he has committed. The biblical word for repentance, however, simply means a change of mind. There is nothing wrong in feeling sorry for one's sins: in fact, every truly saved person must feel sorry for acts which necessitated the death of Christ. But the question that arises in the mind of the sinner is, have I felt sufficiently sorry for my sins, and have I catalogued all of my sins? If repentance is a separate work before salvation, how can one be certain he has done enough to have the assurance of salvation? When one sees repentance as a change of mind he is no longer faced with this problem. When one becomes a Christian he changes his mind about sin and about Christ and about himself and he turns to God in faith. Now it may seem strange that Paul who elsewhere places such great stress upon believing that Christ died for our sins, does not even mention faith or believing in this passage. However, from a careful study of Paul's epistles on the subject of salvation it will be seen that repentance, turning, receiving are simply different aspects of the one act of believing. One cannot believe on the Lord Jesus Christ without changing his mind and without turning to God. Dispensationally we must see the difference between John's preaching to Israel of the baptism of repentance for the remission of sins, and Paul's preaching of repentance to the Gentiles. People who stress salvation by grace through faith apart from every kind of work often shy away from the idea of repentance because of the confusion which surrounds the subject. Such people are sometimes accused of preaching against repentance. What they are opposing is not repentance as Paul uses it and means it, but the imposition upon unsaved sinners today of the message of repentance which was preached to God's covenant nation of Israel. Israel was the chosen people of God and near to God by reason of the covenants; whereas the Gentiles were aliens and strangers and far off from God (Eph. 2:12). Failure to distinguish these two groups and the messages preached to each has resulted in much misunderstanding and confusion.

Paul's statement in verses 22 and 23 has been quoted by ultra-dispensationalists as proof that Paul had not, up to this point, preached the mystery, or the truth about the One Body of Christ. Paul stated that he had continued with God's help to that very day, witnessing to both small and great, saying none other things than those which the prophets and Moses did say should come, that Christ should suffer, and that He should be the first that should rise from the dead, and should show light unto the people of Israel and to the Gentiles. Since the truth of the Mystery cannot be found in the prophets and Moses, how could Paul have been preaching it if he were preaching only what was stated in the prophets and Moses? First of all, it should be remembered what Paul was doing. He was not giving a theological discourse on the Body of Christ. He was defending himself against the charges of the Jews. He was not preaching anything contrary to what Moses and the prophets said would come. The prophets clearly foretold the salvation of the Gentiles, as well as the death and resurrection of the Messiah. Therefore the Jews had no basis for condemning him for preaching these truths. James recognized this use of Scripture when he quoted about Gentile salvation from Amos (Acts 15:14-18). He applied this prophecy to the then present Gentile salvation, although the passage clearly indicates that its actual fulfillment will not come until after the return of Christ and the reestablishment of David's house.

At this point Festus interrupted Paul as he shouted with a

loud voice, "Paul, you are out of your mind. Your great learning is driving you insane!" Paul's words were all foolishness to him (cf. 1 Cor. 1:18-25). But Paul answered: "I am not insane, most noble Festus, but I am speaking the sober truth." And then turning to Agrippa, he said, "The king is familiar with these things and I can speak freely to him. I am convinced that none of these things has escaped his notice, for this thing was not done in a corner." And then addressing the king, Paul asked, "King Agrippa, do you believe the prophets?" And Paul answered for him, "I know you do." Paul's answer put Agrippa on the spot. As a ruler of the Jews he knew better than to say he didn't believe the prophets, but if he did believe how was he to answer to Paul's message about Christ?

Agrippa was apparently insulted by Paul's act of bringing him into this controversy. Who did this leader of this heretical sect of Christians think he was, trying to persuade the great King Agrippa? There is no doubt that he answered Paul in a contemptuous tone of voice. The "almost thou persuadest me to be a Christian," of the *King James* is not an accurate translation. The Greek word "oligo," translated "almost," means either little or few words, or little or short time. The exact expression is found in Eph. 3:3: "As I wrote afore *in few words.*" Agrippa apparently said, "Do you think that in such a short time, or with such few words, you can persuade me to become a Christian?" We are aware that this more accurate translation spoils the basis for the hymn of invitation, "Almost Persuaded," but it seems evident that Agrippa was not almost at the point of conversion. Paul's reply was, "Whether short or long, I would to God, that not only you but also all who hear me this day might become such as I am—except for these chains."

That ended the hearing. Agrippa, Festus, Bernice, and the other dignitaries arose and left the room, and as they discussed Paul's case they agreed that he had done nothing worthy of death or even of imprisonment. And Agrippa said to Festus, "This man might have been set at liberty if he had not appealed to Caesar." But the appeal had been made. The die was cast. There was no other course for Paul or Festus. Nothing remained now, but to await a convenient opportunity to send Paul to Rome. We might question, would it have been better had not Paul appealed to Caesar, for now he could have been set free? But had he not appealed to Caesar he might not even have been alive. But the way it worked out Paul was given a free trip to Rome; he doubtless turned many of the 276 on board the ship to faith in Christ; he made such an impression on the island of Malta that even today Paul's name is connected with everything on the island and he was given considerable liberty during the two years he was in Rome, so that he could meet with the Jewish leaders and minister to all who came to him, even though he was bound to a Roman guard. If he had not appealed to Caesar and if he had escaped death at the hand of the Jews in Jerusalem, and if he had gotten to Rome as a free man, he would never have had opportunity to testify before the Emperor.

VIII. PAUL'S TRIP TO ROME, 27:1-28:10.

A. *From Caesarea to Fair Havens,* 27:1-12. It is clear that Luke was with Paul when he arrived at Jerusalem in Acts 21:17, for we read: "When *we* were come to Jerusalem." However, from that point to chapter 27:1 the narrative is given in the third person. No doubt Luke remained in Jerusalem and then in Caesarea with Paul, for we find him sailing with Paul to Rome: "And when it was determined that *we* should sail into Italy . . ." Luke is completely silent on what he did during this time. He tells us nothing of what happened to the men who accompanied Paul to Jerusalem with the offerings from the Gentile churches. Some writers have criticized James and the Jerusalem elders for deserting Paul and doing nothing to help him after he got into trouble, basing their argument upon Luke's silence. But upon the same basis we would have to conclude that Luke and all of his other friends deserted him, and we do not believe for a moment that they did. After Paul was arrested and in the hands of the Romans there was nothing any one could do, except as the Romans permitted Paul's friends to minister to his needs, and we know that this happened but we are not told who the persons were (cf. 23:16; 24:23), except for Paul's nephew. It is altogether possible that James and others of the Jerusalem saints ministered to Paul as they were allowed to do so. We are sure that Luke did everything possible to help him during his two year imprisonment.

Paul and certain other prisoners were turned over to one Julius, a centurion who belonged to the Imperial Regiment. They boarded a ship from Adramyttium which was bound for the seaports along the coast of the Province of Asia. Luke tells us that Aristarchus of Thessalonica was with them. Apparently he was the only companion of Paul besides Luke who was with him. The next day they stopped at Sidon, a distance of about 65 miles, where Julius gave Paul the liberty

to visit friends and accept their hospitality. Then they left
Sidon, and because the winds were contrary, they were forced
to sail under the lee of Cyprus. From there they sailed north
and skirted the coasts of Cilicia and Pamphylia until they
came to Myra, a distance of about 400 miles from Sidon.
There they had to change ships and Julius found an
Alexandrian ship bound for Rome. Boarding it they
embarked, but for many days they made little headway and
finally with great difficulty arrived off the island of Cnidus.
The wind would not allow them to go on, so they sailed south
under the lee of Crete off Salmone and struggled along the
coast until they came to a place called Fair Havens, which was
near the town of Lasea.

B. **The Storm,** 27:13-38. A great deal of time had been lost and
navigation was becoming hazardous. It was already after the
Fast, that is, Yom Kippur, the Jewish day of atonement,
which came on the tenth day of Tisri, corresponding to the
end of September or the beginning of October. Paul warned
them it would be disastrous to proceed and that they would
run the risk of losing not only the cargo but the ship and their
lives as well. But the centurion, instead of taking Paul's advice,
listened to the pilot and the owner of the ship, and since the
harbor was unsuitable to winter in they decided to sail on to
Phoenix, a harbor at the west end of Crete, which faced both
southwest and northwest. A south wind sprang up and they
thought this would be a perfect day to make the trip. They
weighed anchor and sailed along the southern coast of Crete,
but suddenly a wind of hurricane force, called the North-
easter, swept down on them. They could not head the ship
into the wind, so they had to give way and be driven by the
wind. They were blown behind a small island called Clauda,
where they had great difficulty in hoisting aboard the life boat
which was being towed behind. Then they strengthened the
hull by tying ropes around the ship to hold it together.
Fearing they would run aground on the sandbars off the coast
of Lybia they, shortened the sail and let her drift. The next
day they lightened the ship by throwing the cargo overboard.
The next day they threw the ship's tackle overboard with
their own hands. When neither sun nor stars appeared for
many days and the storm raged on unabated, they gave up all
hope of being saved.

After the men had gone a long time without eating, Paul
stood up before them and said: "Men, you should have taken
my advice, not to sail from Crete, then you would have spared
yourselves this damage and loss. But now I urge you to keep

up your courage, because not one of you will be lost; only the ship will be destroyed. Last night an angel of the God whose I am and whom I serve stood beside me and said, 'Do not be afraid, Paul. You must stand trial before Caesar; and God has graciously given you the lives of all who sail with you.' So keep up your courage, men, for I have faith in God that it will happen just as he told me. Nevertheless, we must run aground on some island" (N.I.V.).

It was about midnight on the fourteenth day as the ship was being driven up and down in the Adriatic Sea that the sailors sensed they were coming near to land. They took soundings and found the water was 120 feet deep. Some time later they tried again and found it was 90 feet deep. Fearing they would be dashed upon the rocks they dropped four anchors out of the stern and then hoped for daylight. The sailors wanted to abandon the ship and got as far as letting down the lifeboat into the sea as though they were going to put out anchors from the prow. But Paul saw what they were up to. He told the centurion and the soldiers that unless these men stay with the ship no one could be saved. So the soldiers cut the ropes and let the lifeboat fall away.

At daybreak Paul urged them all to eat, since they had been fasting for fourteen days. He promised them that not a hair of their heads would be lost and then took some bread and gave thanks to God before all of them, broke it and began to eat. Then they all took courage and began to eat. In all, Luke tells us, there were two hundred and seventy-six persons on board. This must have been a fair sized vessel to carry that many people besides cargo. Josephus tells us that he was in a ship-wreck that had six hundred on board from which he and about eighty others escaped. We are not accustomed to thinking that the ancients had such large ships. After they had eaten enough they lightened the ship by throwing the grain overboard.

C. **The Ship Wreck,** 27:39-44. When daylight came they did not recognize the land but they saw a bay with a sandy beach, so they decided to run the ship aground if they could. Cutting loose the anchors they left them in the sea, loosed the ropes that held the rudders (ships had two paddle-like rudders tied together), hoisted the foresail to the wind and made for the beach. But the cross-currents carried them into a sandbar. The bow stuck fast on the shoal, while the stern began to break up by the pounding of the surf.

The soldiers decided to kill all of the prisoners to prevent them from swimming ashore and escaping. But Julius was determined to save Paul, so he stopped them from carrying out their plan. Instead, he ordered all the men who could swim to jump overboard and make for the shore; the rest to follow, clinging to planks or other floating debris. In this way everyone reached the shore safely.

D *Paul on the Island of Malta,* 28:1-10. Once on land they discovered they were on the island of Melita (modern Malta). The ship had been driven a distance of about 460 miles from the little island of Clauda during the fourteen days of the storm. The traditional place of their landing is Cala di San Paolo (St. Paul's Bay), on the N.E. end of the island. The natives of the island are called barbarians, but the Romans called everyone barbarian who did not speak Greek or Latin. The islanders were not uncivilized, in fact, they showed unusual kindness to the cold, shivering and drenched survivors. They lit a huge bonfire to warm them. Paul himself had gathered a bundle of sticks and as he was putting them on the fire, a viper was driven out by the heat and fastened itself on Paul's hand. When the islanders saw the venomous snake hanging on his hand, they said among themselves, "No doubt this man is a murderer, whom, though he has escaped the sea, yet vengeance will not allow him to live." But Paul shook the snake off into the fire and felt no harm. The natives watched him, expecting him to swell up or suddenly fall down dead, but after watching him for a long time and seeing no harm was done to him, they went to the other extreme and said he was a god. How fickle is human nature! Back at Lystra the people were ready to worship Paul as a god after he had healed the crippled man, but after the Jews came condemning Paul as an evil man they stoned him and left him for dead. Here the people started out thinking he was a murderer and the next moment they were ready to worship him as a god.

Near to the place of the shipwreck were lands belonging to Publius, the chief official of the island. He welcomed them to his home and for three days entertained them hospitably. His father was sick in bed with fever and dysentery and Paul went to his bedside, prayed for him, laid his hands on him and healed him. When others on the island heard of this, they brought their sick to Paul and were healed. Miraculous healing was one of the characteristics of both the ministry of the Lord Jesus and of the Apostles during the Acts period. Healing was one of the signs of an apostle (2 Cor. 12:12, cf. Rom. 15:18,19). Besides this there was the gift of healing which was given to certain believers. Paul had written that these miraculous gifts of the Spirit were to pass away, and the time was drawing to a close when they would pass away with the conclusion of the transition period. What happened here was not the exercise of the gift of healing but the exercise of the signs of an apostle. It is the last recorded miraculous healing. In epistles written after this we find Paul prescribing remedies for sickness (1 Tim. 5:23), and even having to leave a faithful fellow-worker sick (2 Tim. 4:20).

E. *On to Rome,* 28:10-16. The shipwrecked travelers remained on Malta for three months during the winter weather. There was an Alexandrian ship which had wintered in the harbor which was bound for Italy and which bore the sign of Castor and Pollux. In the Greek text the word for Castor and Pollux is "Dioskourous." The Dioscuri were the twin sons of Zeus or Jupiter in Roman and Greek mythology, whose names were Castor and Pollux. These are the names of the two brightest stars in the constellation of Gemeni, often called "the Heavenly Twins." Many hundreds of years before the birth of Christ these two stars served to mark the beginning of the new year by setting together with the first new moon of spring. The constellation of The Twins was supposed to be especially favorable to sailors and ships were often placed under the protection of these twin gods. Our modern ejaculation, "By Gemini," is a swearing by these two gods.

When the party boarded the ship at Malta the islanders honored them in various ways and provided them with supplies they needed. This must have been an even larger ship than the one that was wrecked, in order to take on an additional 276 passengers. Of course, some of the seamen may have stayed behind or hired out to other ships. Their first stop was at the historic city of Syracuse on the eastern shore of Sicily, where they stayed for three days. Their next stop was Rhegium, at the "toe" of the Italian boot, where they were detained for a day waiting for favorable winds. The next day the south wind sprang up and carried the ship some 180 miles to Puteoli on the northern edge of the bay of Naples. As they sailed across the bay the prominent part of the landscape was Vesuvius, that sleeping giant which, eighteen years later, was to explode and snuff out all life in Pompeii, Herculaneum, and Stabiae. Little did Paul realize, as he viewed that peaceful scene on his right, that a fiery rain like that which destroyed Sodom and Gomorrah would rain down upon Pompeii and snuff out the life of that Jewish princess, Drusilla, with whom he had conversed shortly before leaving Caesarea. From excavations of Pompeii, it is evident that it was perhaps as immoral as Sodom and deserved the destruction which came upon it.

Upon disembarking at Puteoli Paul found a group of believers who invited him to stay a whole week with them. The liberty which the Roman centurion gave to Paul is remarkable. He had permitted Paul to go ashore at Sidon to be refreshed by his friends. He had kept the soldiers from their purpose of killing the prisoners in order to save Paul's life. Now at Puteoli he permitted Paul to spend a whole week with his friends, and then as they went on their way to Rome he permitted him to meet with the brothers who had heard he was coming and who had gone down as far as Appii Forum and the Three Taverns to meet him. The Forum was sixty miles from Rome and the Three Taverns some ten miles closer. It must be remembered that Paul had written a letter to the saints at Rome while he was on his last visit to Jerusalem. They were looking forward to meeting him. No doubt the believers at Puteoli got word to those in Rome that Paul was on his way. They had hardly expected to see him come as a Roman prisoner, but when Paul saw their loving regard for him, he thanked God and took courage. Finally, when they arrived at Rome Julius turned the prisoners over to the captain of the guard, but Paul was permitted to dwell by himself in his own lodging with a soldier to guard him. It was no doubt through the influence of Julius that this liberty was granted to Paul.

It is commonly taught that Paul was shut up in a dark, dank Roman dungeon during the time he wrote his prison epistles. However, it is plain from Luke's account that during this imprisonment while he was awaiting his trial he was permitted to live in his own hired house under guard, where his friends had liberty to visit him and minister to him. If it was unlawful to punish a Roman citizen before he had been tried and found guilty, and if this law was observed so meticulously in the far reaches of the empire, it is certain that Paul's citizenship would be respected in Rome itself. Apparently in his second imprisonment in Rome, as recorded in 2 Timothy, he had been condemned to death and was under much different treatment and circumstances.

Although Luke is silent on the subject, we are sure that some of those 276 souls who accompanied Paul to Rome must have been saved through his life and testimony. We would not at all be surprised to meet Julius in glory, along with some other centurions who are mentioned in Scripture. At last, the long journey of over two thousand miles was ended.

F. *Paul Meets With Jewish Leaders in Rome,* 28:17-24. Paul wasted no time in calling a meeting with the chief Jews in Rome. After three days they met with Paul, who said to them: "My brothers, although I have done nothing against our people or against the customs of our ancestors, I was arrested in Jerusalem and handed over to the Romans. They examined me and wanted to release me, because I was not guilty of any crime deserving death. But when the Jews objected, I was compelled to appeal to Caesar—not that I had any charge to bring against my own people. For this reason I have asked to see you and talk with you. It is because of the hope of Israel that I am bound with this chain" (N.I.V.).

There are at least two things in Paul's statement which deserve our closer attention. The first concerns his declaration that he had done nothing against the customs of the Jewish people. It will be remembered that Paul had gone into the temple at Jerusalem to prove that he had not taught the Jews of the dispersion to forsake Moses, or to cease circumcising their children or keeping their customs. If Paul was shading the truth or misrepresenting his ministry to the Jews, as some commentators have charged, it is evident that Paul is still doing the same thing in Rome. Surely the great apostle, after all of the bitter experience he had been through, and with over two years in prison to reconsider all of his actions, would not continue this deception, if, indeed, it was a deception. We believe that Paul's statement here and in Jerusalem, is a truthful representation of his ministry among the Jews scattered among the Gentiles.

The other matter concerns his statement that it was for the hope of Israel he was bound with chains. Ultra-dispensationalists who teach that Paul's ministry all during the book of Acts was one of offering the Kingdom to Israel and not one of ministering to the Church which is the Body of Christ, have used this verse to support their teaching. They claim that the truth of the Mystery was not made known until after this final meeting with the Jews at Rome. But what does Paul mean by "the hope of Israel?" They say "the hope of Israel" is the earthly, millennial kingdom, and they say it was because Paul was preaching this kingdom message he was arrested and put in chains. However, Paul states in one of his letters written from the Roman prison that it is because of the mystery of the Gospel that he is an ambassador in bonds (Eph. 6:19,20). He must have preached the Mystery before this in order to be in bonds for preaching the Mystery. No, it seems quite evident from Paul's statements before the Sanhedrin in Acts 23:6, and before Felix in Acts 24:15, and before King Agrippa in Acts

26:6-8, that Paul's definition of the hope of Israel is the resurrected Lord Jesus Christ. One has but to turn to Jer. 14:8 and 17:13 to see that the Lord, the Saviour of Israel is called "the Hope of Israel."

After Paul's opening statement, the Jewish leaders replied that they had not received any letters from Judea against him, and that none of the brothers who had come from there had brought any news about him. But they said they wanted to hear his views because they knew that people everywhere were talking against this sect.

G. *Final Pronouncement of Blindness Upon Israel,* 28:25-31. So the Jews arranged for a meeting with Paul on a certain day and an even larger number of them came to the place where he was staying. All day long, from morning until evening, Paul explained to them his message about the Kingdom of God and did his best to persuade them about Jesus from the law of Moses and from the prophets. Some of the Jews believed and some did not believe. When they could not agree among themselves and started to leave, Paul spoke this one final word to them: "Well spoke the Holy Spirit through Isaiah the prophet unto our fathers, saying, 'Go to this people and say, Hearing you shall hear and shall not understand, and seeing you shall see and not perceive: for the heart of this people is waxed gross (has become calloused), and their ears are dull of hearing, and their eyes they have closed; lest they should see with their eyes, and hear with their ears, and understand with their heart, and should be converted, and I should heal them.' Therefore I want you to know that the salvation of God has been sent unto the Gentiles, and they will listen to it."

This final pronouncement of judicial blindness upon the nation of Israel brings the Book of Acts to a close (cf. Isa. 6:9,10; Matt. 13:14,15; Mk. 4:12; Lk. 8:10; John 12:39-41; Rom. 11:8). But what is the significance of closing the book at this point? Why does Luke simply tell us that Paul dwelt two whole years in his own hired lodging, receiving all who came to him, preaching the kingdom of God, and teaching with all confidence those things which concern the Lord Jesus Christ, no man forbidding him? Why does he not tell us why his trial before Caesar was delayed so long? Why does he not tell us of the verdict of that trial? We are sure that Paul was acquitted and had further missionary journeys, perhaps going as far as Spain (Rom. 15:24). Why is Luke silent about the last days of Paul's life and his final imprisonment and death? Luke was with him to the end (2 Tim. 4:11), and could have told us all of these things, had his purpose in writing been simply to portray the life and ministry of Paul. If this was not Luke's purpose, what was it?

IX. THE PURPOSE OF THE BOOK OF ACTS

We believe the purpose of the Book of Acts is to show the how and the why of Israel's fall: why the nation of Israel to whom the promise and the offer of the Messianic Kingdom was made, did not enter into that Kingdom; why "Israel has not obtained that which he sought after" (Rom. 11:7). We must understand this before we can rightly understand the epistles of Paul which follow the Book of Acts. The book begins with the offer of the Kingdom to Israel and ends with the pronouncement of blindness upon the nation and the complete turning over of the salvation ministry to the Gentiles. We see all of this happening progressively throughout the latter half of the book. Acts 28:28 does not mean that the salvation of God is only now being sent to the Gentiles, as the King James seems to imply and as some have taken it. The verb "sent" is in the second aorist, indicative passive, and should be rendered as it is in many of the newer versions, "has been sent." This sending of salvation to the Gentiles and the turning away from Israel under Paul's ministry began in Acts 13:46: "It was necessary that the word of God should first have been spoken to you (Israel): but seeing you put it from you, and judge yourselves unworthy of everlasting life, lo, we turn to the Gentiles." We see the same thing in Acts 18:6: "And when they (Israel) opposed themselves, and blasphemed, he (Paul) shook his raiment, and said unto them, Your blood be upon your own heads, I am clean: from henceforth I will go to the Gentiles." Practically the same thing happened in Paul's great ministry in Ephesus, for he separated his disciples from the synagogue ministry after that the Jews became hardened and believed not and moved his ministry to the school of one Tyrannus, a Gentile (Acts 19:9).

Therefore Acts 28 does not mark the beginning of a completely new dispensation, but the end of a transition from the old to the new, and emergence into the full-blown operation of the new. Some students of the Word believe that the dividing line comes in the year 70 A.D., with the destruction of Jerusalem, instead of some eight years earlier with the end of the Acts. However, it seems to us that apart from the long-suffering of God the destruction of Jerusalem would have coincided with the end of the Acts period. But God is long-suffering, not willing that any should perish, and He did give to individual Jews a few more days before the judgment was executed. This destruction of the city of Jerusalem was threatened by the Lord Jesus if they rejected God's message (Matt. 22:7; Lk. 21:24), and we know that there will yet be another destruction of that city before the return of Christ (Zech. 14:1-3).

The Book of Acts reveals little of the political turmoil between the Jews and their Roman rulers. There was a constant smouldering of unrest among the Jews towards the Romans which occasionally broke out in riots and rebellion. In 66 A.D. the criminal incompetence of Gessius Florus precipitated a rebellion in which palaces and public buildings were burned and the Antonia itself was captured and the garrison of Roman soldiers was slain. Cestius Gallus hastened down from Syria and was at first successful in his seige against Jerusalem, but for some reason he made a partial withdrawal which turned into an inglorius retreat and defeat. After that Vespasian commenced his conquest from the north by slow and well-planned steps. He was recalled to Rome when he was appointed Emperor, and his son Titus took charge of the war. The seige of Jerusalem began on the 14th of Nisan, 70 A.D. and lasted 134 days. It was Passover time when the seige began, and besides the crowds who had assembled for that feast, there were multitudes who had fled before the advancing Roman army. Jerusalem had been beseiged on numerous occasions in the past, but none of those destructions could be compared with this terrible onslaught. It is reported by Josephus that 600,000 Jews were slain, although many authorities believe it impossible that so great a number of people could have been within the walls of the city. At no time in the past had the city been so magnificent and its fortifications so powerful, but as the Lord had predicted, not one stone was left standing upon another. The temple was burned and completely demolished. The Romans left three of the great towers and the western wall standing, both to protect the camp of the Tenth Legion and to show to posterity what kind of city it was. The remainder of the city was dug up to its foundations.

Thus ended the possibility of the ceremonial practise of Judaism, for apart from Jerusalem and the temple there could be no offering of sacrifices or the carrying out of other aspects of the Mosaic law (Deut. 12:10-14 cf. 2 Chr. 6:5,6).

SECTION THREE

Note Page

1 107. – Marvin R. Vincent, *Word Studies in the New Testament* (New York, Charles Scribner's Sons, 1914) Vol. I. 536.

2 113. – Ibid., Vol. I, p. 546.

3 116. – Ogg, op. cit., p. 107.

4 125. – Donald Guthrie, *New Testament Introduction* (Downers Grove, Ill., Inter-Varsity Press, 1973) pp. 472-478; 526-536; 555-558, discusses the Roman and Ephesian imprisonment views.

5   134. – C.R. Stam, *Acts Dispensationally Considered* (Chicago, Berean Bible Society, 1960), Vol. IV, pp. 13-37, 58, 72; also Vol. II, pp. 126-128, 260, 261, 270-272, 288, Vol. III, pp. 142, 178, 230-241, 261-265.

6   134. – Donald Grey Barnhouse, *ACTS, An Expositional Commentary* (Grand Rapids, Zondervan Publishing House, 1979), pp. 168, 169.

7   135. – Ibid., p. 170.

8   135. – Ibid., pp. 185, 186.

9   135. – Ibid., p. 186.

10   136. – Ibid., p. 189.

11   136. – Ibid., p. 189.

12   136. – Ibid., p. 190.

13   136. – Ibid., p. 191.

14   136. – Ibid., p. 193.

15   136. – Ibid., p. 194.

16   137. – Ibid., p. 195.

17   137. – Ibid., p. 199.

18   137. – Ibid., p. 196.

19   138. – F.F. Bruce, *The Acts of the Apostles* (London, The Tyndale Press, 1951) p. 385.

20   138. – Homer A. Kent, Jr., *Jerusalem to Rome, Studies in the Book of Acts* (Grand Rapids, Baker Book House, 1972) pp. 158, 159.

21   139. – George Williams, *The Student's Commentary of the Holy Scriptures* (Grand Rapids, Kregel Publications, 1949) p. 895.

22   139. – Alford, op. cit., Vol. II, p. 235.

23   147. – Conybeare and Howson, *The Life and Epistles of St. Paul* (London, Longman, Brown, Green, Longmans, and Roberts, 1857), Vol. II, p. 297.

24   149. – This statement needs to be qualified by the fact that Paul states that although the New Covenant was made with the house of Israel and with the house of Judah (Jer. 31:31; Heb. 8:8), the Gentiles in this dispensation have been made partakers of all of the spiritual blessings of that covenant (Rom. 15:24 cf. 2 Cor. 3:6). The covenant also contains physical and material blessings which Israel will realize in the Millennial Kingdom, but which are not shared by the Church today.

25   159. – *International Standard Bible Encyclopedia*, op cit., Vol. 2, p. 1105.

26   159. – Vincent, op. cit., Vol. I, p. 582.

27   160. – *International Standard Bible Encyclopedia*, op. cit., Vol. II, p. 1105.

Scripture Index